The Best
INSTRUCTION
BOOK EVER!
EXPANDED EDITION

Some of the material in this book was
previously published in *Golf Magazine*, and
is reprinted with permission by Time Inc.

Published by Time Home Entertainment Inc.
135 West 50th Street
New York, N.Y. 10020

Time Inc.
1271 Avenue of the Americas
New York, N.Y. 10020

ISBN 10: 1-61893-021-4
ISBN 13: 978-1-61893-021-7
Library of Congress Control Number: 2011945987

We welcome your comments and suggestions
about Time Home Entertainment Inc. books.

Please write to us at:
Time Home Entertainment Inc. Books
Attention: Book Editors
P.O. Box 11016
Des Moines, IA 50336-1016

If you would like to order any of our
hardcover Collector's Edition books,
please call us at (800) 327-6388
(Monday - Friday, 7:00 a.m. - 8:00 p.m. or
Saturday, 7:00 a.m. - 6:00 p.m. Central Time).

Cover and book design by Paul Ewen
Cover photographs by Angus Murray

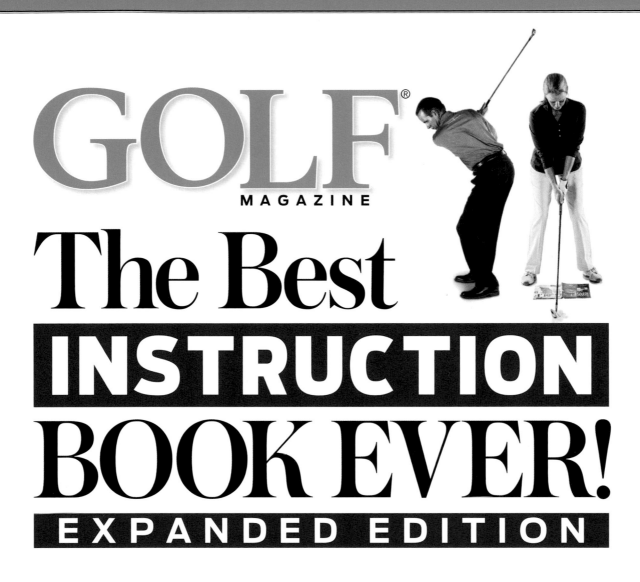

GOLF
MAGAZINE

The Best
INSTRUCTION
BOOK EVER!
EXPANDED EDITION

From the Top 100 Teachers in America

EDITED BY DAVID DeNUNZIO

GOLF
MAGAZINE
TOP 100
TEACHERS
IN AMERICA

Time
HOME ENTERTAINMENT

A SPORTS ILLUSTRATED PUBLICATION

YOUR BEST GOLF EVER!

Despite any success you've had in the past, the book in your hands is going to help you shoot lower scores and better enjoy your golf experience. Confident claims, no doubt, but they're easily made considering the source of the more than 1,000 tips, drills and lessons contained within. Each one comes straight out of the pages of *Golf Magazine*. With a 50-year-plus legacy of award-winning instruction, *Golf* has become the leader in the way the game is taught and played. Moreover, our instruction is driven by the single greatest collection of teaching experts in the game: the Top 100 Teachers. Members of this elite group are chosen not only for their swing knowledge and experience, but also for their teaching skills and knack for developing methods that make the game easier to learn. Some of the Top 100

Teachers you know by name—the ones that work with the major stars on the professional tours. Others are teaching legends with hall-of-fame status. But all of them are dedicated to helping golfers just like you get better, and to making sure these changes stick.

Since their debut in 1996, the Top 100 Teachers have produced more than 3,500 pages of instruction in *Golf Magazine* and the *Golf Magazine* tablet editions (as well as hundreds of videos on Golf.com). This revised edition of the original *Best Instruction Book Ever!* represents their greatest hits, organized to help you hit the ball farther, putt better, score lower and beat anything the course throws at you. With the help of the Top 100 Teachers, your best golf ever is just around the corner.

DAVID DeNUNZIO MANAGING EDITOR (INSTRUCTION) *GOLF MAGAZINE*

WHAT'S INSIDE

SECTION 6

Your Short Game
p. 124

Whether it's an approach to a par 5 or a greenside chip to help save par, here's how to get it close.

LEARN HOW TO:
- Chip the ball close without chunking or skulling it
- Hit pitch shots that bite
- Master flop shots and lobs
- Chip it high or low from the fairway or rough

SECTION 7

Escaping the Sand
p. 146

Bunker shots come in all shapes, sizes, lies and levels of difficulty. Here's how to play them all.

LEARN HOW TO:
- Get out of any bunker on your first swing
- Play from hard or wet sand
- Choose the right club to blast from the sand
- Pull off impossible escapes

SECTION 8

Holing Out
p. 160

It all comes down to the most perplexing part of the game. Here's the smart way to make every putt you see.

LEARN HOW TO:
- Aim your body and putterface at your target
- Determine speed and break
- Find the right putter for you
- Lag closer
- Avoid three-putting

SECTION 9

Trouble Shots
p. 182

Even the best-made plans sometimes go awry. Here's how to get out of any predicament on the course.

LEARN HOW TO:
- Control trajectory to hit the ball over or under obstacles
- Putt from off the green
- Save par from the rough
- Hit the ball straight from sidehill and sloping lies

SECTION 10

Flaws and Fixes
p. 192

How to make sure you don't make the same mistake twice when bad habits creep into your swing.

LEARN HOW TO:
- Cure your putting yips
- Stop slicing and hooking
- Fix fat or thin contact
- Avoid popping up tee shots
- Stop pulling or pushing your approach shots

What you do before your rounds and in the time between them determines the scores you shoot and how quickly you can lower them.

SECTION 1

PREPARING TO PLAY

How to get your round motoring out of the blocks even before you hit your first shot

There are two parts to the game: the playing part and the part that occurs between your rounds. While your typical day on the course lasts roughly four hours, the time from the moment you make your last putt on 18 to when you place your tee in the ground on the first hole of your next round is significantly longer. For some golfers, weeks longer. And although you judge your game by the scores you shoot, it's really what you do between rounds—and just before you tee off—that determines the numbers you mark on your card.

The fact that you're holding this book in your hands means you're serious about your game and about improving. The majority of these pages are dedicated to helping you get around the course in as few strokes as possible. This section, however, focuses on what you need to do between rounds to make sure the lessons stick.

With the help of the Top 100 Teachers, you'll learn how to warm up before play to get off to a good start, how to pinpoint areas of your game that require the most work, how to make your practice time serious learning time, and how to make your lessons more effective. Armed with this knowledge, you'll optimize the non-playing part of your game so you can put your swing on autopilot and shoot the scores you want.

5 THINGS YOU'LL LEARN IN THIS SECTION

- *How to get your swing warm before you play, whether you have an hour to get ready or just 15 minutes.*
- *How to practice with a purpose, make effective practice swings and groove the right moves quickly.*
- *The flaws you must fix first.*
- *How to select a teacher and get the most out of a lesson.*
- *How to change your attitude on Improvement and adopt new, proven strategies to make swing fixes stick.*

Learn more about the basics you need to play your best at **golf.com/basics**

HOW TO BE A "PLAYER"

Here are three tricks to posting the lowest score possible that only pros know

● Play with the right ball. Most golfers don't know what that is. As a general rule, choose the ball that works best for you when putting and chipping, not the one you can hit the farthest.
—Bruce Patterson

● Learn to adapt to different weather conditions with your gear. For instance, if it's cold, use a driver with a lower loft and move the ball a bit back in your stance. When the weather turns, the optimum launch angle isn't 12 degrees. It's more like 8 degrees.
—Peter Krause

● You've probably been told to finish your swing with your hands high. But if you want to hit the ball farther, consider finishing low. If you observe the big hitters on Tour, you'll notice that their hands never get much higher than their left shoulder in their finish. This is the result of unhinging, or releasing, the wrists fully through impact. It provides a powerful snap to the swing and produces a low finish.
—Mike Adams

HOW TO GET WARM

Easy ways to get loose before practice and play—and avoid injury while doing it

INSTRUCTION

The 15-Minute Warm-Up

A quick and effective routine to jump-start your round

THE SITUATION

You've arrived late to the course and have only 15 minutes to warm up.

THE SOLUTION

Get your short game and putting warm because you'll need them more than ever while you work out the kinks in your full swing.

WHAT TO DO

This plan calls for six two-minute segments and allows for three minutes to pick up balls and move between drills. First, stretch your hamstring muscles and twist your trunk all the way right and left to loosen up a bit.

STEP 1

Take five swings each with your 7-iron, 5-wood and driver at 3/4 speed. Don't hit balls, just swing the clubs.

STEP 2

Grab three balls and your 8-iron, 60-degree wedge and putter, and hightail it to the practice green.

STEP 3

Hit the short-game shots described at right in order (*Nos. 1 - 5, right*). If you can squeeze in one full swing before you tee off, hit a 4-wood out onto the range. You'll be ready to start your round with a smooth 4-wood into the first fairway.
—Dave Pelz

Hit three lofted pitch shots over a practice bunker with your lob wedge (or highest-lofted club) to learn how your ball reacts upon hitting the green.

Jump into the bunker and hit three short sand shots to a greenside target to activate your hands.

Hit three running chips with your 8-iron to a hole 50 feet away to get a feel for distance.

Stroke three long lag putts well across the putting surface to dial in the speed of the greens.

Hit six three-foot putts to become comfortable with the short ones—these are the score-breakers.

Start with Your Short Game

Most golfers warm up with their longer clubs first. Not good.

Statistical averages show golfers score better on the middle 10 holes than on the first and last four. It's easy to see how the pressure to shoot a certain score might make you nervous and result in poor scores at the finish. But poor play on the first four holes? Perhaps this is because **you're not prepared to scramble when you miss the first few greens.** This data emphasizes the importance of warming up your short-game feel and touch before heading to the first tee. A complete-game warm-up is optimal, but when you're short on time, warm up your scoring game first! —**Dave Pelz**

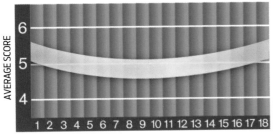

Golfers score better on the middle holes than early or late. Warm up your short game first to buck this trend.

How to Customize Your Warm-Up

Find the pre-round prep that works best for you

On Tour, I notice that some players take just 40 minutes to get ready, while others warm up for several hours. My point is this: Your pre-round preparation must be tailored to your personality and body conditioning. What gets one player ready to play their best may tire you out. **Optimize your scoring potential by trying different warm-up times and techniques** and keeping track of the scores you shoot afterward. Once you learn what works best for you, use it for all of your rounds in the future. —**Dave Pelz**

How to Loosen Up Your Body

Follow these steps for peak performance

Whether your pre-round warm-up time is an hour (ideal) or 15 minutes (typical), you have time to get ready for one of your best rounds. Here's the sequence to follow:

STEP 1
Walk briskly to the driving range to get your blood moving, then warm up. Hold two clubs together and swing them in circles, doing 10 repetitions with each arm. This prepares your shoulders for the demands of the swing.

STEP 2
Rest the clubs on the ground and hold them vertically, securing your hands on top of the grips *(above)*. Keep your hands there and do 10 squats to warm up your knees, calves and hips.

STEP 3
Hit your short irons for a solid 10 minutes. Start with slow, three-quarter length swings and gradually build to full swings. After 10 minutes of hitting balls you can tap your arm, leg and core muscles however you like without risking a visit to the chiropractor the next day.

Even if you don't hit another ball after this last step, your body will be primed to hit a good drive on the first tee and sustain high performance throughout your round. —**Dave Phillips**

Another Way to Loosen Up Your Body

Go from trunk slam to swing-ready in a matter of minutes

Despite your best intentions to arrive early for your Saturday morning tee time, you once again pull into the club parking lot about 10 minutes before your scheduled starting time. But all is not lost. Here are some quick tips to help you get your game and body ready if you're running late.

STEP 1: LIMBER UP

As soon as you get out of your vehicle, loosen up your arms and torso with a few stretches. Put one foot up on the bumper with your arms extended forward and hands resting on the trunk or inside of your car. Slowly bend forward to stretch out your lower back, glutes and hip flexors, all of which are vital to achieving good body rotation and posture throughout the swing. Make sure to change legs, and hold each stretch for 15 seconds.

Next, stretch your shoulders by pulling one arm across your chest toward the other shoulder. Hold for a count of five then switch arms. If you know you're going to be late, loosen up your hands and fingers by squeezing an exercise ball or even just the steering wheel as you drive. This will help relieve any stress or tension you have in your hands.

Use the rear bumper of your car to help stretch your back, glutes and hip flexors.

Keep an exercise ball in the car and use it to loosen up your hands and fingers as you drive to the course.

STEP 1: HEAD FOR THE PRACTICE GREEN

If you have a few minutes to spare, drop a couple of balls down and putt them to various spots on the edge of the practice green, not at a hole. Try to get a feel for the speed of the greens, which is key to avoiding three-putts.

STEP 2: HANG BACK

When you arrive at the first tee, ask the other players in your group to hit first so you can stretch your shoulders, mid-back and hamstrings a few more times. As you're stretching, visualize the best tee shot you've ever hit on this particular hole, or see the ball soaring down the center of the fairway. Think positive—you want that first tee shot to set a good tone for the rest of your round.

Try to get a general feel for the speed of the greens by putting a few balls to the edge of the practice green. Don't worry about making these putts.

Before you tee off, make a couple of full swings with a mid-iron. All you're trying to do here is groove a smooth, even tempo.

TEMPO

Don't Forget! The 10-Second Slice Fix

Keep your right leg flexed and shift your weight

THE FAULT

You take the club back with a steep shoulder turn and strand your weight on your front leg. This is called a "reverse pivot," and it's one of the most common causes of a slice.

THE FIX

Follow this simple drill before you tee off to make sure your first shot isn't a crooked one:

1: Take your address and hold a club across your chest.
2: Make your backswing, keeping your right leg slightly bent so you can transfer weight to it as you turn.
3: Stop when you can't turn your shoulders any farther. If you've done it correctly, the shaft will point to a spot that's behind the ball and on the other side of the target line. You'll be able to make a fuller, less-steep turn when you shift your weight correctly (*photo, above*).
4: If the shaft points at the ball or even in front of it, then you're still reverse pivoting. Try again until you can keep your back knee bent and shift your weight into it every time.
—E.J. Pfister

HOW TO PRACTICE
The best advice and drills to keep your swing skills fresh between rounds

DRILL

How to Practice Like a Tour Player

Improve your rhythm—and look cool doing it!

START HERE
Tip over a bucket of balls and, with your club in your right hand, pull a ball out of the pile and drag it over to a spot where you can hit it.

Now "present" the handle of the club to your right hand, release your left hand, and go back to Step 1. Now you're practicing like a pro!

THE PROBLEM
You go through a bucket of range balls like a wave of locusts through a cornfield.

THE SOLUTION
When you beat balls at a machine-gun pace you're not helping your game much. You need to set up to the ball correctly every time, and also take the time to follow through completely, study your ball flight and landing patterns, and then decompress and get ready for the next shot. In other words, you need to practice like you play.

HOW TO DO IT
Watch Tour players on the driving range. Most pros follow a six-step procedure that takes them from ball to ball in a deliberate, measured way that mimics how they approach each shot on the golf course. If you copy that procedure, you're guaranteed to become a better ball striker.
—John Elliott, Jr.

Stand behind your ball and pick your target. Step into address—first with your right foot and then with your left— while glancing at your target.

As the ball comes to a stop, remove your right hand from the grip and allow the club to slide down the fingers of your left hand until it feels light and balanced in your hand.

Make a complete, balanced swing so that you're facing the target and most of your weight is on your left foot. Study the flight of your ball, and stay in this position until it has landed.

Once you're comfortable in your address position and have visualized your target line, waggle the club once or twice to loosen your wrists, and then swing away.

INSTRUCTION

How to Practice Your Putting

Six tips for making your time on the practice green pay off

SAVE TRICK SHOTS FOR POOL
It might be fun to slide a 60-foot putt through a slalom course of tees, but on the course you're more likely to miss the straight 3-footers.

PLAY FOR KEEPS
Have a nine-hole putting contest with a buddy. This is the best way to prepare for a match. You'll be forced to make putts under competitive pressure, just as you will on the course.

NEVER GIVE AN INCH
Ever laugh at a guy practicing 1-foot putts and then lose to him? Practice some short ones. You'll win more matches by assuming you'll never be conceded a putt.

DON'T BE A DRONE
Don't repeatedly drain the same well-trodden putt, as if every one you face will be a 6-footer with the same right-to-left break. Practice putts that vary in length and slope to more accurately match the putts in a typical round.

TALK IS CHEAP
Don't look at the practice green only as a place to unload a new batch of jokes. If you take putting practice seriously, your results will speak for themselves.

SET GOALS
Try to make 10 3-footers in a row along a tee- or coin-marked wheel around the cup. If you miss on No. 9, start over. Then try three in a row from 10 feet. Goal-setting breeds discipline and confidence.
—Gale Peterson

PRACTICE THESE MAJOR KEYS

Q: Other than working on technique, what should I focus on during my practice sessions?

● Practice with the club that allows you to hit the fairway on the most consistent basis, even if it's a 3-wood. Don't feel like your driver is the only club you can hit from the tee box. Also, work on shots around the green, particularly on putts from four feet and in. I've seen it help players drop three strokes in three days.
—Rod Lidenberg

● Hit little punch shots with your 7-iron to ingrain the feel of a correct release. Address a ball and cock the club up so the club shaft is parallel to the ground. Hold it there, then get comfortable and start the swing from this point, taking your hands back to chest height. Start down with your hips and finish at chest height. This drill trains your hands and arms to store the power of the downswing for as long as possible.
—Ron Gring

● Hit shots with the sole purpose of maintaining your posture from start to finish. You can practice this at home, too. Place a pillow against a wall and rest your forehead against it, then make practice takeaways without moving your head off the pillow.
—Mike Bender

GET MORE FROM YOUR PRACTICE

Our Top 100 Teachers pinpoint areas in serious need of attention

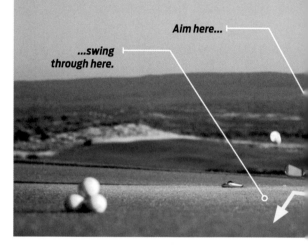
The bad news is you practice wrong. The good news? Our Top 100 Teachers are here to help, with drills that will dramatically improve your game from tee to green.

Lowering scores means paying special attention to where you're throwing away strokes. We asked the Top 100 Teachers in America to each name three areas in which amateurs make the biggest mistakes—that is, to pinpoint the critical elements that are consistently missing from the everyday player's game. We tallied the results and discovered that your No. 1 shortcoming is improper practice, which sets off a card-killing chain reaction that costs you strokes across the board, from your driver to your wedges. This domino effect helps explain why your handicap usually doesn't budge, even when you make positive steps. Lower scores are a total-game event. By practicing smarter with the seven simple drills that we've presented in the following pages, you'll transform your entire game.

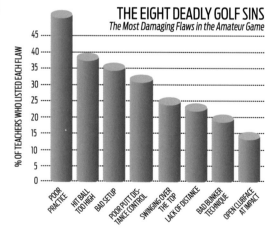

THE EIGHT DEADLY GOLF SINS
The Most Damaging Flaws in the Amateur Game

% OF TEACHERS WHO LISTED EACH FLAW

Categories (left to right): POOR PRACTICE · HIT BALL TOO HIGH · BAD SETUP · POOR PUTT DISTANCE CONTROL · SWINGING OVER THE TOP · LACK OF DISTANCE · BAD BUNKER TECHNIQUE · OPEN CLUBFACE AT IMPACT

BUCKET LIST

Your biggest flaw is that you don't practice correctly. Set aside some range time and try the Top 100 Teachers' No. 1 new ways to practice shown on these pages. They'll give you what your practice time has been missing: proven ways to get better. With a little effort and a few buckets of balls, you'll shoot the scores that you've always known were out there.

THE FAULT

You swing over the top, cutting across the ball (too much outside to in) at impact. When you do square the clubface, you hit dead pulls; when you leave the face open, the ball sails O.B. right.

THE NO. 1 DRILL TO FIX IT

Get in the good habit of swinging more inside-out, especially with your driver. This is difficult to do without a visual reference that helps you adjust your swing path—you may think you're swinging correctly, but you can't know for sure unless you have some guides in place. My "gate" drill does the trick.

STEP 1: Point one of your irons at the target, then lay a second iron parallel to the first. Align your body and stance to the second iron.

STEP 2: Create a "gate" to the right and a few feet in front of your alignment station with two piles of balls, as I've done here. Set one side of the gate in line with the middle of your alignment station and the other side a yard to the right. Tee a ball in the middle of the station and take your

stance—the gate should appear to be noticeably off to your right.

STEP 3: Make half-speed swings with the goal of driving the ball through the gate, not down your target line. After a few attempts you'll get the proper feel of delivering the club from the inside and out—it's like you're hitting to right field on a baseball diamond. Once you can consistently hit shots through the gate, remove the tee and hit balls off the turf. You should see your divots pointing straight down your line and the ball curving back to the center.
—**Tom Stickney**

The No. 1 Way to Add Yards

Try my "step drill" to fix your weight shift and gain power

THE FAULT
You don't drive the ball with the power you deserve because you don't get your weight moving to your front leg early enough in your swing, and as a result your sequence fails to max out your available speed. To maximize your driving distance, you need to feel the correct order of movements.

THE NO. 1 DRILL TO FIX IT
The drill at right is an easy way to ingrain the feeling of a proper sequence so you can pick up big yards quickly.

STEP 1: Set up with your weight distributed equally between both feet and your heels and toes.

STEP 2: Swing back, exaggerating your weight shift—feel as though you're pushing off your left foot.

STEP 3: Allow your left foot to come off the ground and move a few inches closer to your right foot, like you're trying to click your heels together. You should be fully loaded on your right leg before you reach waist height in your backswing.

STEP 4: Just before you transition to your downswing, drive off the inside of your right foot and then step in and plant your left foot ahead of the ball—this should all happen as you end your backswing. If you've ever played baseball, this should feel as though you're stepping into a pitch. Once you plant, the key is to swing aggressively through the ball. You should feel a whiplike sensation as you transition to your downswing, which will create more leverage—and speed—at impact.
—**Ron Gring**

Exaggerate your weight shift going back...

...then shift aggressively forward before you end your backswing to max out your downswing sequence and speed.

SLIDE IT DOWN
The key to consistency is to swing the clubhead and the shaft down on the same plane.

DRILL

The No. 1 Way to Stay on Plane

Use the image of a door to hit purer shots

PUSH DOWNSWING
Club on plane — Hands off plane

PULL DOWNSWING
Club off plane — Hands on plane

PERFECT DOWNSWING
Club on plane — Hands on plane

DRILL

The No. 1 Way to Get It Square

Learn to use your left hand and arm to control the clubface

THE PROBLEM

You're swinging either under the desired plane (see hooks and pushes) or above it (see by slices and pulls). You need to swing on the proper downswing plane if you want to hit straight shots and make consistently solid contact.

THE SOLUTION

The ultimate fix to your plane issues is to construct a training aid like I have (pictured above), but if you can't, a pair of golf shafts or alignment sticks set at a 45-degree angle will do the trick. Your goal is to swing down to the ball with both the shaft and the clubhead on the door the entire way. If the clubhead pops off the door as you near impact, you'll know you're coming over the top. If your hands and shaft come off the door but the clubhead stays on, you're swinging too far from the inside. Practice keeping the shaft and clubhead on the door and your shots will start flying straight on a consistent basis.
—**Charlie Sorrell**

THE FAULT

You tend to make contact with an open clubface (i.e., your shots fly right).

THE NO. 1 DRILL TO FIX IT

Most golfers who have difficulty squaring the clubface at impact struggle because they try to square

Your left arm and hand are the keys to squaring the face.

DRILL

The No. 1 Way to Fix Your Slice

This easy drill shows you the correct right-arm action to square the clubface

THE PROBLEM

You're a lifelong slicer, mostly because you try to square the face at impact. While it's true that that's what you want, you can't think of it that way. Solid hits result from closing the face through impact—squared contact is simply a moment between the time the face is open and the time it's closed.

THE SOLUTION

I fix slicers by telling them to forget about contact and do whatever it takes to make sure the clubface is closed after impact. This means that you're properly releasing the club, which is the only way to ensure you'll catch the ball square. The trick to releasing is in your right arm—it needs to rotate as you power through the hitting zone (think of your right palm pointing away from you in your downswing, and then facing the ground after you make your strike). But even this isn't enough. The move that pulls it all together is to straighten your right arm as you rotate it. **Straightening and rotating your right arm is a guaranteed slice buster.** To get a feel for these moves—and automatically release the club and get the face to close after impact—try the following drill.

If you can get the clubface closed after impact, chances are good it'll be square at impact.

the face either by rotating their hands just before impact, or by moving their shoulders to the left. Good golfers control the clubface with the left hand and forearm together, and they begin squaring up sooner rather than later in the downswing. The following drill will help you copy their action.

STEP 1: Swing to the top and stop.

STEP 2: Take your right hand off the grip, then slowly bring the club down with your left arm only. Don't move your shoulders or your right arm.

STEP 3: As you bring the club slowly back to the ball, use

your left hand and forearm to rotate the clubface to a square position (with the clubface pointing at the target) before impact—it should be dead square as the clubhead reaches the impact zone.

WHY THIS WORKS:

Using only your left arm and leaving your shoulders and right arm behind lets you feel the left-forearm rotation needed to square the clubface. When you re-create the same feeling when you swing for real on the course, you should notice a completely new sensation at impact. The more slowly you do the drill, the more you'll benefit.
—Shawn Humphries

Swing back...

...then roll and straighten.

STEP 1: With your right arm only, make a full backswing, then swing down to a spot at which the right forearm is level with the ground and stop. Look back at your hand and the club—you should see that your right arm is bent, your wrist is still hinged and the clubface is open in relation to your target.

STEP 2: Swing down past impact and stop before your hand reaches waist height. As you do this, focus on both straightening and rotating your right arm. If you've done it correctly, your right palm will face the ground and the clubface will look closed.
—Keith Lyford

The No. 1 Way to Upgrade Your Sand Attack

"Hit the wall" for a better bunker swing

THE FAULT
You struggle with greenside bunker shots because you either hit up on the ball and blade it across the green, or you chop down too steeply and get your clubhead stuck in the sand.

THE NO. 1 DRILL TO FIX IT
You need to correct your angle of descent so that it's neither too steep nor too shallow. Use this simple drill.

STEP 1: In a practice bunker, set two shafts or aiming rods (available at most golf shops and D.I.Y. stores) in the sand about two feet apart and parallel left of your target line (*bottom left*). Take your address while using the shafts or rods to simulate setting up with your back against a wall.

STEP 2: Make a few practice swings with the goal of getting the palm of your right hand—as well as the shaft of your club—to touch the "wall" formed by the two shafts (*bottom right*). Your palm should touch at about hip height.

STEP 3: Make the same swing, but this time hit the shot for real. You should soon notice a much crisper contact with the sand, with the ball easily flying out of the bunker. Keep practicing until you get the hang of it.

WHY THIS WORKS
Getting your right palm to touch the wall gives your bunker swing the perfect blend of steepness (so you can swing under the ball) and shallowness (so you can motor all the way through the sand). It's that simple.
—Chuck Winstead

The best bunker swings are neither too steep nor too shallow.

Set up with a "wall" to your left...

...then hit the wall with your right palm.

The No. 1 Way to Gain Expert Putt Control

Here's the pro way to practice your stroke—and never three-putt again

THE FAULT
You don't know how long a stroke to make—or how much force to put into it—on long putts. As a result, you typically leave your first putt too far from the hole for a realistic shot at making your second. This failure to knock it close from long range is the most typical cause of three-putting.

THE NO. 1 DRILL TO FIX IT
On the practice green, set up about 50 feet from a hole. Lay a 5-iron on the ground and point it parallel to the line you want the ball to start on. Set the ball in the middle of the shaft. Then simply roll putts to the hole, with your goal not to make it but to hit it "hole high." As you do this, use the 5-iron as a guide.

It's essential that your stroke be the same length on both sides of the ball— to one end of the 5-iron on your backstroke, and to the other end on your through-stroke. Over the

Getting good at long putts will make shorter ones seem easy by comparison.

The truest measure of your aim comes from your shoulders, which should be parallel to your starting line.

years I've found that a 5-iron provides the perfect stroke length for a 50-foot putt, and that practicing long putts teaches you how to control distance better than practicing short ones does. If you're consistent from 50 feet, 15- to 30-foot putts will seem easy by comparison.

If your putts come up short or roll too far, your tempo is off. Don't change your length (keep matching your 5-iron), but instead make your stroke faster or slower. When you start nailing this distance, your tendency to three-putt will disappear.
—**Keith Lyford**

Swing back to the end of your 5-iron...

...and then through to the other end for a perfect lag.

The No. 1 Way to Aim Like a Pro

LET YOUR SHOULDERS POINT THE WAY

Most people check their alignment by laying clubs on the ground, usually off their toes. But all this does is show you where your feet are pointing. The truest measure of your aim is your shoulders, because the arms and hands are connected to them and it's the arms that swing the club. **As you set up, make sure your knees, hips and shoulders are all lined up square, or parallel, to your start line.** To check this on the range or the course, lay the club on the ground and set up to your starting line. Without moving your shoulders, pick the club up and hold it with both arms hanging straight down. The club should mirror the position of your shoulders, parallel to the starting line.

Get ready for your "major" by practicing your short game—a lot!

DRILL

How to Train for a Competitive Round

Prep like a pro for your lowest scores ever

It's summertime, and while the best players in the world are preparing for the British Open and the PGA Championship, you're getting ready to tackle your own "major." Whether that happens to be your club championship or a buddy-trip match, you'll want to bring your "A" game and take home the hardware—or at least bragging rights for the following year. Here's how to get your game "championship" ready.

FOCUS ON THE SHORT GAME

You're not going to change your swing in the weeks leading up to the big event: There's just not enough time to make a substantial difference. Besides, the critical scoring shots—the ones that make the difference between winning and losing—are those inside 60 yards. Spend at least 75 percent of your practice time putting, chipping and pitching. Work on the par-saving shots, like the high flop shot from just off the green, the mid-range bunker shot, or the 30-yard pitch-and-run. Chip from various lies (ball down in the grass, up against a collar of rough, etc.) and distances, so there are no surprises out on the course. On the greens, roll some 10-foot putts with your eyes closed to improve your feel, and practice your lag putting: If you can avoid costly three-putts, you'll be tough to beat.

INCREASE YOUR COMFORT LEVELS

To play championship-caliber golf, you have to be comfortable with shooting lower scores. If you have trouble stringing a few birdies together in your normal Saturday foursome, it stands to reason that you won't be able to do it when the pressure is ratcheted up in your tournament. In the weeks leading up to your major, play a few rounds from the forward tees and try to birdie every hole. Don't hold anything back: Go for the par 5s in two and seek the pins on the par 3s. Going low requires an aggressive, confident attitude, which you can only get from having done it before. Also make sure to play a couple of rounds from the toughest conditions (i.e., the tips), so that whatever you encounter in the tournament will seem easy by comparison.

Train yourself to go low by playing a few rounds from the forward tees.

HOLD A STRATEGY SESSION

Book a playing lesson with the club pro to discuss the best strategy for each hole, based on the format and your skill level, preferred shot shape, etc. Make sure to figure a few different scenarios into your preparations—i.e., one shot down with two holes to play, one up with three to play, etc. Your pro can help you decide when to be aggressive and when to play more conservatively, and can also tell you how to best make par or birdie when it's absolutely necessary.

Your club pro can tell you when it's best to play conservatively or aggressively.

6 Ways to "Think" Your Way to a Win

Playing your best isn't just about the swings and strokes you make on the course

Here's some advice I lend my more famous students in the weeks leading up to the game's four majors. Use it to score your best or win the tournament you covet most.

1. Go with what you've got. As you get closer to your event, it's time to accept your game for what it is and play to your strengths. Example: If you tend to slice the ball off the tee or with your irons, stop trying to fix your slice now. Play it by aiming down the left side of the fairway (or green) and fading the ball back.

2. Make meaningful preview strokes on the greens. Every putt you face is critical, so get into the habit of dialing in the right touch with a focused preview (practice) stroke until you can almost see the ball roll at perfect speed to the hole. Once your stroke feels right, step into the putt and repeat your preview stroke.

3. Develop an "I can make this putt" attitude. If you don't feel this way now, flip a mental switch and start turning your attitude around. You don't have to make every putt to win your major. You just have to putt better than your competition does.

4. Stay calm. If you get nervous, start tossing a ball into the air and catching it. Use this to remind yourself about what you can—and can't—control. You're in control of your swings and your strokes (like you are the balls you're tossing into the air). You can't control good and bad bounces, wind, spike marks, and the rest. Nerves are normal and should be embraced.

5. Believe. While belief alone won't make you win, believing in yourself will at least let you play your best and put you in the best position to pull off a victory.

6. Learn from the experience. Once your major is over, reflect on where your game needs improvement. Take a good look at your scoring for the tournament and notice where you lost strokes. Then plan to address your weaknesses during the off-season.
—Dave Pelz

HOW TO LEARN & IMPROVE

You can do it yourself and take years to get better. Or you can seek out a qualified teaching professional and improve faster than you imagined.

CHECKPOINT

How to Get the Most From a Lesson

Six ways to get what you pay for: a better game

CHOOSE YOUR CLASSROOM
Decide whether you need a range lesson or a playing lesson. If you're looking to improve your swing and ballstriking, the range is the best place. But if you want better course management, take a playing lesson.

SET EXPECTATIONS
Before the lesson, tell your instructor what you're looking to improve and how much you'd like to accomplish. Don't expect to drop 10 strokes after one lesson and don't expect 300-yard drives if you're just learning to grip the club.

FIND THE RIGHT PRO
Ask your pals for suggestions—or find one of our Top 100 teachers at golf.com. Call the pros and interview them. Ask them about their teaching style—what you can expect—then pick a teacher who appeals to your needs.

HIT REWIND
Start every practice session with a review of what you've been taught. Start with the basics then go through your last lesson. Don't abandon the teachings if you're not getting perfect results—keep at it and you'll start to see the payoff.

COOL DOWN
Spend another 15 minutes on the range after your lesson. Work on your own to relax and apply what you've just learned from your teacher. You should take notes, and if your pro tapes the lesson, taking home a video is even better.

DON'T RUSH
Whether you're coming from home or the office, don't blaze into the parking lot and quickly throw on your spikes. To get your mind and body in optimal condition, arrive at your lesson 15 minutes early to loosen up.
—Rick McCord

INSTRUCTION

THE NEW WAY TO IMPROVE

While you've been looking for a new way to get better and shoot lower scores, scientists have unearthed something far more important—how we learn to get better. Here are seven new ways to become the golfer you were always meant to be.

1. Elevate Your Goals
The more precise you aim, the higher you'll climb

When it comes to setting goals, make a long-term commitment to achieving them.

THE PROBLEM
You have a strong desire to improve, but you're not really doing anything concrete to get there. Setting a goal of simply "playing better" won't get the job done.

THE SOLUTION
Research shows that if you commit to improving by defining specific and moderately challenging goals, you'll learn a motor skill (like releasing the clubhead) faster. It also suggests that the longer you commit to playing the game, the better you'll perform.

THE SCIENCE THAT PROVES IT
Dr. Gary McPherson, a professor of music education at the University of Illinois School of Music, asked 157 children picking up an instrument for the first time a simple question: "How long do you think you'll play your new instrument?" He sorted the children based on their answers and tracked their performance over several years using a standard musical-skill scale. McPherson discovered that progress in learning the instrument wasn't dependent on aptitude, but by the goal set by the child. With the same amount of practice, the kids who voiced a long-term commitment outperformed those who intended to play only through the school year by 400 percent. Although the benefits of goal-setting haven't extensively been studied in golf, the McPherson data and research with other motor skills suggest that they'll translate very well to what you do with a club in your hands.
—*Golf Magazine* learning consultant Dr. Robert Christina

2. Take a Lesson

Learn from a pro to play like a pro

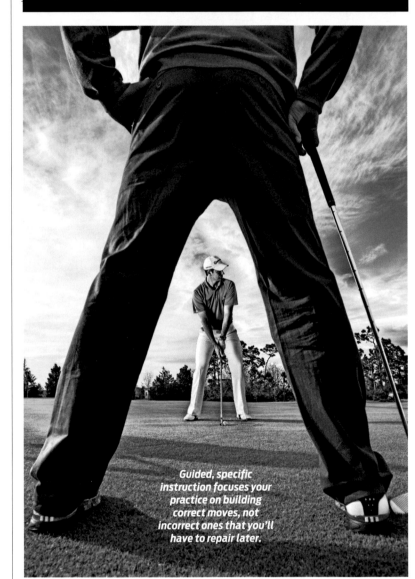

Guided, specific instruction focuses your practice on building correct moves, not incorrect ones that you'll have to repair later.

COLD HARD FACT

Wondering why the average amateur handicap hasn't dropped in the past 50 years? Here's why...

Q: Have you taken a lesson in the past 12 months?

No: 88%

Yes: 12%

Source: GOLF Magazine reader survey

THE PROBLEM

Since you know your swing better than anyone, you choose to navigate your own path to enlightenment. You never take lessons and think all you need is some extra range time.

THE SOLUTION

Book time with a pro—it's that simple. Whatever your skill level, it's highly unlikely that you can recognize swing or putting-stroke flaws, let alone prescribe an appropriate fix. Taking lessons from an experienced teacher or mentor helps you learn motor skills the right way, and learn them more effectively. An instructor won't allow you to perform or ingrain errors when you practice—he or she is interested only in getting you to do the right things, and getting you to do them over and over.

THE SCIENCE THAT PROVES IT

Golf Magazine looked at the handicap changes of 318 amateur players. These were no ordinary golfers—each had studied with our Top 100 Teachers in America between September 2007 and September 2008. The numbers on the opposite page illustrate their startling progress—these students lowered their indexes by an average of 35 percent! The golfers who are improving are the ones who are taking lessons.
—Dr. Robert Christina

GO OUT AND LEARN!

Not enough golfers are taking lessons, and there's a reason for it: lame excuses. Consider our rebuttal to the five most common cop-outs.

1. I DON'T HAVE THE CASH

Play one less round a month, and apply that money toward a lesson with a qualified PGA teaching pro. You can make up for the missed on-course experience by playing an imaginary round on the range, or bring your favorite foursome and make it a group learning session.

2. I DON'T HAVE THE TIME

See the answer to No.1, or simply make time. Get up an hour earlier on your day off—most teachers start their lesson day at 7:00 a.m. This works on weekdays too—you can easily make a 9:00 a.m. meeting.

3. I JUST NEED A TUNE UP

Fine. Your instructor can build a lesson plan, or even a single lesson, to match your schedule, time, goals and wallet.

4. I'M TOO EMBARRASSED

That's like saying your teeth are too rotten to go see a dentist. Calm your fears: Your teaching pro—and dentist—have seen worse than you. Plus, they need your business as much as you need theirs.

5. MY HOME LIFE IS TOO BUSY

C'mon! Make your lesson a family event. You should be introducing your kids to the game anyway. Have your spouse take the kids over to the practice putting green during your lesson, then swap if he or she needs lessons, too. Your kids will get a kick out of rolling the ball into the cup, and there isn't a course in the world that discourages young golfers.

Visit golf.com to find a Top 100 Teacher near you.

In one year, 318 Top 100 Teacher students lowered their handicap by an average of 4.5 strokes:

12.8
Average established handicap of Top 100 Teacher students on September 1, 2007

8.3
Average established handicap of Top 100 Teacher students on September 1, 2008

35%
Average decrease in Top 100 Teacher students' handicaps over one year

.01%
Average decrease in average handicap in the USGA database, 2007–'08

3. Practice for Transfer
How to stop leaving your best swings on the range

The transfer of learning from the range to the course is enhanced when you practice a drill or skill more like you do when you play.

THE PROBLEM
You hit it beautifully on the range. Then you head to the first tee and reality bites.

THE SOLUTION
When you hit balls at the range, you typically aren't thinking about a specific hole, the conditions, the score you need to stay in the match, the pressure, etc.—but you do when you play. Practicing your technique within the context of where you'll apply it is called "Transfer Practice," and it makes all the difference in the world to your game."

THE SCIENCE THAT PROVES IT
With Top 100 Teacher Eric Alpenfels (*above*), I asked 30 students to perform the "feet-together drill." Half the group performed the drill as though they were on the course, going through pre- and post-shot routines, hitting to targets and grading their shots. The other half simply performed the drill. We measured driver distance and accuracy at the beginning and end of each practice day, and a final time on the tee of a hole. The test subjects who practiced for transfer—those who imagined it was a real shot on the course—hit 33% more drives in the fairway on the course than the practice-only group (*graph, right*).
—Dr. Robert Christina

COLD HARD FACT
Q: Do you make your best swings on the range or on the course?

Both: 9%
On the range: 81%
On the course: 10%

Source: GOLF Magazine reader survey

PRACTICE FOR TRANSFER

1. DIG SOME DIRT
To work on your irons and wedges, find a grass range. The perfect lies you get on a mat are rarely found on the course, and the secret to transfer practice is creating actual conditions of play.

2. WORK THROUGH YOUR BAG
Hitting 25 drivers in a row is skills practice. Hitting driver, then 7-iron, and then wedge is transfer practice—it mimics how you play on the course. Regardless of what part of the swing you're working on, do it with a different club after every swing.

3. STOP PRACTICING AT THE RIGHT TIME
Call it quits when you're no longer able to concentrate on the task at hand. Beyond that point, you're just going through the motions. But you should also stop when you're swinging well or have the skill you're grooving in a good place. The danger in continuing practice is that you'll get sloppy or get lost in misguided experimentation.

PRACTICE LIKE YOU PLAY

Dr. Robert Christina and Eric Alpenfels' data suggests that practicing while creating actual playing conditions—Transfer Practice—improves the ability to transfer practice skills from the range to the course.

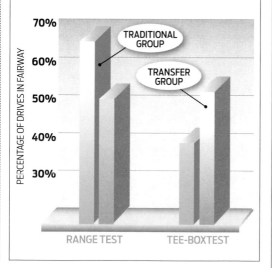

PERCENTAGE OF DRIVES IN FAIRWAY

70%
60%
50%
40%
30%

TRADITIONAL GROUP
TRANSFER GROUP

RANGE TEST TEE-BOX TEST

4. Just Do It. Do It Again.
No one has ever learned a motor skill without practicing it

THE PROBLEM
You marvel at the way Tour pros make the game look so easy, and ask, "Why can't I do that?"

THE SOLUTION
Um, keep practicing. Dr. Anders Ericsson, a renowned professor of psychology at Florida State University, estimates that it takes 10,000 hours of practice to become an expert at any motor skill. Similar studies show that it takes 10 years before you can reach an elite level in any sport.

THE SCIENCE THAT PROVES IT
Carnegie-Mellon researchers Drs. William Chase and Herbert Simon originally devised the 10-years-to-become-elite rule back in 1973. Numerous studies since have supported that theory and Ericsson's 10,000-hour benchmark. In the 1990s, veteran golf writers David Barrett and Al Barkow examined the careers of nine top PGA Tour pros and found that each had won their first major approximately 16 years after picking up a golf club for the first time (an updated study by *Golf Magazine* in 2009 shows that it takes today's pros even longer). Only one golfer has significantly beaten the 16-year time frame required to transition from novice to major winner: Gary Player, who won the 1959 U.S. Open after only seven years of practice and play. The Player phenomenon doesn't necessarily refute the 10,000-hour rule. He likely was engaged in other sports—rugby, cricket—that allowed him to train motor and mental skills that translated easily to golf, or he had uncovered some powerful external swing cue that allowed him to bypass the required motions. That's like finding the magic bullet.
—Dr. Robert Christina

23.6
The number of years the last 11 major winners had played the game before their victory

5. Find a Role Model
Copying is allowed when learning new skills

THE PROBLEM
You're an expert at following orders. You digest information easily, and don't have to be told things twice. This skill has paid off at work, but not in your quest for a better swing and lower scores. Nothing your buddies tell you seems to sink in.

THE SOLUTION
Ditch the verbal instructions and study the moves you're trying to learn in a video or a photo. "Using your eyes can help you learn a lot faster than using your ears or imagination," says Dr. Penny McCullagh, a professor of sport and exercise psychology at California State University–East Bay. "Watching an expert perform the skill you're trying to learn— what performance experts call 'modeling'—allows you to acquire the idea of the movement patterns of the skill in question, giving you a blueprint to guide your motions."

THE SCIENCE THAT PROVES IT
Dr. McCullagh asked 60 female college students to balance on a stabilometer (a platform situated on a fulcrum). A quarter of the test subjects, none of whom had ever tried to balance on the device, listened to instructions that painted a picture of the exercise ("Imagine yourself standing with your feet shoulder-width apart"). Another quarter were shown a silent video of a woman balancing on the device with perfect form. A third group was given both types of instruction, while a final group performed the drill cold. The modeling group significantly outperformed the others (*graph, right*).
—Dr. Robert Christina

35%
percentage increase in skill learning when using a model (i.e., a picture or a video) to guide your movements

MODEL BEHAVIOR

WATCH & LEARN
Dr. Penny McCullagh's research shows that watching an expert perform the skill you're trying to learn is the fastest way to make that skill your own.

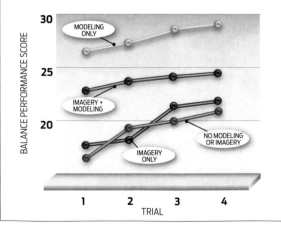

6. Make a Neural Shift
Get better—biologically

THE PROBLEM
You empty bucket after bucket on the range, but the new swing change you're trying to ingrain just won't stick. In fact, you find yourself repeating the fault you're trying to lose over and over.

THE SOLUTION
Work on one change only, or you'll short-circuit your brain. Repeating a movement causes changes in your central nervous system that increase the efficiency of the circuits controlling the muscles involved. One of these changes is myelination, the production of a fatty tissue called myelin around your neural circuits. Each time you use a circuit, this myelin cocoon gets thicker and increases the timing and speed of the signal traveling through the circuit, making it more efficient. Here's the problem: Myelin doesn't recognize a good move from a bad one. This means each lousy swing you make creates myelin and makes that bad move easier to repeat. The key is to practice while someone qualified is watching you, or with drills or training aids that provide you with feedback to ensure that you are performing the skill correctly.
—Dr. Robert Christina

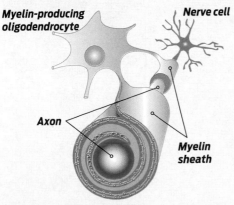

Myelin-producing oligodendrocyte

Nerve cell

Axon

Myelin sheath

Repeating movements—like a golf swing—causes a fatty tissue called myelin to form around the circuits in your brain that guide the motion and make them faster and more efficient.

Lessons work better if they're structured to complement your preferred way of learning

7. Get the Most Out of Your Lessons
Structure your learning time to optimize the way you prefer to process and digest information

THE PROBLEM
You take lessons, but you don't improve.

THE SOLUTION
Check out the cheat sheet on learning the do's and don'ts at right so that your practice sessions alone and with your pro don't go sour.
—Dr. Robert Christina

1 Hitting the same club over and over isn't good transfer practice. Rather, it's the fast track to grooving flaws.

2 Video is a form of feedback (critical to learning) and a way to model your movements. When trying new moves, watch a Tour pro. When fixing flaws, watch yourself.

3 Feedback works best after several swings, so you can engage in the learning process by trying to solve the problem on the non-feedback swings. Feedback after every swing can become a crutch that won't be there when you play.

4 Unsupervised instruction rarely leads to increased motor-skill learning.

5 Practicing like you play—which is the essence of a playing lesson—is the cornerstone of successful transfer practice, something that has been proven to improve skill retention.

6 Adding an element of pressure is another example of practicing within the context of play, a very real benefit.

7 Learning to shape shots or hit different trajectories usually involves imagery and feel, or external cues instead of internal cues.

8 While it's always best to work with an instructor, some studies suggest that learning peaks when you also struggle on your own to discover the solution to your swing problem.

Elite golfers base their swings on the principle that good positions lead to better positions in the segments of the swing that follow. Do likewise and the lasting improvement you're looking for will come more easily and more quickly than you expect.

SECTION 2

UNDERSTANDING YOUR SWING

How to make it simple and repeatable for consistent success

The swing is a complex beast. This statement is no surprise to anyone who has tried to build one. Those that excel at it are the ones who commit to constant practice and study to turn the complexities into simple, repeatable actions. Unfortunately, you can't simply learn a swing and expect it to take your game where you want it to go. You must understand it. Only when you grasp how your setup and every motion affects what happens next in your swing will you truly be able to hit effective shots, stop bad ones when they occur and own the ability to self-correct and improve.

Like most instruction books, this one starts at the beginning with your address. But unlike the rest, the Top 100 Teachers break down every facet of the swing that follows and provide insights and checkpoints you can use to improve every inch of your motion. It's a simple approach because correcting even just a few positions—or learning how to get into them correctly for the first time—automatically improves each and every position that follows.

Follow this guide and you'll quickly become a true student of your swing and learn to recognize breakdowns in your technique. That's when the game you've always wanted will begin to take shape.

5 THINGS YOU'LL LEARN IN THIS SECTION

- *How to stand at address and hold the club correctly so it can swing itself.*
- *How to swing on the proper plane and make powerful contact on the sweet spot.*
- *Myths to avoid and swing secrets that every golfer should know to hit successful shots.*
- *Drills to turn your practice time into quality learning time.*
- *A checkpoint at each moment of the swing to make sure you're doing it correctly.*

Improve your swing at every position with the Top 100 Teachers at **golf.com/contact**

YOUR GAME

CAN YOU REALLY GET BETTER?

YES! More than 90 percent of the Top 100 Teachers reported you can drop your handicap by a third in three months. The exact way to accomplish this, however, varies.

LESSONS PER WEEK

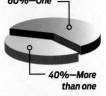

60%—One

40%—More than one

PRACTICE (HRS/WK)
48%—6

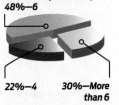

22%—4

30%—More than 6

● Practice six hours a week—four of those hours dedicated to the short game and the other two to tee shots. You'll shoot much lower scores if you can hit the fairway more often and get the ball close from short range. —Dr. David Wright

● Regardless of your practice structure, use the following rule of thumb: 60 repetitions for each new motor skill learned, repeated for 21 days in a row. —Dr. T.J. Tomasi

THE FIRST STEP

A fundamentally solid grip allows you to make a natural motion and stops swing errors in their tracks

IT ALL STARTS HERE
Your hands are your only connection to the club, so you'd better make that connection a good one. As a general rule, hold the club in your fingers, not in your palms.

The New Way to Take Your Grip

This step-by-step plan gives you a perfect hold in five seconds flat

In a recent poll of Top 100 Teachers, 81 percent acknowledged that the grip is one of the first things they work on with new students. I'm not suprised. Most golfers see the grip as simple—grab the handle and squeeze. But there's a lot more to it, and making even the slightest error can have serious ramifications in your swing. (By the way, the 19 percent who said their students' grips don't need work admitted to coaching only pro players. See a pattern?) If you're concerned about your grip, then follow the steps at right. This is the method we teach at the Pinehurst Golf Academy, and it's sequenced to set your hands in the correct positions and avoid the most common grip errors. It's a five-second procedure that will give you the power and control you've been missing.

TOP 100 TEACHERS ON: **AMATEUR GRIPS**

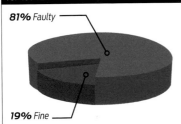

81% *Faulty*

19% *Fine*

"For most amateurs a correct grip feels strange. There'll be a tendency to return to your old 'comfortable' hold, but stick with it and trust that it will pay huge dividends." —**Ed Ibarguen**

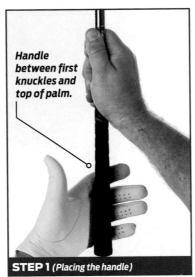

Handle between first knuckles and top of palm.

STEP 1 *(Placing the handle)*

With your right hand, grab the shaft where it meets the grip and hold the club out in front of you at a 45-degree angle. Turn your left palm toward you and then set the grip in the area between your first knuckles and the top of your palm.

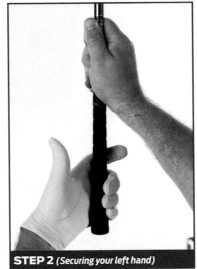

STEP 2 *(Securing your left hand)*

Without changing the position of the grip in your left hand, curl your left-hand pinkie, ring and middle fingers around the handle. If you've done it correctly, it should feel as though every part of the undersides of these fingers is in contact with the grip.

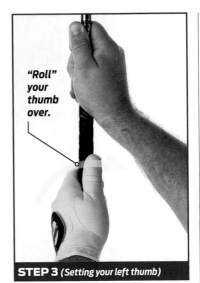

"Roll" your thumb over.

STEP 3 *(Setting your left thumb)*

Again, without changing the grip's position, "roll" your left thumb over to the right side of the handle while curling your left index finger around the grip. Make sure that the fatty portion at the base of your thumb is pressing directly down on the handle.

STEP 4 *(Positioning your right hand)*

Slide your right hand toward your left and, just as you did with your left hand, allow the shaft to sit between your first knuckles and the base of your palm.

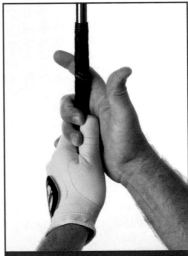

STEP 5 *(Securing your right hand)*

Wrap your right pinkie into the fold between your left middle and index fingers (or interlock them—see page 85) and your right ring and middle fingers around the handle. Your connection here is critical—add pressure to the handle with these last two fingers.

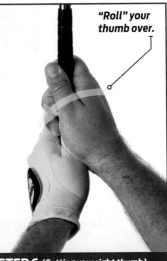

"Roll" your thumb over.

STEP 6 *(Setting your right thumb)*

Place the lifeline on your right palm directly over your left thumb by "rolling" your right thumb to the left while curling your right index finger around the handle. You should feel pressure from the fatty pad at the base of your right thumb on your left thumb.

CHECKPOINT

Strong, Neutral or Weak?

Face it—you're not sure. This new test gives you the definitive answer.

FACT

The faster you turn your hips on your downswing, the more your hands will be ahead of the clubhead as you swing into impact, which has a tendency to open the clubface.

WHAT IT MEANS TO YOUR GRIP

The more your clubface tends to turn open as a result of hip speed, the stronger you need to make your grip so that you can get the clubface back to square at impact. Players with slower hips don't have to worry about the face turning open because slower hips fail to produce this dynamic hand/clubhead action.

CHECK YOUR ACCURACY

Set up with the leading edge of your 7-iron pressed against the side of a chair (or desk, etc.). From this position, turn your body into a mock impact position—the one you want to be in when you strike the ball. If the clubface rotates open, you need to strengthen your grip and try it again. Keep strengthening your hold (turn your hands to the right) until you can rotate into your mock impact position with the face remaining square.

HOW TO MATCH GRIP STRENGTH TO YOUR SWING

Without a club, stand at address, make a mock backswing with your right arm only, then swing back to impact and stop. Feel like you're giving an imaginary ball teed up to your waist a solid slap with your right hand. Now check your belt buckle.

YOU HAVE SLOW HIPS...

...if your belt buckle points only slightly ahead of the ball and your right foot is still planted on the ground. The chances of your hands leading the clubhead are nil, as is the likelihood of the clubface rotating open.

USE A WEAK GRIP

Left hand rotated more to the left on the handle with the Vs formed by the thumb and forefinger pointing toward the left side of your chest.

WEAK GRIP

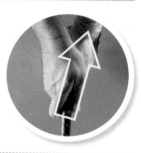

YOU HAVE MID-SPEED HIPS...

...if your belt buckle points slightly in front of your left foot and your right heel is off the ground. You tend to get your hands a little ahead of the clubhead on your downswing with the face rotating open slightly, especially with longer clubs.

USE A NEUTRAL GRIP

Minimal hand rotation, with the Vs formed by the thumb and forefinger pointing straight up or slightly right of your chin.

NEUTRAL GRIP

YOU HAVE FAST HIPS...

...if your belt buckle points at the target and you're all the way up on your left toe. You need max control of the club to offset the fact that your hip speed causes the clubhead to lag behind your hands and open the clubface.

USE A STRONG GRIP

Left hand rotated more to the right on the handle, with the Vs formed by the thumb and forefinger pointing toward your right shoulder.

STRONG GRIP

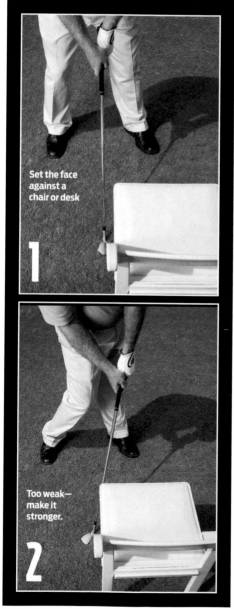

Set the face against a chair or desk

1

Too weak—make it stronger.

2

Pressure Pointers

The secret to securing your hold is applying force where you need it the most

THE PROBLEM
You feel good about your grip, but you don't know how hard to squeeze the handle.

THE SOLUTION
This one's tricky. Ask a dozen teachers how tightly, on a scale of 1 to 10, you should squeeze the handle on your clubs and six will say "8" and the other six will respond with "3." That's because grip pressure is relative to hand strength. Most Tour professionals admit to using a light grip pressure (the "3"), which they can get away with because of the tremendous strength they've built up in their hands and wrists over the years (if you've ever shaken a PGA Tour player's hand, you know what I mean). Most amateurs' hands aren't that strong, which explains the "8" recommendation.

MY BEST ADVICE
The secret to nailing your grip pressure is to squeeze the handle as hard as you can without affecting your wrist movement. Think "firm hands, soft wrists," which will enable you to control the face yet release the club fully. Try that, along with these other grip-pressure recommendations.

Pressure Point No. 1
Wrap your left ring and middle fingers tightly around the grip, pinching the handle into the crease at the top of your palm. Do it correctly and you should be able to hold the club out in front of you using just these two fingers.

Pressure Point No. 2
With downward pressure, the lifeline on your right palm should fit snugly over your left thumb. If there's space between them, you'll suffer.

Pressure Point No. 3
Whether you use an overlapping or an interlocking grip, make sure that your right pinkie is applying downward pressure on your left hand, rather than simply resting on top of it. Just that little bit of pressure unifies your hands.

Pressure Point No. 4
Notice how in a good grip your right palm faces the side of the grip. Apply pressure in this direction to activate your wrist hinge before you swing back.

Pressure Point No. 5
If you see any voids between the thumb and forefinger on either hand, pinch those digits together. Pressure there ensures a more connected grip and greater control.

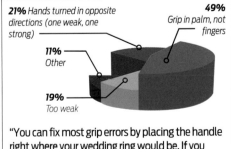

TOP 100 TEACHERS ON: THE WORST GRIP FLAW

21% Hands turned in opposite directions (one weak, one strong)

49% Grip in palm, not fingers

11% Other

19% Too weak

"You can fix most grip errors by placing the handle right where your wedding ring would be. If you can't remember that, you've got real troubles."
—**Top 100 Teacher Jason Carbone**

You're Playing The Wrong Size Grips!

After analyzing 1,440 swings, we discovered that 9 out of 10 golfers play the wrong-sized grips, and that finding a perfect match can make you longer and more accurate—without having to change your swing.

"Relying on standard grip-fitting procedures—or even your personal preferences—will inhibit your ability to hit your best shots."
—Eric Alpenfels

THE CONVENTIONAL WISDOM
Unless your hands are unusually big or small, you can get away with playing standard-size grips. You can also use a static fitting chart like the one below to match grip size to your hand size.

OUR NEW THEORY
Finding the correct grip size has little to do with the size of your hands, or even personal preference. It has everything to do with the dynamics of your swing.

HOW WE TESTED IT
Twenty-four golfers (ranging in handicap from +1 to 7) hit their own 5-iron and five identical 5-irons (Titleist AP2s with Dynamic Gold S shafts), each with a different-sized Golf Pride grip (undersized, standard, slightly larger standard, midsized and jumbo). All markings were covered to prevent any previous size bias. While blindfolded, each golfer was asked to choose the grip they preferred simply by holding each club in their hands. They were then measured for grip size using a fitting chart similar to the one below.

After sufficiently warming up with their own 5-iron, each golfer hit two practice shots out to a target on the range, then hit 10 additional shots that were measured on a Trackman launch monitor. This was repeated for each club (assigned in random order), concluding with their own 5-iron, which served as a control club. The test results [*opposite page*] were very surprising.

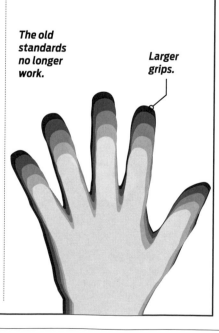

The old standards no longer work.

Larger grips.

HOW MUCH SQUEEZE DO I NEED?

Q: Is the old adage true that you should squeeze the handle like you're holding a little bird? That's a tough one—not many have ever held a little bird.

● I recommend that you grip the club as though you were gluing your hands to it. You want complete contact. Every bit of the insides of your fingers should be touching the handle. No gaps, no air pockets and no spaces.
—Bob Toski

● Hold your club over your right shoulder and pretend to throw it end over end without letting go of the club. The feeling you have when holding your club and going through the throwing motion is a good fit for your grip and grip pressure.
—Craig Harmon

The Shocking Results!

After tallying the results of the pre-hit tests and the data collected by the launch monitor, we know three things for certain:

1

Hand Measurements Don't Work

● 16 of the 24 blindfolded golfers (67%) preferred a grip size that was different than their measured grip size in the pre-test.

● After hitting shots, 22 of the 24 players (92%) preferred a grip size that was different than their measured grip size.

CONCLUSION:
Determining grip size through static fitting procedures isn't a very good predictor of the grip size that golfers prefer.

 ## 2

Neither Does Relying on Your Feel Senses

● 21 of the 24 golfers (88%) had standard-sized grips on their own 5-irons, yet less than half of these players (10 of 21) were measured for standard-sized grips.

● Only slightly more than half (11 of 21) of the test group preferred the standard-size grips on their 5-iron after hitting test shots with the other 5 test clubs.

CONCLUSION
If you're playing off-the-rack clubs with standard-sized grips, there's only a 50% chance that these grips match what you'd be measured for in a static fitting, or what you'd actually prefer.

 ## 3

You're Playing the Wrong Grips!

● Only 5 of 24 golfers (21%) hit their best shots with the grip size that matched their measured grip size in terms of left/right accuracy. These weren't always the grip size the golfers preferred, either.

● Only 3 of these golfers (13% total) hit the best shots with the grip size that matched their measured grip size in terms of distance control.

● Only 1 golfer (4%) hit the ball straighter and with greater distance control with the grip that matched their measured size.

CONCLUSION
You grips are costing you at least 5 strokes per round.

92%
Preferred grip different than measured grip

8%
Preferred grip same as measured grip

21

11

Players with standard grips

Players who preferred standard after testing

96%
Hit best shots with grip other than measured grip

4%
Hit best shots with measured grip

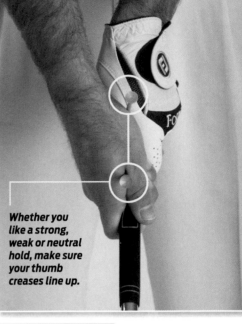

Whether you like a strong, weak or neutral hold, make sure your thumb creases line up.

CHECKPOINT

Do Your Hands Work Together?

A lot of golfers can't hit the ball squarely because their hands work against each other, not with each other. To make sure that doesn't happen to you, take the following test.

● Grip any club and have a friend insert two tees in the creases formed by the base of your thumbs and the back of your hands as shown above. If one tee points to the right of your grip and the other points to the left, you've created opposing forces in your hands and you'll limit their ability to square up your clubface and release the club with authority.

● Your goal is to position your hands on the handle so that the two tees line up [photo, above]. In this position your hands can work as a single unit and deliver your clubhead to the ball with zero wasted energy.

● If you slice, line up the tees over the right side of the grip. This gives you more power to square up the clubface through impact. Line the tees up over the left side of the grip to keep the face from closing too quickly and reel in your hook or hit a purposeful fade.
—Jason Carbone

LOOK, MA—NO WEAR SPOTS! THE RIGHT-SIZE GRIPS WON'T LEAVE A MARK

If you wear down gloves fast, you've got trouble. You shouldn't see much wear and tear at all—even after a few rounds and practice sessions—**because glove breakdown is a result of the grip moving around in your hands,** which you get when your hold is incorrect or your grip is the wrong size.

If you tend to wear down the part of the glove covering the base of your thumb or anywhere in your palm then you're not holding the handle in your fingers. If you're wearing down your glove where you hold the handle in your fingers, it's a sign that your grip is too small. You shouldn't see any black marks or even blisters if you've nailed your grip and grip size.

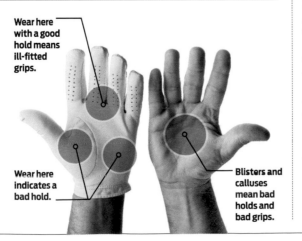

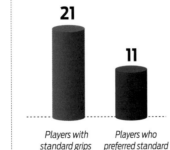

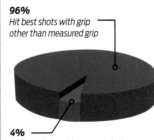

Wear here with a good hold means ill-fitted grips.

Wear here indicates a bad hold.

Blisters and calluses mean bad holds and bad grips.

SETUP BASICS

The majority of your swing errors—and the need to make compensations—are the result of mistakes in your setup. Get it right here and your swing will take care of itself.

How to Step Into Your Shot

Here's a reliable way to get your stance width correct every time

STEP 1
Aim your clubface at your target, then step in with your right foot, pointing it behind the ball. This cue is a reminder that you're starting to position the ball. You might even repeat that objective to yourself ("inside left heel," "center of stance," etc.).

STEP 2
With your right foot in place, step in with your left. Position it relative to where you want to play the ball. The above is a 5-iron, so the ball goes four inches inside your left heel. A driver, played off your left heel, would require a smaller step.

STEP 3
Step out with your right foot, widening your stance until you feel comfortable and stable. With your stance and ball position set, take a quick final look at the target, then return your eyes to the ball and begin your swing.
—**Kip Puterbaugh**

Rock Your Feet to Find Your Balance

A quick way to get more athletic at address

Balanced swings are good swings, and good balance starts at address. Start by standing tall with your arms at your sides, then bend forward and flex your knees, like a linebacker ready to pounce in any direction. Keep your neck in line with your spine, and hinge so that your hips remain over your heels and your arms dangle freely below your shoulders.

After you settle into the above position, **rock gently forward on your toes, then back onto your heels and forward again so that your weight is evenly distributed across each foot.** This simple drill places you in perfect balance and in position to make a controlled swing.
—**David Glenz**

How to Fix a Faulty Setup

A magazine is all you need

THE PROBLEM
It happens every time you address the ball: You're not sure how far apart your feet should be, where to position your hands, or where to play the ball in your stance. As a result, your swing and your shots are inconsistent to the point where you have no idea where the ball is going from one round to the next.

THE SOLUTION
Lay a magazine on the ground with both covers face up and follow the checkpoints below.

3 *Eyes over the top edge of the magazine.*

4 *Hands over the bottom edge of the magazine.*

1 *Align the insteps on both feet with the magazine's edges.*

2 *Ball and hands aligned to the magazine's spine.*

1. STANCE WIDTH
Take your address with a mid- or long-iron. Set the instep of your right foot even with the edge of the front cover, and your left instep with the edge of the back cover. This is the perfect stance width for an iron.

2. HAND/BALL POSITION
Position the ball even with the magazine's spine and set your hands directly above the spine. You should see a slight lean in the shaft toward the target. Perfect. Also, make sure that your hands are over the bottom edge of the magazine. You don't want them extended too far away from your body, or too close to it.

3. POSTURE
Bend from your hips, keeping your back nice and flat until your eyes are over the top edge of the magazine. This will help you settle into the correct posture for an iron. You don't want your head too far out in front of your toes, nor do you want to address the ball while standing straight up and down.
—**Carol Preisinger**

Nail Your Stance Width

Take a walk to fine-tune your address position

THE PROBLEM

You might take it for granted, but the wrong stance width can inhibit your ability to create power and maintain balance. Most amateurs set up with their feet too far apart, a mistake that strands body weight on the back foot during the downswing while also preventing a full shoulder rotation. A stance that's too narrow is just as damaging.

THE SOLUTION

The most surefire way to find your correct stance width is to simply take a relaxed walk. **The length of your stride during a comfortable walk is typically the same as what your stance width should be for a dynamic motion, like making a golf swing.**

Stand where you are, walk a few paces and stop with your right foot ahead of your left. Now pivot to the left a full 90 degrees—this is how you should feel at address. What I'm betting is that your feet are probably pretty close to shoulder-width apart. Whatever stance width your natural gait gives you in this exercise, use it on every swing from here on out. It's the one that best allows you to consistently produce a free-flowing backswing and follow-through.
—**Mark Hackett**

The distance between your feet when you walk at a comfortable pace...

...is the same distance you should set your feet at address when hitting an iron.

How to Take Aim

Use close targets to prevent shots that fly off line

STEP 1

Once you've decided on a target, pick out a divot or another obvious spot on the ground about a foot in front of your ball. The spot should sit on the line that runs from your ball to the target. Now imagine a track that extends out from the entire clubhead, toe to heel, along your line [*inset photo*]. Thinking of it as a lane instead of a line makes it easier to check that you're aimed correctly.

STEP 2

Once you have your aiming lane, hold your club steady and stand with your feet nearly touching. Position your feet so that the leading edge of the club is perpendicular to your toe line. Now your body can accommodate a swing that travels on a plane that correctly matches your line to the target. Widen your stance to address the ball and swing with confidence.
—**Nancy Quarcelino**

Build Confidence at Address

Nail your setup by standing the correct distance from the ball

THE FAULT

Your swing is pretty solid, so you're often at a loss to explain your inability to play consistently and score like you should. The problem might very well be your setup, which for most players is inconsistent and often incorrect. If you learn to nail your address, your shots—and overall game—will be much more predictable.

THE FIX

Consistency in your swing starts with a consistent setup. Instead of simply going by feel, follow these simple steps to make sure you have the right amount of forward bend and to ensure you're the correct distance from the ball—two of the most damaging amateur setup errors.

STEP 1: Assume your setup position.

STEP 2: Check where the butt of the golf club is pointing—it should be aimed at the center of your zipper. If it's pointing at your stomach you're standing up too tall, and if it's pointing at your inseam you're bent over too much.

STEP 3: Now hold your position but take your right hand off the club and open it wide. Use your open hand to measure the distance from the butt of the club to your legs. Get this distance correct every time and you'll know you're set up correctly.
—**Jim Murphy**

Your Right Foot First

Another way to make sure you're aimed at your target

STEP 1: As you approach the ball, set the middle of your right foot perpendicular to your target line and even with the back edge of the ball with no knee flex. Set your left-hand grip.

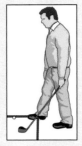

STEP 2: Place your club on the ground behind the ball without trying to aim the clubface. The shaft should line up with your left forearm. The clubface will look open, but don't change it.

STEP 3: Add your right hand to the club and bring your left foot even with your right. Notice that your hips and shoulders are parallel to each other. Swivel your head, fix your eyes on your target and spread your feet into your regular stance width. When you look back down at the ball, your clubface will still look open. Again, don't change it—that's the adjustment you need to combat what's called "hidden offset," which occurs when the toe of your iron sits up at address. Trust it, and you'll enjoy more accurate shotmaking.
—**Dr. David Wright**

You're set up correctly when the shaft points at your zipper and you can fit your open hand between the butt of the club and your legs.

Pick the Right Ball Position

The trick? Know where your nose is.

Each club in your bag features a unique length and lie angle (the angle the shaft creates when the clubhead is soled on the ground). Because of this, you must vary where you play the ball in your stance to accommodate the dimensions of the club in your hands. As a general rule, the longer the club, the more forward you should position the ball in your stance, but the ball should never be left of your left shoulder or right of your nose, regardless of which club you're using for full swings. This photo shows an easy way to remember exactly where to position the ball for every shot.

"You stand taller with a 3-iron than with a 7-iron, so it will bottom out later in your swing—that's why you play the ball forward in your stance with longer clubs."
—Michael Breed

Putter

PW-7

3-6 iron

Hybrid/Fairway wood

Driver

Use Your Body to Position the Ball

Line up the ball correctly in your stance with this anatomical guide

DRIVER
Position the ball even with the outside of your left shoulder.

HYBRID/WOODS
Position the ball even with the center of your left armpit.

3- THROUGH 6-IRON
Position the ball even with your left ear for long and mid-irons.

SHORT IRONS
Play the ball off your left cheek for short irons and wedges.

PUTTER
Play the ball even with your nose to sink more putts.

Once you have your ball position set, make two final checks at address: your weight distribution and your shaft position.

CHECK 1
For standard full swings with every club, make sure your weight is evenly spread over both of your feet. This provides you with a stable platform to help you maintain balance throughout your motion.

CHECK 2
If you have difficulty making clean contact consistently, press the shaft slightly forward by moving your hands toward the target (be careful not to move the clubhead as well). This gives you the best chance for ball-first contact and solid strikes.
—**Michael Breed**

The ball position in both photos is exactly the same, but my incorrect weight distribution in each photo changes the position of the ball in relation to my head. For the short iron I'm using here the ball should be positioned off my left cheek. This underlines the need for even weight distribution.

WRONG! **WRONG!**

WHEN IS IT TIME FOR A NEW BALL?

The modern ball is pretty durable and will hold its properties for a long time. A top-tier ball will last for about three rounds and a lower quality ball will last slightly less. Even if you hit down on the ball hard and hit a lot of bunkers and cart paths, the only damage you'll really see will be a duller finish. When the finish wears, your ball flight will be affected and replacing it wouldn't be a bad idea. However, most modern urethane covers make this a slow process and most golfers will lose the ball long before serious wear occurs.

● If you're not hitting many greens in regulation, switch to a ball that's a bit softer to help you more around the greens.
—**Steve Bosdosh**

How High Should You Tee the Ball?

Our exclusive test provides the rock-solid answer

THE EXPERIMENT

Twenty-seven golfers, aged 25 to 71 with handicaps ranging from scratch to 29, were divided into three groups of nine by handicap level: 0-9, 10-19, and 20 and above. Each golfer hit 10 drives at each tee height (low: top edge of the ball even with top of clubhead; medium: equator of the ball even with the top of the clubhead; and high: bottom of the ball even with the top of the clubhead). Each group hit from the three tee heights in varying order to ensure that fatigue and motivation were balanced. Only the best five out of each player's 10 drives at each tee height were recorded so that mis-hits would not skew the data. Participants used their own drivers, with clubheads ranging from 410 cc to 460 cc.

THE ANALYSIS

Carry distance and other data were measured by a launch monitor. Accuracy also was recorded: drives that landed in the fairway were scored higher than those that landed in the rough or beyond the rough.

THE RESULTS

Carry distance for mid and high tee heights was significantly longer than the low tee height, largely an effect of the higher tees promoting higher launch angles and less spin. The high tee height provided the most distance, giving players an average of 12 yards more carry per drive than the low tee height.
—Eric Alpenfels

HANDICAP	Low tee	Mid tee	High tee
Low (0-9)			
Carry distance (yards)	211.64	219.62	222.92
Launch angle (degrees)	10.5	13.04	13.17
Ball spin (rpm)	4,051	3,875	3,434
Clubhead speed (mph)	98.32	97.08	97.36
Ball speed (mph)	138.59	138.13	138.95

AVERAGE CARRY: 218.06 yards

HANDICAP	Low tee	Mid tee	High tee
Mid (10-19)			
Carry distance (yards)	171.46	177.84	179.84
Launch angle (degrees)	12.4	14.4	14.04
Ball spin (rpm)	3,844	3,794	3,529
Clubhead speed (mph)	86.04	85.76	85.24
Ball speed (mph)	120.9	120.93	120.93

AVERAGE CARRY: 176.38 yards

HANDICAP	Low tee	Mid tee	High tee
High (20 and up)			
Carry distance (yards)	160.85	174.15	178.24
Launch angle (degrees)	11.23	13.7	14.75
Ball spin (rpm)	3,834	3,801	3,591
Clubhead speed (mph)	85.39	85.87	85.01
Ball speed (mph)	120.15	120.92	120.39

AVERAGE CARRY: 171.08 yards

The perfect tee height—bottom of the ball at top of clubface. Tee your ball slightly above the crown.

HOW TO TEE UP FOR A...

SCORING IRON

For a 6-iron through wedge, bury the tee in the ground so you can see only its head.

LONG IRON

For longer irons, leave about 1/4-inch of the tee above the ground.

HYBRID CLUB

For hybrids and fairway woods, leave 1/2-inch of the tee above the ground.

CHECKPOINT

The Moment of Impact

What happens when you do it right

Catching the ball on the beginning of the upswing produces a higher launch angle and less spin, leading to greater distance.

At impact, the ball compresses because of the force transferred to it from the clubhead. The ball actually sticks to the clubface, sliding and rolling on it for about .0004 seconds.

After impact, the ball leaves the clubface with whatever launch angle, speed and spin your swing has imparted to it. About 1 to 2 percent of deformation in the ball remains, causing tiny vibrations inside.

Once clear of the clubface, the vibrations are dampened out, and the ball is on its way.

Striking the ball above the center of the face—the new "sweet spot"— promotes a higher launch angle and less spin. These conditions result in a longer, more efficient ball flight that more than makes up for the clubhead rotation (and loss of ball speed) caused by hitting the ball above dead center.

WRONG! *Only half the ball is above the crown.*

Results from the mid tee height came in second to the high tee height.

WRONG! *The entire ball is below the crown.*

All three handicap groups lost distance on the low tee.

QUICK TIPS TO
IMPROVE YOUR ADDRESS

THE TOP 100 SAY

KIP PUTERBAUGH
Set up for a level turn

"Take your normal address, and then point your chin toward your right foot. Keep your head in that position and swing back so that your left shoulder turns to your chin. This promotes a stronger move away from the ball and guards against reverse pivoting."

MICHAEL BREED
Kink your right side

"Get your upper body over your right foot at address with your spine tilted slightly away from the target. This places your head behind the golf ball and lowers your right shoulder. You know you're doing it right if the left side of your body forms more of a reverse "k" than a straight line."

SHAWN HUMPHRIES
Keep your chin up

"Posture is an easy thing to overlook on the course. So when you feel your shoulders start to slouch, take your index finger and push your chin back up. That should get you nice and tall again."

SCOTT MUNROE
Relax your attack

"Tensing your jaw tenses up much of your upper body, which will slow you down. Move your jaw forward, open your mouth slightly, and stick your tongue lightly to the roof of your mouth. I personally use a mouthpiece to position my jaw correctly, and when I do I consistently pick up about 5 mph of clubhead speed!"

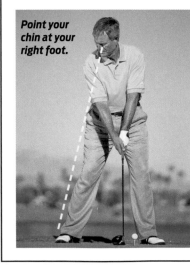

Point your chin at your right foot.

NO!   *YES!*

Push your chin up for better posture.

Letting go of tension in your jaw will allow you to swing faster.

ADDRESS

Your hands start in a box...

TAKEAWAY

...and stay in the box during your takeaway.

Keep Your Hands "In the Box"

It's a key to getting your swing off to a good start

At address, notice how your hands fit nicely into a small rectangle *[above]*. This is your "hands box," and you'll know it's in the right place if you take your stance by bending from your hips so that the shaft is perpendicular to your spine. Make sure that your hands don't leave the box during your takeaway. If they move to the right of the box, you took your club back too far to the inside *[right]*.
—Michael Hebron

WRONG!

MAKING YOUR SWING

A solid address position sets the stage for you to create a powerful impact. Here's what to do in each segment of your swing to make good on that promise.

Get Your Takeaway Right

A good start always leads to a good swing

Get the club in a neutral position every time you make your backswing. The best checkpoint is when the club is parallel to the ground. In the large photo you can see that the clubhead is actually blocking the view of my hands from this down-the-line view. This is ideal. From here you have a much better chance of getting the club into a solid position at the top of your swing, and you'll be much less likely to rely on compensations in your downswing.

The best way to ingrain this neutral position is to simply practice with a friend or your pro watching. Once you know you can get the clubhead in the same spot every time, go ahead and make full swings from this position until it becomes comfortable to you.

—Brady Riggs

NO!

Clubhead picked up too quickly outside the hands.

NO!

Clubhead dragged too far inside the hands.

How to Turn Your Shoulders

Tilt as well as turn and get more yards

WHAT YOU'RE TOLD TO DO
Make a big shoulder turn to increase your swing power. However, testing indicates that turning your shoulders too much results in a flat shoulder plane. Flat shoulder turns don't deliver as much speed to the ball as those that are on plane.

WHAT TO DO INSTEAD
Tilt your shoulders *and* turn them. The right amount of turn and tilt will position your shoulder line on the preferred plane line, helping you apply maximum force and speed to the ball.

HOW TO KNOW YOU'RE TILTING CORRECTLY
Place your driver across the front of your shoulders and turn to the top of your backswing. Check the angle of the shaft after you've fully stretched your upper back muscles against your hips. If you've done it right, the shaft (and your shoulders) will point toward the ground slightly above the ball [*large photo, below*]. Now you're set for power and prepped to deliver all of it to the ball.

—Jon Tattersall

WRONG!

If the shaft looks horizontal, then your shoulder turn is too flat and you'll hit a weak shot.

DRILL

How to Groove a Solid Backswing

Start your swing like a pro with these three drills

A bad backswing is often due to one of three things: a sway away from the target (causing a loss of power), a reverse pivot where you strand weight on your left leg (increasing the chance of a slice) or straightening your right leg (increasing the likelihood of thin contact). Each of these errors makes it nearly impossible to bring your club into the ball on the correct path, giving you little chance for a successful result. Before you spend hours bashing balls on the practice tee or invest your hard-earned money on the latest training aid, try these three drills. A shaft without a head on it can help you determine which problem is affecting your backswing and then show you how to correct it.

—Brian Mogg

RIGHT!

RIGHT!

RIGHT!

FAULT:
Swaying
FIX: Push the shaft into the ground outside your right leg, angled so that it touches your foot and leg up to your knee. Now take your normal backswing. If your right leg pushes the shaft back, you're swaying. Practice until you can turn without moving the shaft.

WRONG!

FAULT:
Reverse pivoting
FIX: Angle the shaft so that the grip touches your inner right thigh as shown. Now take your backswing. If your right leg pushes the shaft forward toward your front leg, you're reverse pivoting. Practice until you can turn without moving the shaft.

WRONG!

FAULT:
Losing right-knee flex
FIX: Position the shaft behind you so that the grip presses against the back of your right knee. If your right leg pushes the shaft upward into the back of your thigh on your backswing, you've lost your flex. The grip should remain behind your right knee.

WRONG!

QUICK TIPS TO
IMPROVE YOUR TAKEAWAY

THE TOP 100 SAY

SCOTT SACKETT
Play the angles

"Practice swinging back to hip height while keeping the logo on your glove pointing out. The toe of your clubhead should tilt slightly toward the target line and the leading edge should match your spine angle. That's square."

BRAD REDDING
Use pad power

"Turn your left hand clockwise on the handle to get the fleshy pad of your hand more on top of the club. This will cup your left wrist and push the club more into your fingers. The resulting grip allows for a better wrist hinge on your backswing and a straighter takeaway."

CARL RABITO
Turn, don't sway

"Take away the club with your right shoulder while keeping your chin and knees still. This will get your body properly behind the ball and eliminate swaying."

BRAD BREWER
Smooth out your takeaway

"Your takeaway should be natural and free-flowing. Practice it by holding the club with only your thumbs and forefingers. This will keep you from whipping your club to the inside or swinging up too steeply."

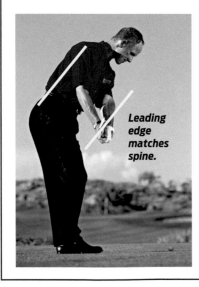

Leading edge matches spine.

Get your pad on top.

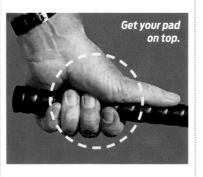

Keep your chin and knees quiet.

A two-finger hold grooves a smooth takeaway.

TAKEAWAY

Keep your head steady...

BACKSWING

...and brace your right hip to accept weight.

Don't Lose Your Balance

Brace your right hip to make a stable turn

As you move from your takeaway into your backswing, your main priority is to stay balanced. This means turning *[above]* instead of swaying *[right]*, indicated by the fact that your head hasn't moved much from address. Also, monitor your right hip position—keep it in place and braced to accept your weight as it moves from left to right. Think of it as the hub around which your body turns.
—**Michael Hebron**

WRONG!

How to Hinge Your Wrists

Do it right and you'll produce power and accuracy

THE PROBLEM
You know you're supposed to hinge your wrists, but you're not sure how to do it.

THE SOLUTION
Use the image of a door hinge to guide each of your wrists in the right direction.

Left wrist hinges up.

Right wrist hinges back.

Your wrists hinge in two directions, either up and down or back and forth. During your takeaway, your left wrist should hinge up, not back. Picture a door hinge on top of your left forearm and thumb with the hinge rod at your wrist to remind you that your left wrist cocks up and down.

Your right wrist does the opposite— it should hinge back on your backswing and forward on your downswing. Imagine a door hinge on top of your wrist and forearm, with the hinge rod in the middle of your wrist. Use that as a guide to direct your right wrist cock both back and through.

Correct hinge keeps your club on plane.

During your backswing, picture hinges on both wrists and cock your left wrist up and your right wrist back. That sets your club on the correct backswing plane. If you hinge your right wrist up, your swing will be too steep; if your cock your left wrist back, your swing will get much too flat.
—**Martin Hall**

Q: Should I think about hinging my wrists on my backswing, or should it happen naturally?

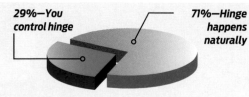

29%—You control hinge

71%—Hinge happens naturally

● Your wrists can and will hinge in response to the momentum of the club, but if you grip the club too tightly, that's not going to happen.
—**Scott Sackett**

The One-Step Power Move

Make an "L" and then move it up to achieve maximum width and power

At the end of your takeaway, rotate your forearms and hinge your wrists to create an L. Then, simply move the L to the top by turning your shoulders. This maintains the width of your swing and increases your power. Check the swing of PGA Tour star Dustin Johnson, who makes this move as well as anyone.
—**Shawn Humphries**

Your left wrist should be flat and your right wrist bent—the perfect anti-slice position.

Make an "L" in your backswing.

Once you make the "L," simply move it to the top.

1

Set the club parallel to the ground and your target line by rotating your forearms and hinging your wrists.

2

Keep turning your shoulders and make sure the back of your left hand matches the angle of the clubface.

3

Lift your arms as you continue to turn—this is what maintains the L.

KEY MOVE

4

You've done it right if the angles of your left hand and clubface still match and you've created separation between your right side and your right elbow.

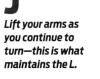

DRILL

How to Sync Up Your Backswing

Try this quick drill to match your arm swing to your turn

TRY THIS!
Take an ordinary car-wash sponge and place it under your right arm at address. Imagine that the sponge is full of water and that any tension placed on it will spill the water all over your shirt. Hold the sponge with this very light tension all the way up to the top of your backswing, and all the way down to just before impact. The real goal of this drill is to teach you the feeling of a wide-to-narrow swing—**as you take the club back you should feel that your swing arc is wide, and when you swing down and squeeze the sponge, it should feel narrow.** This will help you create clubhead lag, which is the real key to power.
—Jason Carbone

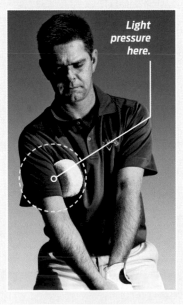

Light pressure here.

INSTRUCTION

Keep Your Tilt to Increase Your Coil

Here's how to power up behind the ball for big-time yards

SPINE-TILT BASICS

In a fundamentally sound setup, your spine should tilt away from the target (to your right) about 5 degrees. This side bend is just as critical as your forward bend from your hips. If you're not bent to the right at address, you're bent left, and that's trouble.

HOW TO TILT FOR POWER

As you swing to the top, increase your side bend by tilting your upper body to the right at least 10 degrees. A good way to think about it is to feel like you're moving the top of your spine farther away from the target than the bottom as you make your backswing turn. If you try to keep your spine constant in this sense—that is, you don't tilt it to the right—you'll end up with a reverse pivot and a possible slice.
—**Martin Hall**

Increasing your side bend to the right on the backswing creates coil and stretch, and guards against a reverse pivot [inset].

WRONG!

Assume the power position: Spine tilted to right.

DRILL

Get Dressed to Get Bent

Tie on a tie to learn how to get behind the ball at the top

1

Put on a shirt and tie, or at least imagine that you have. Now bend forward into your golf stance and bump your hips to the left so that your belt buckle moves to the left of the tie. The idea is to move the bottom of your spine, not the top.

2

Swing to the top and check your tie: It should hang farther away from the target than your belt buckle (if the tie is inside your belt buckle you've made a reverse pivot). As you swing back down, try to keep the base of your spine closer to the target than your tie.
—**Martin Hall**

Use Your Eyes to Build a Better Backswing

Focusing with your left eye is the key to power

THE FAULT

You fail to make a full turn in your backswing, which forces your arms and the club to pop up into the air. The result is a weak, steep swing that produces a glancing impact and drives that slice and lack power. You're afraid to take your dominant (right) eye off the ball, and it's making you a poor driver.

THE FIX

The key is to become accustomed to losing sight of the ball with your right eye and utilizing your left eye to see the ball at the top of your backswing. Once you develop this ability, you'll be able to make a much fuller backswing and swing down to impact on plane.

HOW TO DO IT

1. Put an eye patch over your right eye or simply close that eye. If you do the latter, be sure not to cheat.
2. Hit twenty balls with your driver, keeping your right eye closed on every swing. Make a full turn away from the ball each time, making sure you keep your left eye focused on the ball.
3. After hitting the 20 balls, take the patch off or open your right eye and try to replicate the same swing with a nice full turn. It shouldn't take you very long to feel comfortable using your left eye during your swing.
—Dr. T.J. Tomasi

NO!
Keeping your right eye on the ball restricts your turn.

YES!
Focusing on the ball with your left eye frees up your rotation.

Swivel Your Head for Power

Keeping it still just cheats you of distance

THE PROBLEM

You drive the ball straight, but not very far.

THE SOLUTION

Move your left ear toward the ground during your backswing.

WHY IT WORKS

When you try to keep your head still during your full swing, you restrict your ability to make a full turn. Swiveling your head, on the other hand, allows you to make a bigger shoulder turn, and that's a quick way to hit longer tee shots. Watch Tiger Woods when he swings. As he takes the club back, he moves his chin from left to right so that his left ear is closer to the ground at the top. Jack Nicklaus did the same thing, although he swiveled his head before he began his backswing. The key to this move is to keep it natural—allow your head to be carried along by your body turn.
—Brady Riggs

WRONG!
Keeping your head still blocks your upper body from turning as much as it can.

RIGHT!
Allowing your head to swivel with your body turn actually increases rotation and coil.

QUICK TIPS TO
IMPROVE YOUR BACKSWING

THE TOP 100 SAY

SCOTT MUNROE
Set your right foot back

"Take your normal stance and then pull your right foot back (straight away from the target line). This will help keep your shoulders closed for a longer period of time on your downswing and reduce the degree to which you swing out-to-in."

RON GRING
Turn your "T"

"Notice at address how your shoulders and sternum create a "T." The secret to making a solid turn is turning your spine—and the T—as a single unit. Most golfers simply turn their shoulders, which you can do without turning your spine."

JASON CARBONE
The right path to the top

"Picture and feel how you would throw water from a bucket over your right shoulder. That syncs your arms with your body so you can remain in control of the clubhead."

KEITH LYFORD
Shift right to hit straight

"Set up with your left hip against the backside of a chair. Make a full backswing, being sure to move your left hip away from the back of the chair. This will force you to correcty shift your weight to your right side."

Try swinging with your right foot back.

Set the T at address...

...maintain it as you swing to the top by turning your entire upper body (not just your shoulders).

Use the Chair Drill to learn how to load up on your backswing.

BACKSWING

Keep your elbows level as you take your club up.

TOP

You're solid if your shaft and shoulders line up.

CHECKPOINT

Use Your Elbows to Swing on Plane

They should point down at the end of your backswing

The goal of your backswing is to get your club up and around you. Your turn takes care of the around part and your arms take care of the up. But simply lifting the club skyward won't get the job done [*right*]. To keep your club on plane, **strive for level elbows as you lift your club to the top**. Both elbows should point to the ground when you've completed your backswing. You've done it right if your shoulder angle and shaft angle match up.
—Michael Hebron

WRONG!

INSTRUCTION

Get Square at the Top to Get Square at Impact

Dial in the correct face angle by bowing or flexing your left wrist

Slices, hooks and everything bad in between result from your clubface not squaring up to the ball at impact. This happens because you're not square at the top of your backswing, either. **Good ballstrikers know that if you're square to your path at the top (same clubface and shoulder angles), chances are you'll be square again at the bottom.**

To check if you're doing it right, swing to the top and hold. If you're a slicer, the clubface is probably pointing at the target. Try varying amounts of left and right wrist bend to match the face angle to your swing path. Ultimately strive for a flat left wrist at the top of your swing. This will take care of what's happening at impact.
—Tim Mahoney

SQUARE
With very few exceptions, solid ballstrikers have a flat left wrist position at the top.

OPEN
Adding left wrist cup opens the face and requires perfect timing to get square at impact.

CLOSED
An overly bowed left wrist (or an excessively bent right) closes the face—fore, left!

TOUR TIP

How to Stay on Plane

Turn your shoulders, not your arms

FAULT: You overswing.
FIX: Stop your backswing when your shoulders are no longer able to turn. That's it—end of backswing. The killer mistake is continuing to swing your arms back once your rotation stops. It may feel more powerful, but all you're doing is adding another moving part to your swing and motioning the club off plane. If you want to make a bigger backswing, make a bigger turn, and if you want to make a bigger turn, start stretching. But even if you choose to do that, there's still more potential power in a shorter, tighter backswing than there is in a long and loose one.
—PGA Tour player Nick Watney

NO!
Swinging your arms past the point when your shoulders stop turning robs you of power and creates the need for compensations.

YES!
Make your backswing as big as your rotation can handle. Once your shoulders stop turning, stop your backswing.

Pause for the amount of time it would take water to flow from the head to the grip before starting back down.

INSTRUCTION

Pause at the Top for a Smoother Downswing

Patience leads to power

At address, imagine that your shaft is half-filled with water. Before you begin your swing, all of the water is in the bottom half of the shaft, but as you swing to the top gravity pulls the water toward the grip. Instead of racing back down to the ball, allow the liquid to completely fill up the grip end of your shaft before you begin your downswing. **Just that little pause will keep you from lunging or lurching at the ball and make for an overall smoother motion.** Moreover, it will stop your hands from starting your downward motion and allow your lower body to lead and keep the correct downswing sequence—hips, shoulders, hands and clubhead—intact.
—**Steve Bosdosh**

TOUR TIP

How to Build "Lag Power"

Transition by dropping

TRY THIS!
Drop your arms immediately from the top without doing anything else. **This has been a solid key for me ever since I first picked up a club.** Two things to keep in mind: 1) It's not just your arms that drop, but your arms, hand and clubshaft; and 2) Everything must drop straight down. You can get away with dropping your arms and shaft a little behind you, but never in front of you. Although your weight is shifting forward and your hips are turning while you're doing this, it's nonetheless a singular move to focus on and practice on its own.
—**PGA Tour player Ernie Els**

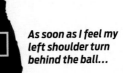

As soon as I feel my left shoulder turn behind the ball...

...I drop my arms and the shaft straight down.

QUICK TIPS TO
IMPROVE YOUR TOP POSITION

THE TOP 100 SAY

DR. GARY WIREN
Swing to your right shoulder

"Try to turn back as far as your flexibility allows, feeling resistance in your left side. If you do this correctly, then all you need to do is get your hands over your right shoulder and the club will be on plane."

MIKE DAVIS
Don't collapse at the top

"Swinging your club past parallel doesn't mean extra power—it just means you're overswinging, usually because you collapse your wrists and left elbow at the top. To fix this, firm up your grip and try to keep your left arm straight. This doesn't shorten your swing—it strengthens it."

STEVE ATHERTON, GOLFTEC
Match your swing to your grip

"If you have a strong grip, you need your left wrist to be somewhat cupped (bent backward) at the top of your swing if you want to have a square clubface at impact. If you have a weak left-hand grip, you need your left wrist to be slightly bowed (bent forward) at the top of your swing. Otherwise, you're asking for trouble."

TOM STICKNEY
Do the bump

"Once you're set at the top, find something to jump-start your move back down. Try 'bumping' your left hip to the right of your target. It's an excellent way to trigger your hip turn as well as keep you from coming over the top."

Hands to right shoulder.

Folding your left elbow is a no-no.

STRONG GRIP
Match it up with a slightly cupped left wrist at the top.

WEAK GRIP
Match it up with a slightly bowed left wrist at the top.

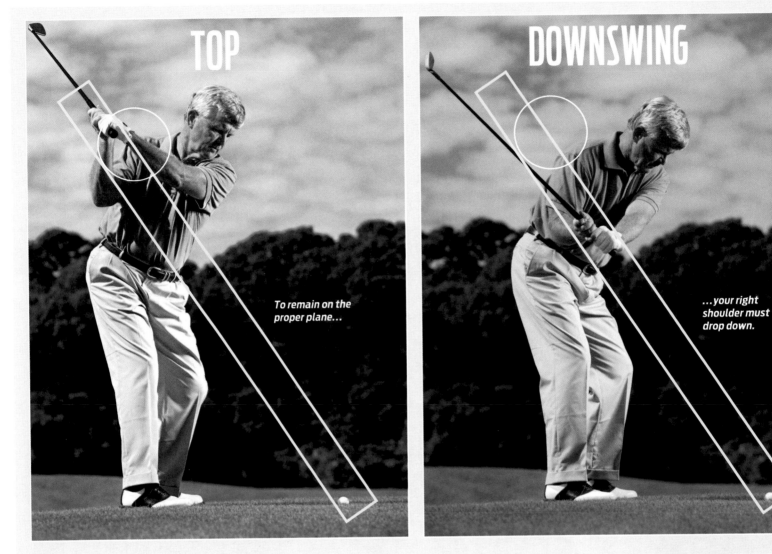

TOP

To remain on the proper plane...

DOWNSWING

...your right shoulder must drop down.

Do You Have the "Magic Move"?

Drop your right shoulder down to keep your club on plane

If you're solid at the top, most of your work is done. But you can lose it all in an instant if you make the wrong first move down. Check what's happening with your right shoulder. Does it drop down at the start of your downswing? If it does, you're in a great position to deliver the club on plane. If your right shoulder stays at the same height [*right*], your downswing will be above plane and your chances of a pull or slice will skyrocket.
—**Michael Hebron**

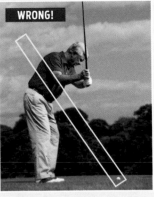

WRONG!

How to Make a Solid Downswing
Keep it simple for sweet contact

Your goal should be to hit the sweet spot more consistently with every club in your bag. The best way for you to achieve it is to properly sequence your downswing. **By that I mean following the four H's: hips, handle, hands and (club)head.** Thinking of your downswing in this order simplifies your thoughts, reduces the amount of effort you make, and produces more yards and purer strikes. The sequence of hips, handle, hands and clubhead is paramount for success. Here's how to get it.
—John Elliott, Jr.

Your hips should stay in line with the tee.

ROTATE YOUR HIPS TO START YOUR SWING

Stick a tee in the butt end of a 5-iron, hold it across your hips and get into your address position. The tee should point toward your target [*inset*]. Now shift onto your left leg, turning the tee to the left [*photo, above*]—this is the motion your hips should take as you start your downswing motion.

LEAN THE HANDLE FORWARD

The handle has to beat the clubhead to the ball in order to get powerful and consistent impact. Again, use your 5-iron with the tee in the grip. Swing to the top and, as you start down, immediately get the tee to point to the ground [*photo, above*]. This will allow the grip to reach the ball first.

CHECKPOINT **3**

KEEP YOUR HANDS COCKED

Your wrists should remain hinged throughout your downswing. A common flaw is to release your hands too early and throw the clubhead at the ball. Instead, keep your hands cocked until after the handle has passed the ball.

DRILL

Drop the Club Down on the Ball

Here's the secret to solid ballstriking

Since the handle of the club leads the way to impact, the clubhead will descend on a slight arc when it contacts the ball. To get a feel for that sensation, try this drill.

1. Push a row of three tees into the ground two clubhead widths behind the ball as shown.

2. Address the ball with a 6-iron and swing. You want to barely nip the tees on the backswing and then completely miss them on the downswing.

3. Swing all the way through to the finish. If you miss the tees coming down, the clubhead correctly lagged behind the handle, and you should be admiring a high, straight shot.
—**John Elliott, Jr.**

TOUR TIP

Hit Correctly From the Inside

Your key is to lead with your hips

Once I complete my backswing I immediately turn my hips as fast as I can while trying to do as little as possible with my shoulders. This happens at a rapid pace—it'd be nice to be smooth and silky like Ernie Els or Fred Couples in the transition, but that kind of rhythm, in my opinion, is very difficult to achieve. I think it's easier to get to the top and then **immediately start rotating your lower body as quickly as possible** like I do, or like Nick Price and Greg Norman did in their primes. It gives you a greater margin for error. Creating separation at the start of your downswing is critical—critical!—for acceleration and swinging on the correct in-out path.
—**PGA Tour player Mark Wilson**

Don't move this...

...move this.

All on-line downswings start with the hips turning first, not the shoulders.

INSTRUCTION

Swing to the one o'clock position on a clock face to groove the right path.

1:00

7:00

Swing From Seven to One

Groove a power-rich inside delivery by picturing a clock at your feet

Imagine your feet resting at the 9 o'clock position on a clock face. As you swing down from the top, try to sweep your clubhead on a path that crosses 7 o'clock on its approach to the ball, and crosses 1 o'clock after impact. If you slice, you're likely swinging from 5 o'clock to 11 o'clock.
—**Michael Breed**

QUICK TIPS TO
IMPROVE YOUR DOWNSWING

THE TOP 100 SAY

MITCHELL SPEARMAN
Swing fast for pure hits

"The simple way to move more dynamically through the hitting zone is to start swinging for the fences. Loosen up your arms, wrists and hands and let them swing freely and quickly with zero tension. Try to get your loose arms and the club to "snap" down through the turf every time."

DAN PASQUARIELLO
Forget your legs

"Too much hip and leg action leads to an open clubface at impact. Your downswing should mirror your backswing, and since your arms take the club away, they should swing it down into the ball, too."

RICK McCORD
Make a heads-down move

"From the top, flex your knees and lower your head to pull your arms down. This pulling motion is what brings the club into impact with the clubhead lagging behind your hands. As you do this, continue to rotate your hips toward the target."

DANA RADER
Keep it tucked

"Tuck your right arm against your right side on your downswing—it helps you drop your right shoulder, putting the club on the correct path into impact. If your right arm stays away from your side, your shoulders will turn horizontally, causing an outside-in swing path and weak slices."

Swing fast through impact and take a nice divot. Feel like you're "snapping" the club at the bottom.

Flex your knees to correctly hit down on the ball.

Stay on plane with a tucked right arm.

DOWNSWING

Shift your weight forward during your downswing...

IMPACT

...so you can catch the ball first and make clean contact.

CHECKPOINT

Bottom Out in the Right Spot

Move forward to make make ball-first contact

If you often hit fat or thin shots, pay attention to how far your lower body moves toward the target on your downswing. **This forward motion allows your hands to get to the ball before your clubhead,** and it moves the bottom of your swing arc toward the target so you contact the ball before the ground. If you hang on your right side [*right*], you'll make contact behind the ball (fat) or after your swing has already bottomed out (thin).
—Michael Hebron

WRONG!

How to Make a Powerful Impact

Strive for these positions and your shots will rocket off the clubface

If you've followed the plan to this point, quality impact will happen by itself, but knowing where you should be when you strike the ball is an important step in improving the other elements of your swing. While they're not mirror images of each other, **address and impact positions do share many common traits.** You'll always make solid contact if your spine and the back of your head are aligned just like they were at address, and if the shaft angle at impact is the same as it was at setup. PGA Tour player Sergio Garcia sets a perfect example for you to follow.
—Shawn Humphries

STAY IN LINE
The butt of the club points at your belt buckle. If it points behind, you released too early.

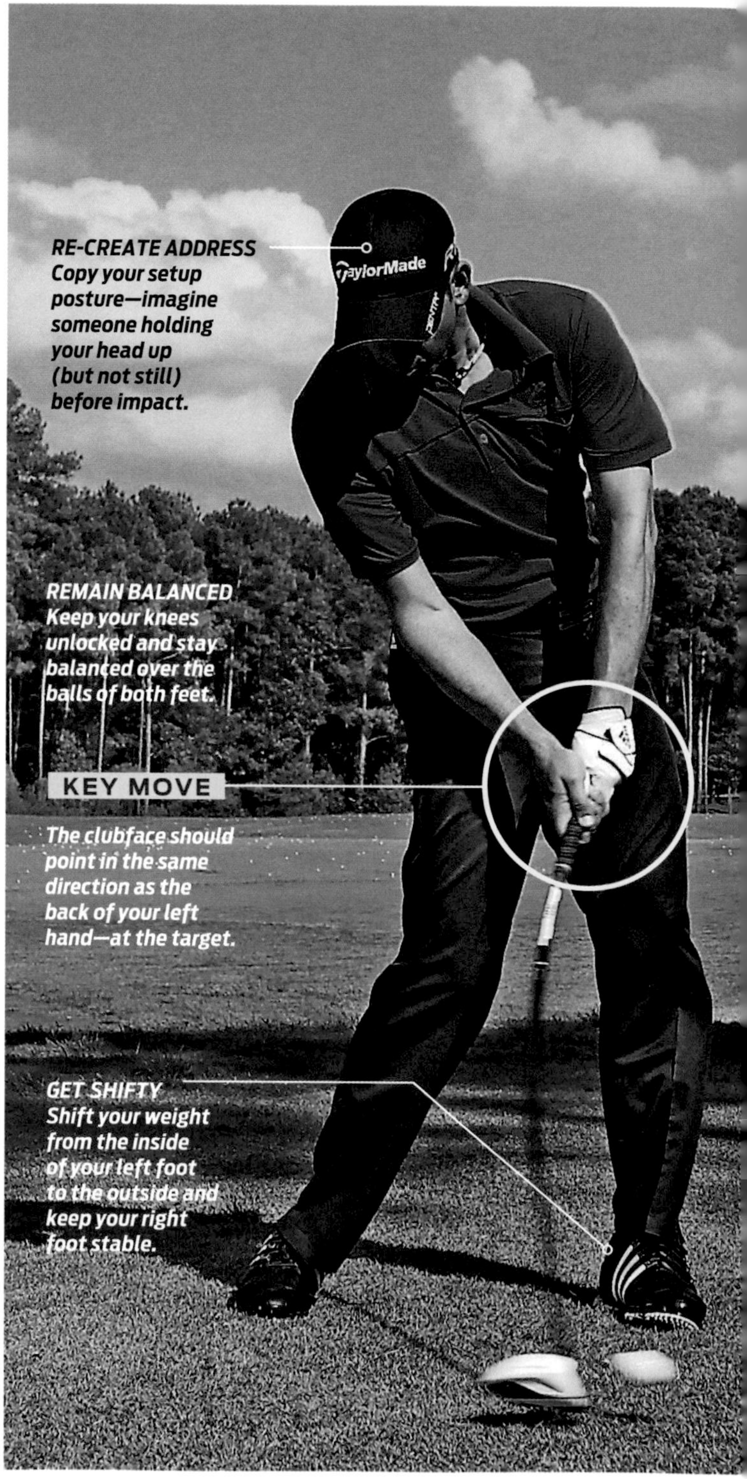

RE-CREATE ADDRESS
Copy your setup posture—imagine someone holding your head up (but not still) before impact.

REMAIN BALANCED
Keep your knees unlocked and stay balanced over the balls of both feet.

KEY MOVE

The clubface should point in the same direction as the back of your left hand—at the target.

GET SHIFTY
Shift your weight from the inside of your left foot to the outside and keep your right foot stable.

Open the Door

Turn your hands like you're opening a door to square up the clubface through impact

Retain the hinge in your wrists deep into the downswing. That saves energy for impact.

Continue to move your hands while keeping your right shoulder back.

Rotate the back of your left hand as if you're turning a doorknob.

Open the door so that the back of your left hand starts facing the target.

Keep your arms extended (so you don't chicken wing).

Maintain the triangle formed by your arms, hands and shaft.

Square It Earlier for Less Spin

Don't wait until impact—square the face way before

THE FAULT

If you consistently slice your drives, it means you have an open clubface at impact. This mistake keeps happening because you're not rotating the clubhead in a counterclockwise direction early enough in your downswing.

THE FIX

To start hitting the ball straight all you have to do is rotate the clubhead in a counterclockwise direction earlier in your downswing. Regardless of whatever else is going on in your motion, if you do this correctly it'll be impossible for you to hit a slice. To make this happen, **rotate the back of your left hand and the palm of your right hand toward the ball as you swing into impact.** I suggest you do this early enough so the clubface is square by the time it gets even with your right foot, or about ten inches from the ball.

—Chuck Winstead

Get the clubface square before it gets to your right foot. Don't be afraid to point the sweet spot at the ball this early in your downswing.

Which Slice Is Your Slice?

Finding the answer is the key to fixing your impact

The predominant ball flight of most recreational players is a slice (a shot that curves wildly from left to right). The first step to stopping your slice is to determine which type of slice is destroying your game. That way you'll know if you have to correct your face angle at impact, your downswing path or both.

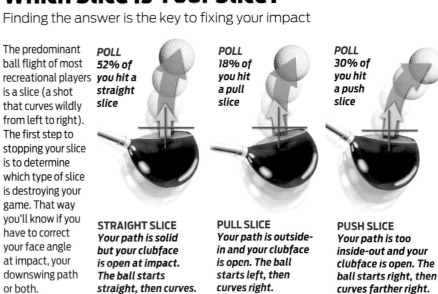

POLL 52% of you hit a straight slice

POLL 18% of you hit a pull slice

POLL 30% of you hit a push slice

STRAIGHT SLICE
Your path is solid but your clubface is open at impact. The ball starts straight, then curves.

PULL SLICE
Your path is outside-in and your clubface is open. The ball starts left, then curves right.

PUSH SLICE
Your path is too inside-out and your clubface is open. The ball starts right, then curves farther right.

QUICK TIPS TO
IMPROVE YOUR IMPACT

THE TOP 100 SAY

TODD ANDERSON
Let your hands win

"Picture a finish line at the ball. Try to get your right knee to that line at impact with your hands leading the clubhead. Shifting your right knee toward the target helps keep your clubhead on a downward path, and if your hands stay ahead of the club, you'll get the most power out of your swing."

MIKE BENDER
Lean the shaft forward

"This drill teaches you to make contact with a forward lean to the shaft. Draw a line in the sand down the middle of your stance. Using your left hand only, swing across the line, blasting out several divots in front of it. The object is to hit the sand and stop, so the grip stays ahead of the clubhead."

BRADY RIGGS
Stack up at impact

"Set up to the ball with a 7-iron, then pull your left foot back 18 inches and rest it on your toe. Make half-speed swings and note how the awkward stance forces your upper body to remain on top of your lower body (otherwise you'll fall off balance). That's the sensation you're looking for."

JIM HARDY
Point your plane to the left

"Try to get your divots to point slightly left of your target. You shouldn't be making a divot until after you contact the ball, and by that time your swing should already be moving back inside the target line. The secret is to use the left side of your body to pull the club to the left earlier in your downswing."

Hands reach the ball first.

Lean the shaft forward.

Stack your upper body over your lower.

Swing to the left through impact.

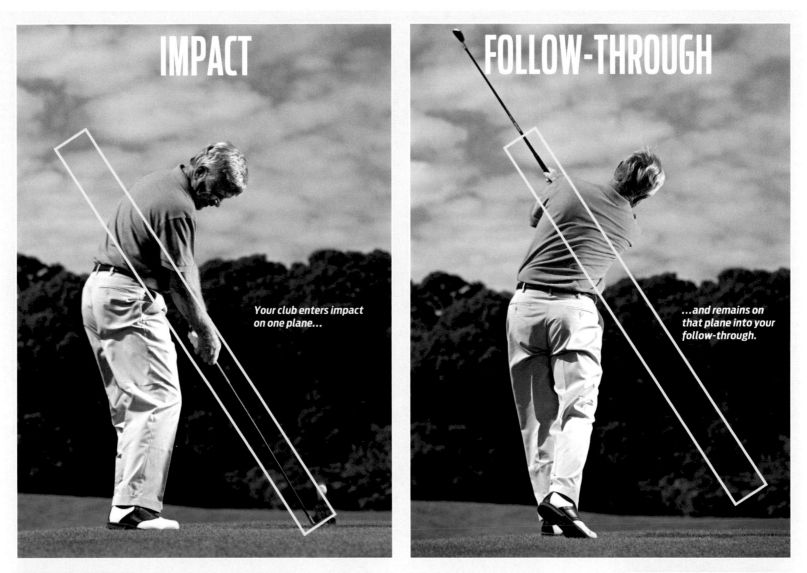

IMPACT

FOLLOW-THROUGH

Your club enters impact on one plane...

...and remains on that plane into your follow-through.

CHECKPOINT

Mirror Your Downswing Path After Impact

Take the right (plane) exit

Very few golfers consider what happens after impact to be very important. But the plane on which your club exits the hitting area says a lot about the path you took on your backswing and downswing. If it's to the left [*see photo at right*], you swung outside-in and hit a slice or pull. **Try to retrace your backswing on your through-swing.** You'll have to maintain your forward bend until the force of your swing causes you to straighten up in your finish.
—**Michael Hebron**

INSTRUCTION

How to Make a Power Release
Give the ball a right-hand slap for explosive contact

ELBOW IN
Your left elbow should hang tight against your torso as your hands release. You can't unhinge your wrists if your left arm bows out (no chicken-winging).

THE STANDARD ADVICE
Try to square the clubface at impact for straighter and more accurate shots.

WHY IT'S MISLEADING
Impact lasts only a few milliseconds, so trying to perfect that moment is nearly impossible.

THE TIP YOU NEED
A solid release guarantees proper clubface rotation through impact, so perfect it instead. Plus, it's easier (and quite possible) to control your release. As you drive through the hitting zone, give the ball a slap with your right hand, changing your right wrist from bent back to bowed. Check these positions here to see what it looks like.
—Laird Small

SHOULDER UNDER
Your right shoulder moves under your chin, not in front of it. This allows your hands to power the clubhead correctly through impact and then around your body.

KEY MOVE

ACTIVE WRISTS
Prior to impact your right wrist was bent. Now it should be bowed. This doesn't happen by itself— "slap" the ball with your right hand to release the club properly.

CLUB ON LINE
A proper release whips the clubhead around your body in a circular motion and into your finish.

DRILL

Wristy Business

Try this drill to improve your release

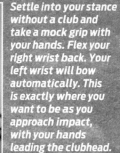

1 Settle into your stance without a club and take a mock grip with your hands. Flex your right wrist back. Your left wrist will bow automatically. This is exactly where you want to be as you approach impact, with your hands leading the clubhead.

2 Create your release by hinging your right wrist into a bowed position at half speed. Notice how your left wrist bends back as a result and how your body turns and opens slightly to the target to support this action.

3 Continue this drill, picking up speed each time. The faster you do it, the more you should feel like you're "slapping" the ball with your right hand, or flexing it forward like you do when you shoot hoops. That's the feel you're after.

INSTRUCTION

Control Every Shot

You can create any ball flight you want by turning your left-hand knuckles either up or down

KNUCKLES DOWN FOR POWER
All full swings, rough escapes and fairway-bunker shots

For maximum speed and distance, gradually rotate your forearms (right over left) and turn your wrists through the hitting zone so that your left-hand knuckles and left elbow point toward the ground in your release.

WHY IT WORKS: Maximum clubhead acceleration occurs when your hands give in to the force of your downswing and turn over to release your clubhead toe over heel. You know you've reached your power threshold when your left-hand knuckles and left elbow point down in your release.

HOW TO DO IT: Through the hitting zone, sling the club smoothly past your left thigh by trying to "flick" an imaginary object off your left thumb. Or, think of how you'd turn your left hand out to hitch a ride.

KNUCKLES UP FOR CONTROL
Greenside bunkers, chips and pitches, knock-downs, bump-and-runs and punch shots.

For shots that require control over raw distance, keep your hands ahead of the clubhead at impact and the back of your left hand pointed up in your follow-through.

WHY IT WORKS: You're basically holding off your release, which is the fastest part of your swing. While you'll lose distance (which you don't need on these shots), you'll gain extra accuracy because you're squaring your clubface with your body turn instead of your hands, and big muscles are easier to control than little ones.

HOW TO DO IT: Through impact, cup your left wrist slightly and lift the back of your left hand toward the sky. This usually produces a scoopy impact, but if you set up with your hands ahead of the ball, your contact will be crisp.
—Robert Baker

When you need full power and speed, point your left-hand knuckles at the ground.

Hit ultra-accurate short-game shots by pointing your left-hand knuckles toward the sky.

DRILL

How to End Your Swing

If you can groove a solid finishing position first, it'll be easier to make the swing moves necessary to finish in balance and eliminate poor ball flight

1 Put on a baseball cap and take your normal address position with an iron.

2 Without moving your feet, stand straight up and bring your club straight up over the top of your head.

3 Make a quarter turn to the left with your face, chest and hips pointing at the target and the butt end of the club pointing to your left. You'll know you're in the ideal finishing position when you feel the shaft lay across the hair on the back of your head where it pokes out from the cap.
—John Elliott, Jr.

Use Your Finish to Shape Shots

Pre-set your club to hit draws and fades on command

HOW TO HIT A DRAW

Get into your address position and swing to waist-high in your follow-through. Move your arms and club so that...

● Your club points 10 yards right of the target.
● Your right arm is fully extended and in line with your clubshaft.
● The toe of your club points up.
● Get a feel for this position and swing back to the top of your backswing. Notice how your club automatically moves to the inside and around you [*inset, below*]. This is the perfect position from which to attack the ball from the inside out.
● When you proceed to play the shot, swing your club in an effort to re-create the feel of the backswing and release that you just rehearsed.

Start here to hit a draw.

Draw top position

HOW TO HIT A FADE

Swing to a waist-high follow-through from address and move your arms and club so that...

● Your left arm is fully extended and creates an "L" with the clubshaft.
● The toe of your club points right.
● The shaft points 10 feet left of your target.
● Ingrain this feel and then swing back to the top of your backswing. This time, your pre-set fade release automatically makes you take the club more up and to the outside [*inset, below*], which is the perfect position to produce left-to-right spin at impact.
● When you proceed to play the shot, swing your club in an effort to re-create the feel of the backswing and release that you just rehearsed.
—**Mike Adams**

Start here to hit a fade.

Fade top position

HERE'S PROOF THAT YOUR FINISH MEANS EVERYTHING

Recently, a Swedish woman came to me to learn how to play golf. She didn't speak English and had never even touched a club. I tried to use pictures and video to explain the swing, but since she only spoke Swedish she couldn't understand me.

STEP ONE was to physically place her into a sound address position. Only when she had ingrained this position into her muscle memory was she allowed to make a backswing.

STEP TWO was to physically take her up to the top of the backswing and pause her there.

STEP THREE was to hit the ball from her static top position. After each swing, I physically adjusted her into a proper finish position and made her hold it for a few counts. I did this for every swing, during every lesson, an hour a day for six days in a row. By the end of the sixth day she was hitting her 7-iron 130 yards with a nice, high draw. It was incredible to see how quickly muscle memory took over her swing. In just under a week she was able to feel if and when she was correct in each spot.

The key to this lesson was pausing at each position. This allowed her to feel what was correct, especially the end point, to give her the feeling of where she needed to be. Most golfers never truly know if what they feel in their swings is right or wrong, especially when they're finishing their swings off balance and out of control.
—**Mike Bender**

SWING SMOOTHER

Follow these tips to swing tension-free and power the ball almost effortlessly

DRILL

How to Swing at Your Speed

Go from too fast or too slow to just right and watch your shots soar high, far and straight

Few swing fundamentals are more overlooked than tempo (the consistency of the pace at which you swing your club). Tempo is a difficult concept to grasp—there's more to it than swinging your club faster or slower. You need to feel it. In the same way that you developed your natural walking pace, you must find your natural swing speed or your motion will lack the smooth, rhythmic feel associated with solid ball striking.

1
Tee up four balls in a row. Address the one closest to you and hit it at 25 percent of your standard swing speed. Immediately move to the next ball. This time, make a swing at 50 percent speed. Hit the third ball at 75 percent speed and the last at full throttle.

2
Perform this drill a few times. Focus on the feel of the different speeds, and keep in mind that your goal is to become familiar with different tempos, not hit the ball longer or straighter.

3
Swinging at different tempos helps you coordinate the movement of your body and your club to produce solid contact in an effortless fashion. It's this level of control that enables you to follow one long and straight shot with another.
—Pia Nilsson

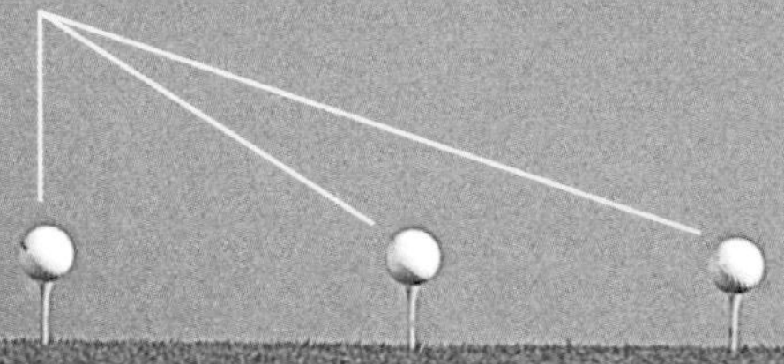

INSTRUCTION

Get Smooth With the Right Hinge

Time your wrist cock with your body pivot

THE PROBLEM
You often lose the timing of your swing because you either delay or quicken your wrist hinge in your takeaway. These errors destroy the natural momentum of your club going back, and can do the same on the way back down via a late release or one that occurs far too early in the downswing.

THE SOLUTION
Hinge your wrists at the correct time, which varies depending on the iron you have in your hands and the shot you need to play. Adjust the timing of your hinge to create perfect rhythm and tempo.
—Dom DiJulia

FOR FULL SWINGS WITH YOUR MID - AND LONG IRONS...
Simply maintain the hinge that you established at address during your takeaway. Full swings require a longer body pivot, so hinge less and turn more as you bring your hands to waist height. You'll know you've done it right if your chest points away from the target and the butt of the club is outside your right leg when the shaft is parallel to the ground.

WRONG!

A late hinge creates a late release and poor tempo.

ERR ON THE QUICK SIDE

You've been told to keep the clubhead low in your takeaway, which is good advice unless you overdo it and remove the hinge in your wrists that was established at address [photo, above]. Now you're late on your hinge going back, which means you'll be early on your hinge going forward, and you'll hit the shot fat. As a general rule, hinge your wrists sooner and you'll hear the sweet sound of crisp contact more frequently.

CHECKPOINT

For half-swing shots inside 50 yards, your right wrist should hinge before your hands pass your right knee.

FOR HALF-SWING SHOTS...
Make a full hinge before your hands pass your right knee. Short swings from 30-60 yards require much less body pivot, which means your wrists must hinge sooner in your backswing. You've done it right if your chest points at your right foot and the butt of the club is on top of your right leg when the shaft is parallel to the ground.

DRILL

Be Loose, Not Lazy

Use "downtime" on the course to your tempo's advantage

THE FAULT: You make casual, right-hand only swings while waiting for the group ahead to clear away. While most of these mini-swings are made with the sole purpose of passing time, they'll ingrain bad habits since you're likely just flipping your club back and through.

THE FIX: Continue to make your mini-swings when the course backs up, but do so with a purpose. Repeat a solid back-and-forth motion with an eye toward removing tension in your arms and hands. Take it a step further and make sure you're rotating your right hand as the club sweeps beneath you. Turn into your follow-through with the toe of your club pointing up. When it comes time to play your shot, you'll be loose and ready to deliver a powerful strike.
—John Elliott, Jr.

Make every swing—even the casual ones while waiting for your turn to hit—count.

HIT STRAIGHTER

Try these teacher tricks to find the fairway or the green with laser-like accuracy

TOUR TIP

The Tour Key for Straighter Shots

Moving forward on your downswing by putting your chest on top of the ball allows you to use every ounce of energy in your swing

THE MOVE YOU NEED

As I start my downswing, I think more about moving forward than I do about moving down, which is kind of counterintuitive but the right thing to do. One of my swing coach Butch Harmon's big things is shifting target-ward as you make your way back down to the ball, so that you can finish your swing with 85 to 90 percent of your weight on your front foot. You can't do that without moving forward.

HOW TO DO IT

My key here is to get my chest on top of the ball just before impact. Of course, this is impossible because the ball is teed so far forward in my stance. The secret is to feel as though the buttons on your shirt are in line with the ball when you make contact.

In addition to ensuring that you transfer as much energy as possible forward into the ball, **this feeling of "chest on top" will at least stop you from hanging back and trying to "lift" the ball into the air,** which almost always results in high, weak shots to the right.

—*PGA Tour player Nick Watney*

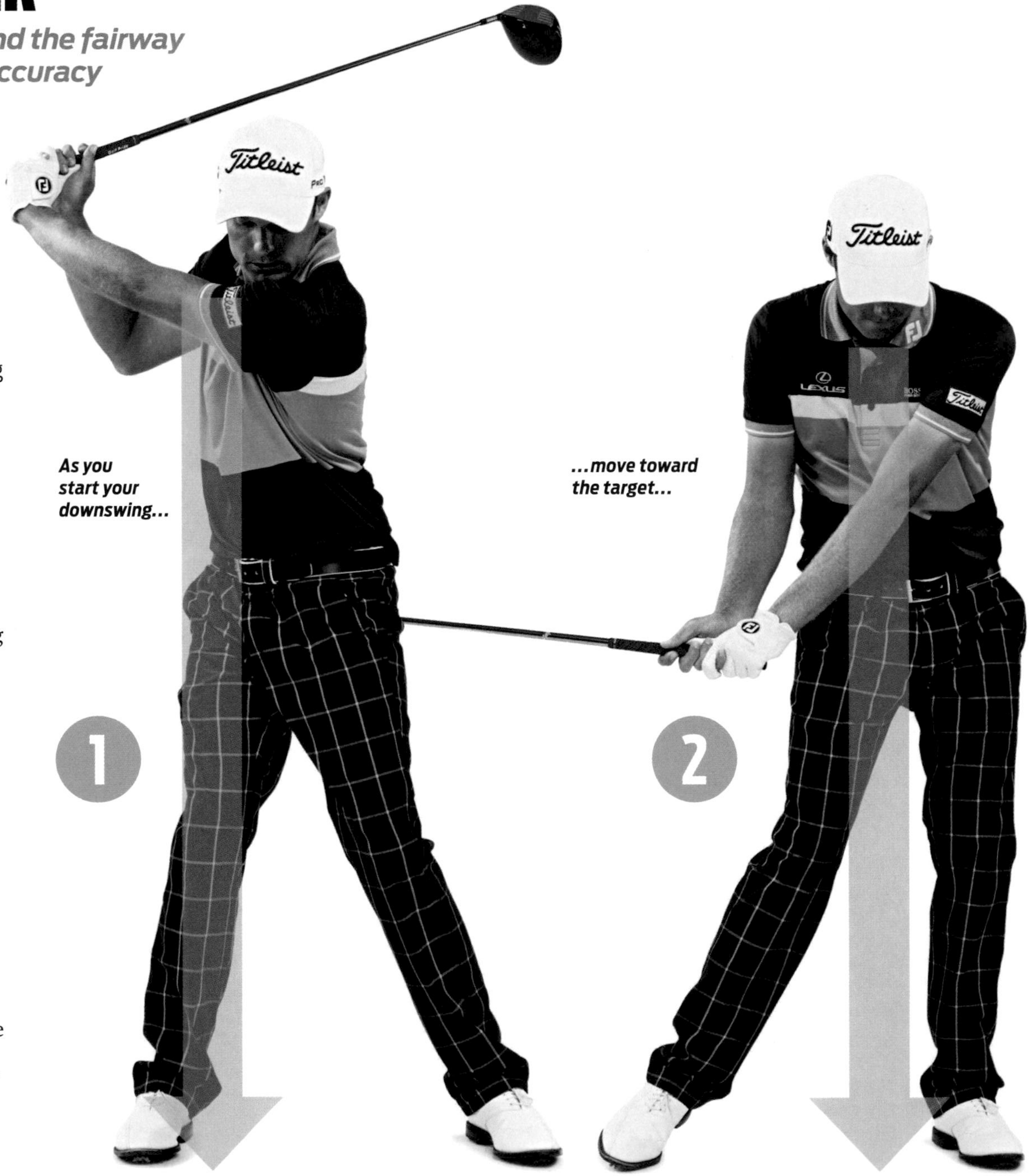

As you start your downswing...

1

...move toward the target...

2

...and reach impact with your chest over the ball.

3

How to Tame Your First-Tee Jitters

Mental tips for getting your round off to a solid start

If you get nervous standing over your first tee shot, relax. Even Tour players feel opening-tee jitters at major tournaments and other big events. The best way to beat first-tee pressure is to use your warm-up time to get into a playing mode rather than just bashing balls with no goals in mind. Here are three keys to becoming a cool customer on the first tee.

1 *Make sure your pre-round warm-up is exactly that, and not practice. Don't work on swing keys or ask for tips when you have 30 minutes or less until your tee time. Any confusion about technique will only heighten the pressure you feel later.*

2 *Vary your clubs and distances often, never hitting more than three shots in a row with the same club. Take a cue from well-coached basketball teams. The players don't take countless free throws before a game, but instead hit shots from various spots around the court.*

3 *Spend the last 10 minutes of your warm-up "playing" the first three holes of the course you're about to tackle. Hit the club you plan to hit off the first tee and then hit the appropriate club for your approach. Go through your pre-shot routine and try to execute the shots exactly as you would on the course. Repeat this for the next two holes. This drill heightens your visualization and helps you narrow your targets. You'll arrive at the first tee ready to play, which will lessen the pressure.*
Richard Coop, Ph.D., *Golf Magazine's* mental-game consultant

Be a Palm Pilot

Your right hand controls the clubface

If you've taken a proper grip, your right palm should mimic the angle of your clubface. So instead of trying to control your clubhead, control your right hand. Make sure your right palm points down at the ball once it reaches your right thigh in your downswing. This forces you to properly hit down on the ball and is a good start to squaring the clubface.
—David Glenz

A square clubface at impact doesn't guarantee success, but it gives you a much better chance for it.

Point your right palm down at the ball as your club reaches the hitting zone to make powerful contact on the sweet spot.

HIT PURER SHOTS

You know when you've crushed it—here's how to get that feeling time and again

How to Hit Piercing Irons

A drill to lower your trajectory and stop pop-ups

THE FAULT
You never get your weight to your left side at impact. Hanging back like this produces a higher ball flight, which may be helpful when you're trying to hit into a green, but keeping the ball low works better in all types of wind and weather. Plus, it's easier to control distance with a lower trajectory than it is with one that balloons.

THE FIX
STEP 1: Address a ball with any iron, then shift into a mock impact position. Make sure your posed impact position features the following:
● Weight over your left foot.
● Upper body bent over (to "cover" the ball).
● Right heel slightly off the ground.
● Shaft leaning toward the target with your hands ahead of the clubhead.
● Right hip pressed in toward the target.

These are the alignments you need to lower your ball flight and avoid hanging back at impact.

STEP 2: Shift back to your regular address position.

STEP 3: Swing, and try to re-create the positions of your posed impact when you strike the ball for real.

This sequence is a great way to practice the impact positions that produce a piercing ball flight. By posing first in the desired impact arrangement, you can feel the correct alignments of both your body and club just before you begin your swing. This works better than making simple rehearsal swings because of the close proximity in time between your posed and real impacts, which allows you to easily transfer the proper feel into your actual motion.
—Brady Riggs

NOTE: Exaggerate each of the positions in your posed impact—students can very rarely get all the way to where they need to be. These positions can't be stressed enough, especially if you hit your irons too high.

Upper body "covering" the ball.

Right hip pressed toward target.

Shaft leaning toward target.

Right heel slightly off the ground.

Weight over left foot.

Pose impact.

Return to setup.

Match your mock impact.

Do You Extend or Flip?

Only one is good for your game

WRONG!

RIGHT!

THE FAULT

If you hit low-flying skulls, chances are your clubhead is whipping ahead of your hands as you try to scoop the ball into the air [*above*]. That puts the leading edge of the club into contact with the ball. You'll know you're doing it if your clubhead is higher than your hands in your release.

THE FIX

Hit a series of balls and stop the clubhead below the level of your waist [*above*]. You'll find it impossible to scoop at the ball—and necessary to hit down on it—to achieve this shortened finish. Don't be afraid to shorten your follow-through if you mis-hit a few irons in the middle of your round.**—Mike Malaska**

Drop Your Foot Back

It helps you get your weight on your front foot

Address a ball in the middle of your stance while holding a 5-iron. Bend your right knee, point your toe into the ground and hit the ball. By dropping your right foot back, away from the target line, you can't lean away from the target—a classic reverse pivot—as you make your downswing. Instead, you will rotate around your left foot and make a descending blow on the back of the ball.
—Mike Malaska

Hit balls with your right foot back to stop a reverse pivot.

Slot the Club for Solid Drives

Keeping your right arm tucked against your side is the key

FAULT: You prematurely release (or cast) the clubhead.

FIX: Take your driver to the top of your swing with your right arm. Hold a plastic bottle against the right side of your torso as shown, then bring your club down to impact. If you squash the bottle before you unhinge your wrists, you delay your release until the moment when it creates the perfect blend of power and accuracy. If you don't, you allowed the clubhead to outrace your hands to the ball, which costs you in yards and missed fairways.
—Robert Baker

Try to squash a bottle against your right side on your downswing to squeeze out a few extra yards.

CHECK YOUR TECHNIQUE

You know what to do, but are you doing it right? Here's how to find out.

Mirror the Perfect Swing

Use your reflection—and hip turn—to stay on plane from start to finish

YOUR GOAL

To create the perfect swing plane. The perfect plane is described as a circle tilted to match the angle of your clubshaft at address. That's a good visual, but you can't attach a hula-hoop to your 7-iron. All you need to perfect your swing plane is masking tape and a mirror.

HOW TO ACHIEVE IT

Let's assume that your address position is solid, with your back straight, knees flexed and ready for action, and your arms hanging underneath your shoulders. Find a full-length mirror and take your address position in front of it. Study your reflection and note the angle of your clubshaft. Place tape on the mirror along this line (we'll call this Line 1), and then another in the opposite direction (Line 2), so that the two lines intersect at 90 degrees. These lines hold the key to grooving an on-plane swing because they help you get your body and club in the correct positions on both the backswing and the follow-through.

—**Mike LaBauve**

CHECKPOINT

1. ADDRESS CHECK

At setup, make sure your shaft mimics Line 1. Your forward bend toward the ball should position your back and head along Line 2. Now you're solid.

Line 1

Line 2

CHECKPOINT

2. BACKSWING CHECK

Take your club back to just above waist high and stop. Look at the mirror and make sure your back and head still lie on Line 2 and that your shoulder turn and wrist hinge have placed the clubshaft along Line 1.

If you're not on the correct backswing plane, it's because you lifted the club with your hands more than you turned your upper body (shaft above Line 1). Or you whipped the club too far to the inside by turning your shoulders too level and not raising the club at all (shaft below Line 1). To get your club correctly on plane, all you need to do is turn your left shoulder under your chin and gently cock your wrists a full 90 degrees.

CHECKPOINT

3. FOLLOW-THROUGH CHECK

Swing through impact and stop when your hands reach just above waist height. Study your reflection to make sure that the shaft rests on Line 1, and your head and back haven't strayed from Line 2.

The common error here is a clubshaft that lies above Line 1, because most golfers don't swing enough to the left, or if they do they don't execute enough hip turn. You really need both: an aggressive and full hip rotation, along with hand movement that brings your club across your chest (not away from it). Although most swings finish with the shaft over the left shoulder (above Line 1), the shaft goes left after impact before it travels up.

CHECKPOINT

6 Plane Errors to Avoid

Do any of these swings look familiar? If so, it's time to get back on plane.

It's very difficult to hit solid shots once your club gets off plane. Make a point to check your swing plane in a mirror often to avoid grooving bad habits.

Upright
Hands way
above shoulders

Hitting under
Shaft below
shoulder plane

Trapped
Club too far
behind the body

Over the top
club above
shoulder plane

Across the line
Shaft points
right of target

Laid off
Club points way
left of target

DRILL

Get the Perfect Finish

Stretch your left hip flexor to the max to maintain proper posture and keep your club on the correct exit plane

With your hands on your hips, make a mock swing and hold your finish. Make sure your weight is over your front foot and your belt buckle faces directly at the target.

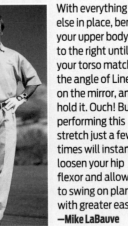

With everything else in place, bend your upper body to the right until your torso matches the angle of Line 2 on the mirror, and hold it. Ouch! But performing this stretch just a few times will instantly loosen your hip flexor and allow you to swing on plane with greater ease.
—Mike LaBauve

Don't expect more distance from swinging harder. Big drives result from widening your swing arc and saving energy for impact. Do both and your swing speed will increase almost automatically.

SECTION 3

YOU AND YOUR DRIVER

How to turn a love-hate relationship into a beautiful friendship—and massive yards

The key to the modern game is to hit the ball as far as you can and then go find it. Technology provides with you the tools to knock it out there, but do you know how to use them? Your driver can't swing itself, nor can you simply move your arms or hips faster to create yardage that isn't there. There are hard, fast rules you must follow. And since your driver is the longest, largest and potentially most dangerous club in your bag, neglecting those rules pays off in a triple-whammy of lost yards, lost balls and lost strokes.

Once you harness the power of your driver, however, you'll find that playing by the big dog's rules makes the game a lot easier. Approach shots become shorter, par 5s become reachable and your confidence soars when you know you can bust one out there anytime you like.

There are three main things you must do to improve your driving distance: increase the width of your swing (especially going back), sequence your downswing to add clubhead speed, and learn how to make consistent contact in the center of the clubface. This section touches on all three, with tips to not only make you the big hitter in your regular foursome, but the most accurate one, too.

5 THINGS YOU'LL LEARN IN THIS SECTION

- *How to widen your swing arc—the primary ingredient in power-packed drives*
- *How to swing faster without swinging out of your shoes*
- *How to hit more fairways—even the narrow ones*
- *Why an expert clubfitting session can give you more yards in an instant*
- *Power drills that give you extra speed at the exact point where you need it the most*

 Watch dozens of lessons on increasing your driving distance at **golf.com/power**

WHAT ARE YOUR WEAK SPOTS?

Here's what *Golf Magazine* readers had to say about their driving game in a recent survey:

Q: What's your most common driving mistake?

Something else: 9%   *Not enough distance: 37%*

Hooking: 21%   *Slicing: 33%*

What club do you replace most often?

Driver: 42%   *Putter: 21%*

Something else: 26%   *Fairway woods: 11%*

● Most golfers struggle on the tee box because they apply the swing motion they use when hitting an iron to their driver. That's a sure way to hit a slice. You swing down and slightly to the left when the ball is on the ground. When the ball is teed up, however, you need to swing slightly up and to the right through impact.
—Dr. T.J. Tomasi

HOW TO WIDEN YOUR ARC

Big swings begin with a big arc, and the wider the path your clubhead traces from start to finish, the more speed and power you can create to launch the ball deep down the fairway

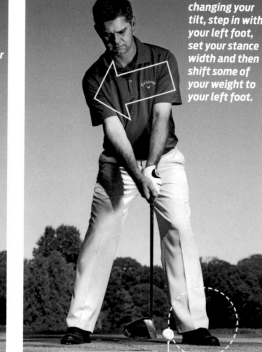

POWER STEP 1
Step in with your right foot and all of your weight on that leg (raise up on your left toe).

POWER STEP 2
In order to hold your balance with all of your weight on your right foot, your upper body should automatically tilt to the right.

POWER STEP 3
Without changing your tilt, step in with your left foot, set your stance width and then shift some of your weight to your left foot.

Try the 3-Step Power Tilt

Set up your swing for a wide arc and ascending strike

STEP 1
Walk into your driver setup with your right foot and 99 percent of your weight on that leg. Your innate ability to balance should cause your upper body to tilt away from the target. If your body doesn't tilt you'll fall over.

STEP 2
Hold your body angle and move your left foot into its normal spot. Now, move your right foot back to set your preferred stance width. As you do, shift some of the weight from your right foot to your left. Now you're solid.
—Jason Carbone

Three Drills to Get Wider

A trio of PGA Tour greats shares their best tips for creating a power-rich backswing

My goal on every backswing: To turn my left shoulder behind the ball.

1. Complete Your Rotation

When you stop your backswing too soon, your body senses that you haven't built enough power, and it speeds up in a jerky rush. The same thing happens when you overextend your backswing: Your body senses that you're too long and steps on the gas. So how do you know when your backswing is full and complete? **For me it's always been when I feel that my left shoulder has gotten behind the ball.** When my turn gets to this point I know it's time to start back down. No indecision, no hesitation, no rush. If your transition isn't as smooth as you want it to be, it's because you never get your left shoulder behind the ball. Most amateurs turn, but hardly any of them turn enough. Spend an entire practice session forgetting about your swing and focusing only on turning your shoulders as far as you can. You'll be surprised at how much power you get without swinging any harder.
—PGA Tour player Ernie Els

Swing wide.

As you take the club back, feel as though you're swinging the clubhead as far away from you as you can.

Keep your weight on the inside of your right foot.

2. Stretch Your Swing

As you start back, feel as though you're swinging the clubhead as far away from you as you can. Don't overdo it and sway off the ball. **The trick is to get wide while still keeping your weight on the inside of your right foot.** My coach, Top 100 Teacher Butch Harmon, is a big proponent of the wide takeaway. When we work together on the practice tee, he'll often stand a few feet behind me on my target line and say, "Hit me with your backswing!" To date, I've missed him every time, but with this drill I've been able to build a consistently wide backswing and pick up more yards than I ever thought possible.
—PGA Tour player Nick Watney

3. Turn Your Back to the Target

I'm built a bit different than most right-handed players—I can turn forward (as in toward the target on my through-swing) easier than I can turn away from the target on my backswing. That's why **I focus on making sure my back is facing the target at the top of my swing.** Even if you can turn easy on the way back, getting your back to face the target is an efficient way to build power in your swing while also keeping your club on plane. The key is to do it while creating a strong foundation in your right leg. Keep your flex and feel your weight transfer into your right thigh and hip as you swing back.
—PGA Tour player Zach Johnson

Point your back toward the target at the top to build maximum energy in your swing.

Spread Your Wings

Go from narrow to wide by flexing your back

Look at any great driver of the ball and you'll see that the space between his shoulders is the same at impact as it is at address. You'll never see hunched shoulders or bent arms as the club swings through the hitting zone.

Maintaining the distance between your shoulders creates the necessary room for you to swing through impact and, more importantly, helps you maintain the width of your swing arc for enhanced speed.

To establish and better retain width, use the muscles in your back. At address, bring both hands to ear height with your palms facing outward. As you do this, sense how the large muscles of your back bring your shoulder blades closer together and pull your shoulders farther apart. Now bend from your hips into your normal address posture, keeping your back engaged and your blades pinched together. You're now set for power.
—Mike Malaska

Pinch your shoulder blades together to get wide at address.

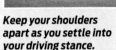

Keep your shoulders apart as you settle into your driving stance.

Re-create wide—not shrugged—shoulders at impact.

Remove your right hand from the grip to get a feel for swinging back with a straight left arm.

DRILL

Hand Yourself Extra Yards

An easy drill to widen your arc

The key marker for correct swing width is the butt of the club, which should remain as far away from your body as possible at the top (like 2010 PGA Championship winner Martin Kaymer is showing here). Here's how to get the right feel.

STEP 1: Take your normal address, but with your fingers on your right hand lifted off the handle.

STEP 2: Swing back by pushing the handle of the club away and behind you using your left hand. As your reach the top of your backswing, push the butt of the club up with your right palm. Continue to push the butt of the club up so that your left arm is perfectly straight.
—Todd Sones

QUICK TIP
For a stronger coil, try kicking in your right knee at address. This makes your right leg a post so you can turn against resistance.

CHECKPOINT

Once you're comfortable with this wider and freer takeaway [*photo, left*], grip the club as you normally do and try to re-create that same feeling of leverage and width as you take the club to the top. Note in the sequence of Martin Kaymer below how this leverage and width is maintained at every point in the swing. That's what you should strive for.
—Todd Sones

> "Create as much leverage between your arms as possible—that is, a feeling of the right arm pushing the left one out."
> **—Todd Sones**

The lie of your club sets the path. | Leverage begins in the backswing. | Hands as far away from the body as possible. | Club re-traces wide backswing arc. | Arms pulled from the shoulder sockets. | Width maintained in the release. | Width is still evident at the end.

INSTRUCTION
Stretch to 10:30
Move the butt of your club far away from your body

The more distance there is between the butt of your club and the ball when you reach the top, the more room your clubhead has to accelerate on the downswing. When the grip is at 10:30, it's the farthest it should be from the ball. **To get it there, swing back while keeping the triangle formed by your shoulders and arms intact.** If your grip hits 12:00, your arms have probably folded, collapsing the triangle and reducing your power. **—Martin Hall**

DRILL
Flex Your Knees for Big Hits
Create width and coil with a simple drill

During your backswing, you need to maintain flex in your right knee. To get a feel for this, assume your address position with a driver and place a ball under your right heel. **The ball will force you to bend your right knee**—it should feel as though you're pushing the ball into the ground with your right foot. This flexed position will allow you to turn your shoulders fully and create more resistance against your lower body. **—Brian Mogg**

DRILL
Take a Hike!
Another way to add leverage

Without a club, set your hands like a quarterback ready to receive the snap from center, with the lifeline of your right hand placed firmly on top of your left thumb. Make a mock backswing and **try to maintain the pressure from your right hand on your left thumb all the way to the top.** You know you've done it right if you feel your right hand push your left arm outward. **—Tim Mahoney**

HOW TO ADD SPEED

Even just a few miles per hour of extra clubhead speed can be the difference between hitting a mid-iron and a long iron on your approach

Nail Drives With the O-Factor

WHAT IS THE O-FACTOR?
The angle of your hips in relation to horizontal.

HOW TO USE IT
Turn your left hip up and to the left of the target immediately at the start of your downswing—and keep turning it!

WHAT IT DOES
The move is so powerful that it literally pulls your shoulders and arms along for the ride. And since your hips move first, everything else must accelerate to catch up at impact. Using your hips like this is what allows you to hammer the ball without swinging hard.
—Robert Baker

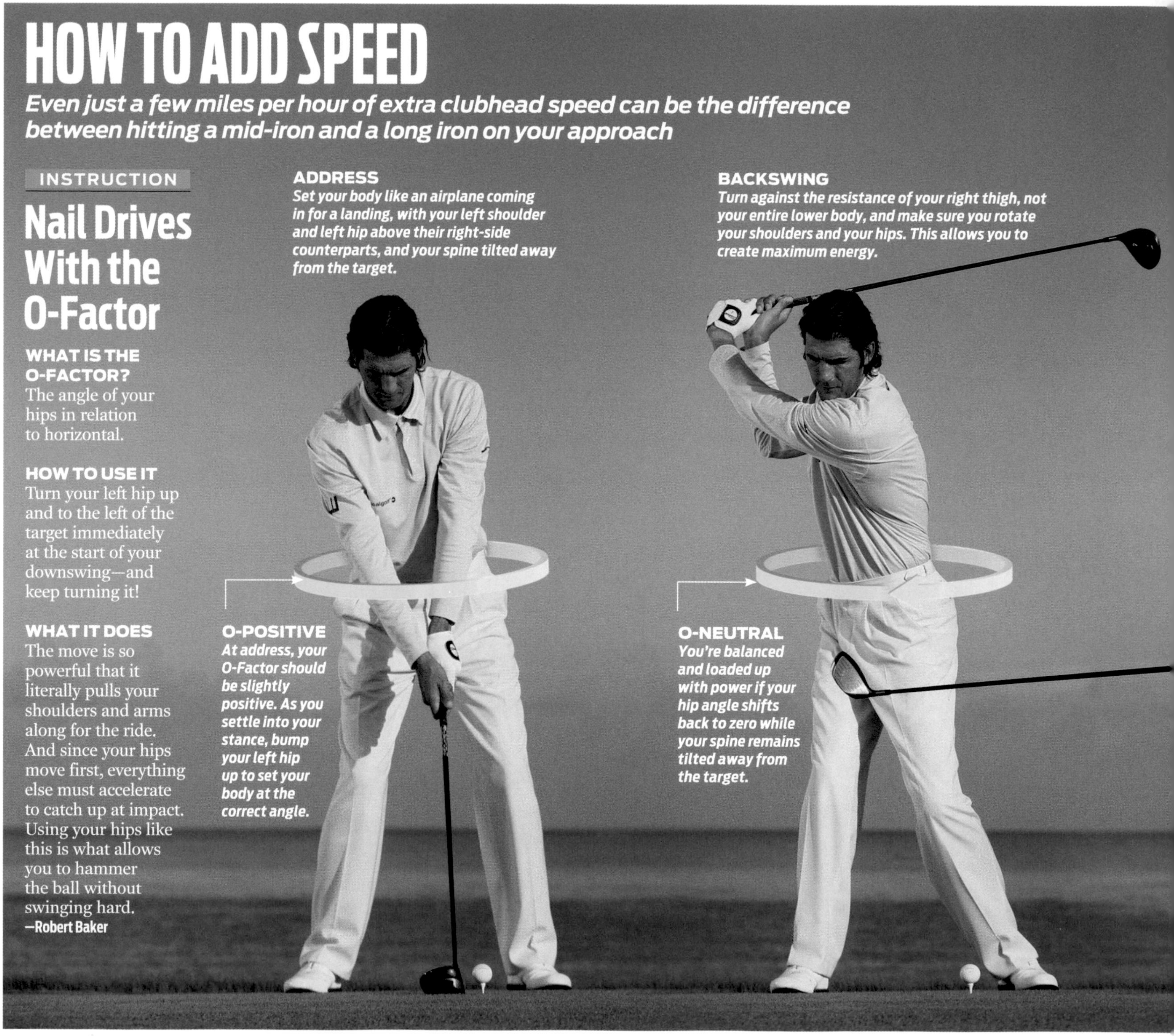

ADDRESS
Set your body like an airplane coming in for a landing, with your left shoulder and left hip above their right-side counterparts, and your spine tilted away from the target.

O-POSITIVE
At address, your O-Factor should be slightly positive. As you settle into your stance, bump your left hip up to set your body at the correct angle.

BACKSWING
Turn against the resistance of your right thigh, not your entire lower body, and make sure you rotate your shoulders and your hips. This allows you to create maximum energy.

O-NEUTRAL
You're balanced and loaded up with power if your hip angle shifts back to zero while your spine remains tilted away from the target.

DOWNSWING
From the top, turn your hips immediately to the left and, as the club approaches impact, pull your left hip up. This creates whip-like speed and helps drop your club onto the correct plane.

O-POSITIVE
Kick in your right knee to get your left hip moving up and your right shoulder moving down.

DRILLS

How to Groove Your O-Factor

Perform these drills to improve your hip action and gas up your swing

MAKE A HIP SWING

To learn the feeling of powering your downswing with your hips, place your driver behind your back as shown, make your backswing turn and, as you rotate through impact, keep your upper body as quiet as possible. Make a level turn going back and use "butt power" to whip your left hip up and around on your downswing.

Whip your hips and let your left arm fold in your follow-through.

Angled shaft matches angled hips.
Level shaft matches level hips.
Left hip up, right shoulder down.

FLING YOUR HEADCOVER

With your left hand, swing a headcover over your right shoulder and slap your back, then use your hips to whip it forward. Keep your left arm in and try to smack your back with the headcover on your follow-through.
—Robert Baker

CHECKPOINT

Fingers First

A palm grip slows you down

Your hands represent one of three power sources in your swing (your arms and your pivot are the other two). To use them correctly, start by gripping the club in your fingers. **Think about a major league pitcher: When he wants to bring the heat, he grips the ball in his fingers.** When he wants to take something off a pitch, he holds the ball in his palm. When you hold the club in your palms it limits your ability to release the club. A palm grip also creates tension because you have to squeeze tighter to hold the club, and that dramatically decreases clubhead speed. How important is a finger grip? It's the first thing you should consider in the search for more power. **—Carol Preisinger**

WRONG!
A palm grip robs you of speed.

RIGHT!
A finger grip adds speed.

INSTRUCTION

Put More Zing in Your Swing

Perform these drills to improve your hip action and ramp up your swing

If you want to hit it big, you need to think small. That's because it's the smaller muscles in your hands and forearms—not the larger, slower chest and shoulder muscles that so many golfers use—that produce the greatest clubhead speed in the golf swing. As your wrists unhinge and the forearms rotate through impact, additional energy is sent down the shaft to the clubhead, increasing your speed where you need it the most—through the ball. Here are a few ways to get these speed producers working for you, so you can add a little zip and pop to your drives.

At address, strengthen your grip but loosen your grip pressure so that your arms are dangling, not pulled tight.

GO STRONG AND LIGHT

Grip the club lightly in your fingers, making sure that the "V" formed by the thumb and forefinger on each hand points to your right shoulder. In this stronger position, you'll have an easier time unhinging and rehinging your wrists, multiplying the speed of the clubhead through impact. The more you hold the club in your palms in a weak position, the tighter your grip will be and the more likely you'll be to use your shoulders on the downswing. Picture two ropes running through your arms at address—they should be dangling, not pulled tight. This image will help you establish the right grip pressure (very light), so that you can accelerate your hands and arms on the downswing without calling on your shoulders.

DRILL: LET 'EM FLY

Here's a drill to help you build more hand, arm and clubhead speed. Stick four tees in the ground side by side and place a ball on the last tee. Set up to the first tee with your feet together and toes turned out, like a duck. Make your normal swing and try to send each tee flying as you shuffle forward with your feet, Charlie Chaplin–style, to reach the next tee. When you reach the fourth and final tee, forget about the ball and focus on launching the tee. It takes a good amount of hand and arm speed to make each tee fly. If you lead with your shoulders and swing too hard on the downswing, you're likely to lose your balance and and fall forward.

When you get to the last ball, forget that it's there and just try to send the tee flying.

Is Custom-Fitting Really Necessary?

Haven't been fit yet? Here's why you need to do it—*stat!*

Q: Have you been fit for a driver?
45%—Yes   **55%—No**

If you read *Golf Magazine* even infrequently, you know that custom-fitting really works. Finding the right loft, lie angle and shaft flex for your swing will trim strokes off your game. The following reader was a classic slicer with a weak grip and poor swing path. Now he hits his driver in the fairway and 34 yards longer.

Age: 29
Handicap before: 25
Handicap after: 22
Old driver: 360 cc, 9.5º, graphite shaft, regular flex, 45.5", standard grip
New driver: 460 cc (draw biased), 9.5º, 65-gram graphite shaft, stiff flex, 45.5", standard grip
This reader switched to an offset, draw-biased head and a lower-spinning ball, and he strengthened his grip. A stronger grip takes some sidespin off the ball and straightens his ball flight. The offset head has extra weight in the heel to promote a right-to-left flight.

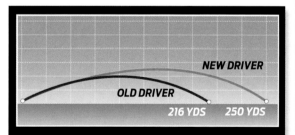

NEW DRIVER

OLD DRIVER

216 YDS   250 YDS

THE CLUBFITTING: Test Result for Driver

	BEFORE	AFTER
Clubhead speed	92 mph	97 mph
Ball speed	137 mph	148 mph
Launch angle°	14°	15°
Height (apex)	89 feet	120 feet
Backspin	3,300 rpm	3,500 rpm
Sidespin	611 rpm	597 rpm
Avg. dispersion	21 yards	15 yards
Carry distance	216 yards	250 yards

Use a towel to get a feel for maintaining the power angle deep into your downswing.

The secret angle to more power.

QUICK TIP
Try to contact the lower inside quadrant of the ball. You'll create a more inside delivery, and maybe hit a draw.

Turn Your Swing Into a Sling

Lock in your "power angle" for big hits

THE PROBLEM

You don't hit the ball as long as you want to because you're not storing up enough potential power during your swing. This usually happens because you're releasing the clubhead too early—a condition also known as "clubhead throwaway"—which is causing you to lose your power angle.

THE SOLUTION

You need to learn the sensation of storing your power angle (the angle between your left forearm and clubshaft) late into your downswing. A great way to accomplish this is to perform my simple towel drill.

Take an ordinary towel and wrap it around your driver shaft. Hold the grip as you normally would with your left hand and the ends of the towel with your right. Now make some swings, being sure to hold the towel tight enough to maintain the hinge in your left wrist and the angle between the clubshaft and your forearm as you swing the club down to the hitting zone each time [*photo, left*]. Everyone develops their own keys for learning this move, so pay close attention to the sensations you're feeling in your body while you perform the drill. Once you've made some swings with the towel, hit a few drives and try to re-create the same sensation you felt during the drill. You should quickly notice a more powerful feeling as you pass through impact.
—**Michael Breed**

DRILL

Use Balance and Rhythm to Add Yards

Get it by hitting drives from a practice bunker

TRY THIS!
Practice hitting your driver in the sand. Learning to swing in a bunker is a good way to improve your balance, rhythm and ballstriking. To begin, find a practice bunker on the range with a relatively low lip and plenty of sand in the bottom. Tee a ball and take your address position with your driver and make a few practice swings at about 60 percent of your normal speed. While you're doing this be certain to maintain your balance. **After a while you should get comfortable hitting solid drives without losing your balance.** When you're done, go to the grass part of the range and hit some drives while maintaining the same feel you had in the bunker. You should feel more powerful, rhythmic and balanced.
—Scott Sackett

If you can rip the ball cleanly while standing in a bunker, then you've achieved the rhythm and balance necessary for consistent driving.

INSTRUCTION

How to Stripe Your Opening Tee Shot

Ask yourself these three questions to find the right fix for you

Don't aim at a target 300 yards away; instead, pick one three inches away.

READER POLL

Q: Do you get more nervous over the first tee shot of the day or a pressure putt late in the round?
53%—First tee shot
24%—Pressure putt
15%—Don't get nervous

1
IS IT FIRST-TEE JITTERS?
It's common to feel nerves on the first tee, which can make you guide your shot instead of making an aggressive swing.

YOU KNOW IF...
You kill it on the range, but you feel like the whole world is watching when you stand on the first tee.

HOW TO FIX IT
Make pre-round range bets with your pals—wager, say, a beer, that you can hit a distant green, or nail the ball picker-upper. That gets you used to playing with pressure so the first tee shot is a piece of cake.

2
AM I TRYING TO MAKE A PERFECT SWING?
The fairway looks extra small on the first tee before you're into the round. You may try to make a perfect swing, which causes tension.

YOU KNOW IF...
Check your recent scorecards. If you struggle on the first couple of holes, you're making the shots harder than they are.

HOW TO FIX IT
Be like Jack. Nicklaus liked to pick a target three inches in front of his ball—a blade of grass, a leaf—and aim at that [*illustration, left*]. Don't even bother looking down the fairway once you're aimed.

3
AM I PULLING THE WRONG CLUB?
Golfers often hit driver with trouble left and right, when a nice little 5-wood would be perfect.

YOU KNOW IF...
Your instinct is to go with a safer club, but you pull driver to keep up with your buddies. You're giving in to peer pressure.

HOW TO FIX IT
Obey your inner caddie, not your inner Daly. Hit the club that gives you the best chance of finding the fairway. Better 220 from the fairway than 180 from the trees.
—Rick Grayson

HIT IT LONGER

A wider swing arc and greater clubhead speed help the yards add up. Here's what you need to put the two together so that you're consistently (and scarily) long off the tee.

NO!
Don't collapse your right leg.

YES!
Push off the ground for max extension and clubhead speed.

Post Up for More Power

Push against the ground for max power, less slide

THE PROBLEM
You slide your lower body toward the target in an attempt to generate more power in your swing. This mistake forces your upper body to hang back, your knees to buckle and your arms to suck into your body rather than extend through the hitting zone. It also prevents you from creating any leverage against the ground because your body weight is sliding forward during the swing. The result is reduced clubhead speed and less overall driving distance.

THE SIMPLE FIX
for this problem is to stop sliding your legs toward the target and instead straighten them as you pass through impact. You should feel kind of like a basketball player going up for a rebound as you swing down through the ball, with your legs pushing hard against the ground and your body weight moving more up than forward. If you do it correctly you'll feel a snap of the clubhead through the ball like you're cracking a whip. If you do it incorrectly, your clubhead will feel dead. If you look at a photo of Tiger or Ben Hogan through impact, you'll notice that the cuffs on their pants are shooting out away from their legs and toward the target. This happens because they both make a fantastic post-up move through impact, which creates tons of leverage. As you read the rest of the instruction in this chapter you'll hopefully learn that leverage is power.
—**Brady Riggs**

Try a Narrow Stance—It Works!

Keep your feet at hip width
to busting big drives

THE PREVAILING WISDOM
A super-wide stance creates the support you need
when you're swinging for the fences.

WHY THE PREVAILING WISDOM IS WRONG
When you take a stance with your feet outside your
shoulders, your lower legs angle in from your feet to
your knees. This is a power-bracing position, not a
power-delivering position.

WHAT TO DO INSTEAD
Place your feet under your hips. This stacks the upper
part of each leg on top of the lower, allowing you to
tap the power of your entire leg.

THE EXTRA BENEFIT
A hip-width stance makes it easier to pivot around each
hip. This is a fundamental of any striking motion. If
your stance is wider than your hips, you'll need to move
laterally to get either hip where you need it, and with all
that sliding you're bound to reverse pivot and hit a
major-league slice. A hip-width stance negates the
need to slide and the likelihood you'll slice.

—Mike Adams

WRONG! **RIGHT!**

An extra-wide stance encourages sliding. *A hip-width stance improves your pivot.*

WHAT'S THE BEST STANCE WIDTH?

**Q: When swinging
a driver, where
should the feet be
positioned?**

Under your shoulders:
58%

Outside your | *Under your*
shoulders: | *hips: 25%*
17%

● A narrow stance
can certainly give you
extra rotation. But if
you're a hard swinger,
place your feet outside
your shoulders.

—Jon Tattersall

Know Your Driver

Look for design
options that can
help your swing

Before you purchase the
same souped-up, high-
performance driver used
by your friends or your
favorite Tour professional,
be aware of the major
design elements that
could help—or potentially
hurt—your swing.

CLUBHEAD
**Most drivers are
460 cc in size.
Smaller heads
are available,
but in general,
larger ones offer
more resistance
to twisting
and added
forgiveness.**

WEIGHTING
**Clubheads with
a low, deep center
of gravity (CG)
produce a higher
ball flight than
those with a
high CG and/or
a CG closer to
the clubface.**

SHAFT FLEX
**Flexes range from
extra-stiff to
ladies. Finding the
proper flex, based
on your swing
speed and tempo,
will help you max
out distance and
improve control.**

BALL FLIGHT
**If you slice, look
for a clubhead
with "draw bias"
weighting. If you
fight a hook, you
may find relief
with a "fade
bias" driver.**

"Start your
downswing by
'firing' your right
side. Kick your
right foot and
knee toward the
target. This shifts
your weight to
your left side and
sets your hip turn
in motion."
—Jimmy Ballard

YES!
Right shoulder closer to the target than the left.

A person standing across from you should see only your right shoulder—not your left—as you swing into your follow-through.

NO!
Left shoulder closer to the target than the right.

"Hide" Your Left Shoulder

Guarantee big yards by rotating all the way through impact

THE FAULT
You don't drive the ball very long because you're not rotating your body enough through impact. You know this is your problem if your left shoulder is closer to the target than your right as you swing into your follow-through [*inset*]. This is a huge drain on your power.

THE FIX
The key is to make sure that your right shoulder is closer to the target than your left as you pass through impact.

In order to make this happen, you need to get your right hip and right lat moving toward the target—if they hang back you'll never be able to get your right shoulder in the desired forward position. Think about your right hip, shoulder and lat all moving in a counterclockwise direction through impact and you'll have the correct feel. If you've done it right, a face-on view [*main photo*] should show your right shoulder blocking the view of your left shoulder, and your right pocket will be clearly visible.
—**Chuck Winstead**

DRILL

Hit the Hot Spot

Make contact high on the face and spot yourself 10 extra yards

You've almost certainly heard Tour players and TV commentators talking about how the sweet spot on drivers has moved from the center to nearer the top of the clubface. **The name for this 21st-century sweet spot is the "hot spot."** The discovery of the hot spot signals a new era in the evolution of the golf swing. It has happened before: Hickory shafts changed to steel, blade irons changed to cavity back, and wood clubheads changed to metal—all these changes produced shifts in how players strike the ball. In short, the way the game is played largely depends on the equipment of the day. The huge-headed drivers are here to stay, so here's how to reap their benefits and start hitting your longest drives ever.

Mark your ball with a dot the size of a shirt button, and place it on the tee so you'll make contact with it.

Note where your longest shots make a mark and tee the equator of your ball to that spot every time.

FIND YOUR HOT SPOT

Why are the world's best players hitting the ball longer than ever before? Their secret is clear—in some cases, contact is being made on the top scoring line of the clubface! This produces the high-launch, low-spin ball flight that translates into extra yards.

No matter which brand of driver you hit, the hot spot is above the center of the clubface. But it's slightly different for each driver. To find yours, take an erasable marker and put a circle on your ball [*top photo*]. Tee it up with the circle pointing straight back at your clubface at address.

Now hit some drives. After each one examine the clubface to see the circular mark [*bottom photo*]. When you catch one flush, the mark will be high. That's your new sweet spot.

Align the equator of the ball with your hot spot every time and you'll hit long drives more consistently.
—Peter Kostis

CHECKPOINT

Long, but not Wrong

Conventional wisdom says the longer your shaft, the longer—but more off-target—your tee shots. Turns out that's not the case.

THE TEST
We gave a foursome of golfers (handicaps: 7, 8, 12 and 14) the following test drivers—460 cc clubhead at 43.5 inches (the old industry standard for shaft length), 45 inches (the new standard), 46.5 inches and 48 inches (the maximum length allowed by the Rules of Golf). Players hit the drivers in a precisely varied order. Shots had to land within the grid (320 yards long x 35 yards wide) to be counted. With the assistance of the experts at Golf Laboratories in San Diego, Calif., we tracked the results with a launch monitor and also measured by hand exactly how far off target each drive landed from the center of the test grid.

THE RESULTS
Holy fairways, Batman! The two longer-shafted drivers were not only long, but also relatively straight. Stunningly, they were actually up to two yards more accurate than the shorter drivers. (In real terms, shots were straight enough to stay in the fairway.) Our suggestion: At the very least, give a longer shaft a try.

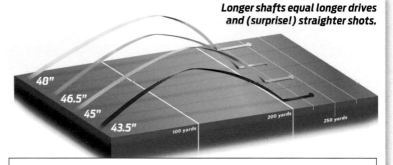

Longer shafts equal longer drives and (surprise!) straighter shots.

SHAFT TEST: TALE OF THE TAPE				
Shaft length (inches)	43.5	45	46.5	48
Head speed (mph)	97	98	99	101
Ball speed (mph)	138	143	144	146
Launch angle (degrees)	10.19	11.97	11.03	12.96
Backspin (rpm)	3,617	3,694	3,289	3,457
Carry distance (yards)	204	217	211	223
Total distance (yards)	241	248	245	252
Dispersion (yards from center line)	15.75	15.93	13.40	14.47

HIT EVERY FAIRWAY

Long drives are good. Long and straight drives are even better.

DRILL

Extend for Accuracy

This drill will eliminate your cut shot

THE FAULT
You miss too many fairways.

THE FIX
Tee up a ball and place a second tee six inches and 45 degrees outside the first tee as shown. Try to sweep the ball off the first tee and swing over the second tee as you sling your clubhead through the hitting area. Performing this drill correctly simulates the feeling of proper extension through impact, stopping you from cutting across the ball (slice) or swinging too much from the inside (push or hook).
—Brian Mogg

Max acceleration occurs after impact, but only if you achieve full extension through the ball.

WHAT STARTS YOUR MOVE BACK DOWN?

Q: On the downswing with a driver, should the legs move the hips or should the hips move the legs?

Hips move the legs:
57%

Hips and legs work together:
7%

Legs move the hips:
36%

● Your backswing and forward swing start from the ground up and, as the old song goes, "the hip bone's connected to the thigh bone." Your legs move your hips, not the other way around.
—Rick McCord

● Your legs are like the legs on a tripod—they hold up the top. Legs react, they do not act.
—Mike Perpich

● Your hips should lead. In fact, they should begin to turn forward before you finish your backswing.
—Jon Tattersall

Shorten Your Finish for Safer Driving

Try this quick tip to split the fairway every time

THE PROBLEM
Not only do you spray your drives, but you take the anxiety over your sprayed drives to every tee.

THE SOLUTION
Instead of swinging into your normal full follow-through, finish your drives when the clubhead reaches about waist high after impact. Call this spot "Checkpoint Charlie," and go through the following list when you reach it:

● *The clubshaft and your left arm are more or less still in line.*
● *Your right wrist is still bent back slightly.*
● *Your right arm is across the middle of your torso.*
● *Your chest is facing the target.*
● *The toe of the clubhead is pointing up, neither too open nor too closed.*

If you work on finishing your driver swings with a short follow-through that satisfies the five conditions above, you may lose a little distance, but you'll also land a lot more shots on the short grass.
—**Martin Hall**

STOP

Release It for Straighter Drives

My "full-overlap" grip works wonders for errant drivers

1. Take your regular grip and slide your right hand up the handle until all the fingers on your right hand overlap those on your left [*Frame 1*].
2. Make your normal swing, but as you approach impact use your right hand to pull the knuckles of your left hand down and under [*Frames 2-4*].
3. As you swing through impact continue to keep pulling the knuckles under all the way to waist high so that your left wrist stays bowed and your right wrist stays bent backward. As the club moves down through the impact zone, turn your knuckles down toward the ground so your wrists flatten [*Frame 5*]. Do this several times without a ball to ingrain the proper feeling.
—**Mike Bender**

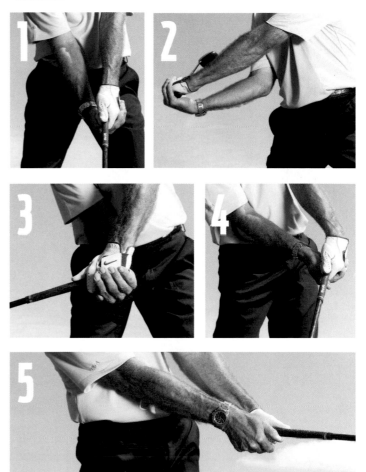

How to Stop Your Overswing

Stay in control and drive it longer at the same time

THE FAULT
In an effort to hit your longest drives you make a backswing that's way too long. Not only does this mistake actually sap your power by forcing your swing out of sequence, it also has a negative effect on the quality of your ballstriking and accuracy.

THE FIX
You need to shorten your backswing, or at least that's how it should feel. The key to driving the ball with power is to deliver the club back to the ball squarely, and a shorter backswing will help you make solid contact and swing in sequence so that

your arms and body are synchronized. The ball doesn't care how long your backswing is when you catch it in the center of the face—it's going to go far. To tighten up your swing, add power and accomplish both of these keys, follow the steps below.
—Brady Riggs

Before you reach shoulder height...

...start turning back to the ball...

...and add lag and tons of swing power.

STEP 1
Make your backswing as you normally would, but don't allow your hands to swing back any higher than shoulder height.

STEP 2
Start turning your hips and torso back toward the ball before you feel like you've completed your "normal" driver backswing.

STEP 3
You should feel a "whip" in your swing through impact, which will create more clubhead speed while promoting solid contact.

How to Build a Go-to Drive

Open your stance and your swing to find more fairways

THE FAULT

Every time you step up to the tee you're taking a big swing and hoping the ball will find the fairway. You don't have a go-to tee shot that you can get in play consistently, and as a result your confidence is at an all-time low. You need to find a shot that you can play with your driver when the pressure's on, or whenever you absolutely must find the fairway.

THE FIX

The best way to solve this problem is to simply learn to hit a high fade off the tee. It's an easy shot to hit consistently, and it shouldn't take long to learn the essentials. To practice this shot so you can take it to the course with confidence and play it on demand, follow these steps:

STEP 1: Set up with your feet aimed approximately 20 yards left of the target line. Place the ball well forward in your stance, which will help you swing out to the left. Don't be afraid to open up your stance—it's critical for playing the high-fade drive correctly.

STEP 2: Take several practice swings but don't move the club directly along your foot line. Instead, swing about 5 yards closer to your target (i.e., if your feet are aimed 20 yards left of target, swing about 15 yards left of the target line).

STEP 3: While making your practice swings, be sure not to strand your weight on your back foot. It's important to strive to make level contact on these shots.

STEP 4: Now pull the trigger. If done correctly, the ball should start out just left of the target line and come back to center, flying on a nice, high trajectory. Practice it until you can do it every time.
—**Brian Manzella**

If you point your stance 20 yards to the left of your target...

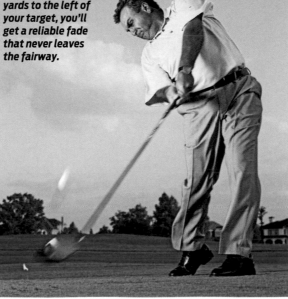

...but swing only 15 yards to the left of your target, you'll get a reliable fade that never leaves the fairway.

Level Out Your Approach

The 5-Wood Drill gets you powerful and accurate in no time

Tee up a ball between your left armpit and big toe, but tee it slightly higher than you would a driver. Then, with a 5-wood or similarly lofted utility club, see if you can sweep the ball off its perch without disturbing the tee. Start with half- and three-quarter swings before giving it a full rip. The only way to keep the tee in the ground and hit the ball solidly is to make a shallow pass at the ball. If you're too steep, you'll pop the ball up and knock the tee out of the ground.

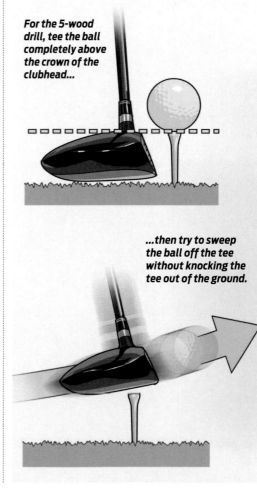

For the 5-wood drill, tee the ball completely above the crown of the clubhead...

...then try to sweep the ball off the tee without knocking the tee out of the ground.

Thanks to technology and our teachers' top tips, you can stretch your scoring zone and get it close with every club in your bag.

SECTION 4

LONG IRONS, WOODS AND HYBRIDS

They're easier to play than ever. Here's how to use them to make more long-range birdies.

You expect to get the ball close to the flagstick with your short irons and wedges. With longer clubs, however, you're happy just getting the ball close to the green. It's time to change that line of thinking. Technology has made long irons, fairway woods and hybrids much easier to play, and the swing to get you to birdie range from long distance is the same you'd use with your 8-iron, minus a few adjustments to your setup to create a more sweeping type of impact. The Top 100 Teachers show you the quick way to make that happen on the following pages, so there's no reason you shouldn't expect to hit shots with longer clubs as close to the pin as you do with your more traditional scoring irons.

The main challenge is to plan your attack in a way that minimizes the damage that occurs when you do miss with your woods and long irons. That means choosing the right landing spot, selecting the right club, and using the lay of the land to shape the shot once the ball hits the ground. The Top 100 Teachers have you covered here, too, with strategic ways to get the most out of your long game.

5 THINGS YOU'LL LEARN IN THIS SECTION

- *How to hit long irons on the sweet spot consistently.*
- *How to get the most out of your hybrids.*
- *The setup and swing changes necessary to sweep the ball powerfully off the turf with your fairway woods.*
- *How to hit long-iron "stingers" off the tee and from the fairway to control spin and trajectory.*
- *Drills to help you hit your long irons and woods farther and with greater accuracy.*

THE LOWDOWN ON HYBRIDS

Q: What confuses you most about golf equipment?

31% — Hybrids
20% — Balls
10% — Wedges
7% — Drivers
7% — Irons
25% — Not confused

What makes a hybrid work

In a word, gravity. The simple physics behind the hybrid's success is its low, deep center of gravity (CG). Because the club's CG is below that of the ball's, the collision of the club and ball at impact produces a higher launch angle and spin rate. A deep CG also directs the clubhead to the ball at a higher effective loft angle, which again increases launch and spin. One other element helps the club get the ball up quickly: a flexible shaft bending forward just prior to impact.

The guts of a hybrid reveal the secret to its success: a low, deep center of gravity.

LONG-IRON SECRETS

Use these special swing adjustments to knock down the flagstick with your 3-, 4- and 5-irons

As soon as you strike the ball, step off the gas and let your arms and body glide into your finish.

SWING ENERGY   **100%**   **60%**

Make Your Finish a "Soft" One

Add accuracy—and look cool doing it

If you're one of those players who tends to fall backward or forward after impact, or to lean to the left or right so far that you lose your balance, then this tip is for you. After you strike the ball, let everything in your body go soft. You should go from swinging your arms as fast as you can through impact to immediately feeling like the only thing pulling them into your finish is momentum. I strive to make the

NO!
Sucking your arms into your body makes it difficult to hit crisp irons.

30% **0%**

YES!
Extend your arms fully through impact.

CHECKPOINT

Reach for It!

Long arms through impact are the key to solid contact

Great iron players have one thing in common: Their arms are fully extended through impact. The key is to feel that your right arm goes from bent to straight as the clubhead passes through impact and into your follow-through. To get the feeling, find a bush on the driving range or in your backyard. Select an iron and take your address position so that the bush is directly in front of you on your target line. You want to be far enough from it so you can just reach it with the clubhead when your arms are fully extended in your release. Make some practice swings, and try to touch the bush with the clubhead as you reach the fully released position. If you pull your arms into your body you won't be able to reach it. If you extend, as you should, the clubhead will just brush the leaves on the bush.
—Keith Lyford

DRILL

Make a Natural Backswing

A simple trick to get on plane

STEP 1: Swing back, allowing your arms to move along your shoulder line and your right arm to fold.
STEP 2: Have a friend lay an alignment stick or club along your shoulder line. You want the club you're swinging and the alignment stick to be parallel to one another.
STEP 3: Move the club until it matches the alignment stick, regardless of where this is. Once you find this spot, hold it for a bit until you can memorize its location.
STEP 4: Hit this spot in your backswing consistently and you'll start swinging more from the inside, your angle of attack will be shallower, and your ballstriking will improve dramatically. Plus, your slice should be gone forever!
—Mike Adams

NO!
A mismatch in shaft angle and shoulder line leads to poor contact.

YES!
Matching the shaft angle to the shoulder line means you're on plane.

end of my swing so soft that my hands and arms automatically fall in front of my chest while I'm tracking the ball in its flight. If your swing energy is at 100 percent capacity at impact, you want to get it to zero by the time your hands reach shoulder height in your follow-through. Finishing soft like this allows you to maintain better balance and control.
—PGA Tour player Hunter Mahan

How to Sting It

Make these three simple changes to hit long irons that fly low, straight and hot

WHAT IT IS
The "2+2+2", a low-trajectory long iron
WHEN TO USE IT
Off the tee on tight driving holes and when playing into the wind.
HOW TO HIT IT
Take your normal address position, then add up the 2s.
—Mike Adams

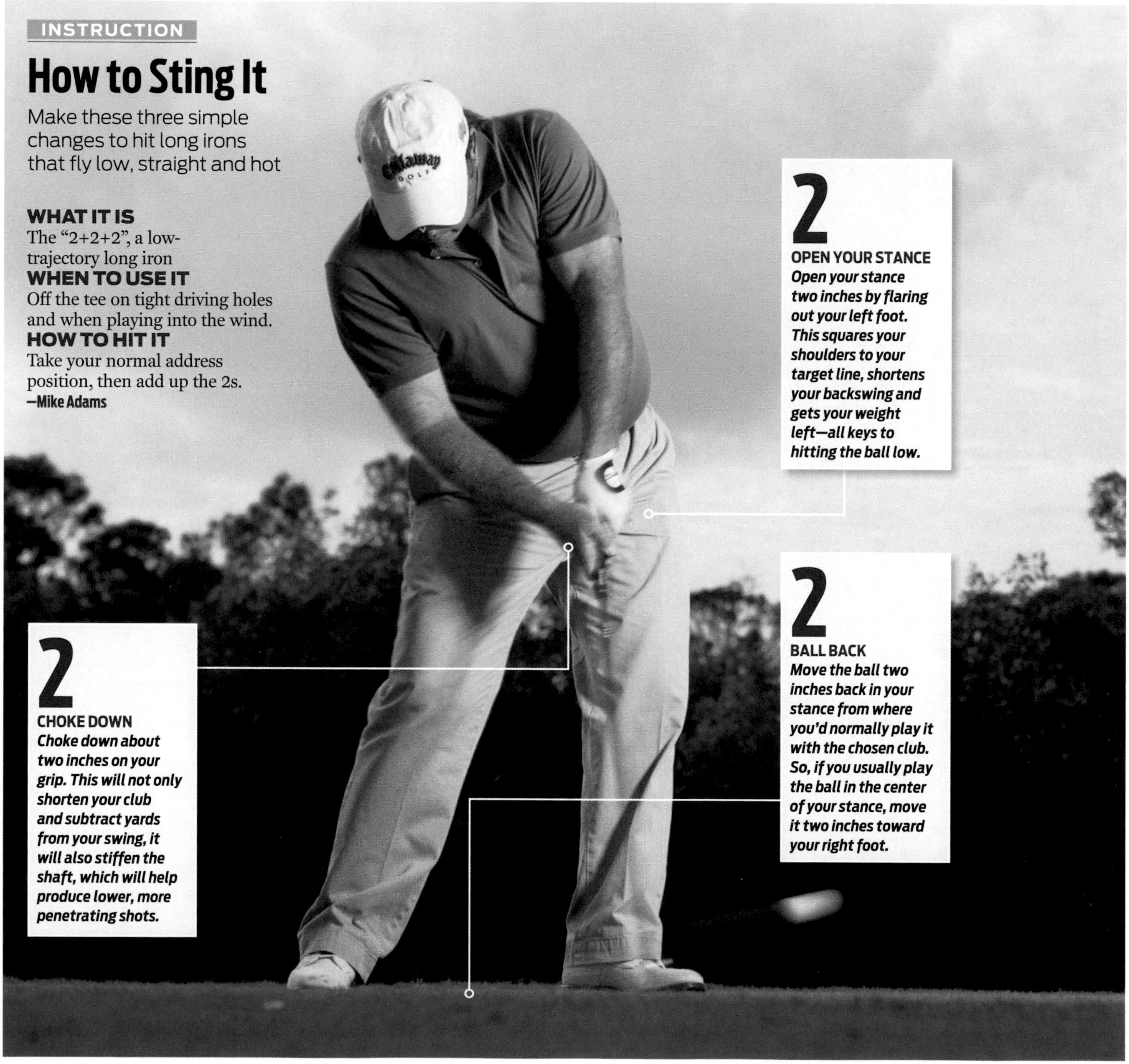

2
OPEN YOUR STANCE
Open your stance two inches by flaring out your left foot. This squares your shoulders to your target line, shortens your backswing and gets your weight left—all keys to hitting the ball low.

2
BALL BACK
Move the ball two inches back in your stance from where you'd normally play it with the chosen club. So, if you usually play the ball in the center of your stance, move it two inches toward your right foot.

2
CHOKE DOWN
Choke down about two inches on your grip. This will not only shorten your club and subtract yards from your swing, it will also stiffen the shaft, which will help produce lower, more penetrating shots.

INSTRUCTION

How to Catch Long Irons Flush

Try this tip to make contact on the sweet spot more often

THE FAULT
You hit long irons super thin.

WHY YOU'RE DOING IT
You're making a big backswing shift to power up behind the ball [*inset photo*], but you're getting stuck there on your downswing. This moves the bottom of your swing arc back so you catch the ball on the upswing.

THE FIX
Get balanced at address and maintain that balance from start to finish. Follow the cues here.
—Tim Mahoney

WRONG!

Keep your head still.

Keep your arms extended as long as you can during your backswing. This will help you maintain your balance.

Turn to the top while keeping your weight evenly distributed over both legs.

INSTRUCTION

Twist the Shaft for Sweet Hits

Here's the easy, amateur way to make a pro-style squaring move

I recommend that you twist the shaft to the left before you reach impact. PGA Tour players typically make this move gradually as they swing the club down from the top. This, however, takes some skill. What you should do is make the twist much earlier, about the time your hands reach belly height in your backswing. All you have to do is turn the grip to the left until the cup in your left elbow disappears, then maintain the twist past impact. You'll know you correctly maintained it if your clubface points at the target in your through-swing.
—Brian Manzella

TWIST!
You can almost guarantee you've hit it solid if the clubface points away from you in your follow-through.

FAIRWAY WOODS

Here's how to hit them sweet to reach par 5s in two and own a go-to option off the tee on short par 4s

Three Musts for Fairway Woods

Follow these rules to sweep the ball powerfully off the turf

1. SETUP: HANDS UNDER CHIN

At address, allow your arms to hang comfortably from your shoulders so that the base of each hand is directly under your chin. The ball should be positioned just inside the crease on your left pant leg. With your hands a good distance from your body, you'll have an easier time turning your shoulders on the backswing, and you'll swing on a more elliptical-shaped path to encourage a level-to-slightly-ascending blow at impact, ideal for a fairway wood.

Keep your hands a good distance from your body, directly under your chin.

A fairway wood requires a level or slightly ascending strike on the ball.

Maintain the triangle formed by your arms and shoulders and brush the club away.

2. DOWNSWING: START FROM THE GROUND UP

Coming down, feel your weight shift toward the target while your upper body remains coiled. Your weight should naturally flow to your front foot, ensuring the proper downswing sequencing and shallow angle of approach you want with your woods. To teach your body to unwind in the correct fashion, stick an orange or spongy object under your left toe and as soon as you start down, squash the orange.

3. BACKSWING:
KEEP THE TRIANGLE INTACT

As you start the club back, maintain the triangle formed by your arms and shoulders at address, winding your midsection over your right hip. The clubhead should nearly brush the grass for the first foot or so of the takeaway, establishing a wide arc and a smooth, unhurried tempo. Many golfers pull the club to the inside with their hands, narrowing the swing arc and significantly reducing their power.

Let your weight flow to your front foot (as though you're squashing an orange) and keep your upper body coiled.

Move away from the target...

...and stay on your right side.

How to Hit High, Soft Woods

Hang back for a little more air

To rip a fairway wood high and long, try the following:
1. Set up with your head slightly behind the ball and your right shoulder a bit lower than normal. This position will help you create a high-trajectory shot that lands softly.
2. Turn a bit further behind the ball than you would normally (move away from the target a bit in your backswing).
3. Stay behind the ball through impact. These three simple adjustments will create a high, soft ball flight and allow you to hit and hold the green.
—Eden Foster

How to Crush Your Woods

This tip turns your clubs into cannons

THE FAULT
You're not hitting your fairway woods as long as you'd like.

WHY IT'S HAPPENING
You're shortening your swing radius in the hope that a more compact swing will help you sweep the ball cleanly off the fairway turf.

THE FIX
Keep your left arm straight during your backswing and feel both arms being pulled from their sockets through impact. Try increasing your right-hand grip pressure. If you maintain pressure from your right hand on your left thumb, your left arm will remain straight. This creates a wider arc and allows you to extend fully and catch the ball powerfully at impact.
—Tim Mahoney

WRONG!

A loose grip makes for short arms and thin contact.

Keep your hands connected for a wide arc and flush contact.

RIGHT!

HOW TO HIT YOUR HYBRIDS

They're the most versatile clubs in your bag, but only if you use the right technique

Hybrid Off the Tee

Think ankles and hips to generate power and control

WHY IT WORKS
A hybrid is shorter than a driver, which makes it inherently easier to control. It also features more loft, and more loft creates more backspin and less sidespin (the spin that sends your ball off to the left or right). A long iron used to be a good driving alternative, but a hybrid beats even that. Its face has the same bulge and roll features of a driver, and these add corrective spin and draw or fade your ball back into the fairway.

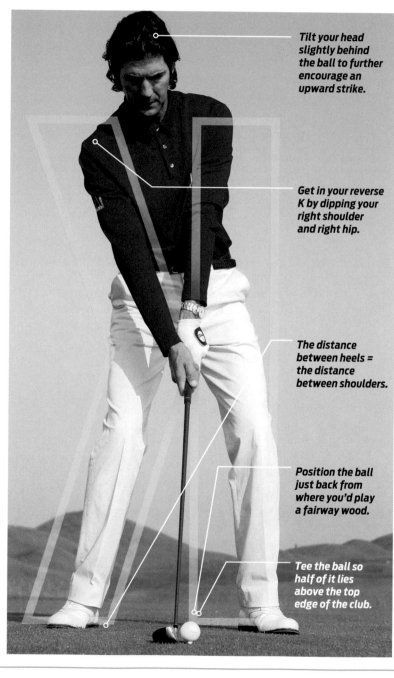

Tilt your head slightly behind the ball to further encourage an upward strike.

Get in your reverse K by dipping your right shoulder and right hip.

The distance between heels = the distance between shoulders.

Position the ball just back from where you'd play a fairway wood.

Tee the ball so half of it lies above the top edge of the club.

ROLL AND SWEEP IT OFF THE TEE
The tilt you establish at address with your "reverse K" [*photo, left*] must be maintained until impact, since it's what allows you to catch the ball on the upswing. Lose your tilt and you'll hit down on the ball—exactly what you don't want.

From the top, roll your ankles toward the target. This simple move has powerful implications. It shifts your weight forward, drops the club into the perfect delivery position, keeps your head behind the ball and saves the energy of your core section for impact. Notice how rolling your ankles whips your knees into action and opens your hips [*sequence, above*]. After you roll your ankles, drive through the ball by turning your right shoulder and hip toward the target. At the same time, pull your left shoulder toward the sky. This move helps you maintain the tilt you established at address so you can catch the ball on the upswing.
—Robert Baker

Roll your ankles toward the target.

Hybrid From the Fairway

Coil behind the ball like you're hitting a driver

GET YOUR PANTS POCKET BEHIND YOU

There's a saying that when the ball is down, hit down. Not so fast. A hybrid from the fairway requires the same sweeping motion as the tee shot. Contact with the ground is okay; divots, however, are not.

To make a solid sweep you must rotate your body behind the ball with your right side on your backswing. Use the classic Greg Norman tip: "Get your right pants pocket behind you." As you turn to the right, feel how your left hip and knee are pulled away from the target. That's the sensation of coil—the stored energy that you release into the ball at impact.

During the takeaway, coil your left shoulder, hip and knee against the resistance of your right thigh.

How to Kick-Start Your Downswing

Your knees are the key to bringing every green into range

Kicking in your right knee on your downswing is an easy move that "breaks" your right leg, making your entire right side shorter and positioning your right shoulder below your left. This sets you up to get your hybrid club under the ball and launch it high toward your target.

To practice this move, place your clubhead with the face slightly open just below your right knee and grab the hosel [*top photo, left*]. Now, kick your knee in (while raising your right heel) and close the face [*bottom photo*]. That's the action you want on your downswing when swinging a hybrid.
—Robert Baker

Nail Your Hybrid Setup

Getting it right at the start makes everything that comes after smooth and easy

I know a lot of you are already using hybrids, but I bet you're not exactly sure if you should swing them like an iron or a wood. Here's my easy guide: If you're more comfortable hitting down on the ball, or have a naturally steep swing, play the ball back in your stance, in the same position you'd use for your long irons. If you're more of a sweeper, or tend to hit your woods better than your irons, move the ball up in your stance closer to your front foot. Get this right and you'll have more freedom to let your hybrids rip.
—PGA Tour player Graeme McDowell

SWEEP SETUP
If you tend to hit your woods better than your irons, play the ball forward. It will help you sweep the ball off the turf without too much ground contact.

SHAFT
It should sit fairly vertical, not leaning unduly toward or away from the target.

BALL POSITION
If you're a sweeper, play the ball just behind your left heel.

LONG-IRON BALL POSITION
Copy this setup if you prefer to swing your hybrids more like you do your irons, or have a naturally steep downswing.

WEIGHT
Make it even. You should feel balanced over both feet, not just over your left foot or right foot.

A Tour-quality short-iron game begins with selecting the correct part of the green to land your ball on and building a swing that favors accuracy over distance.

SECTION 5

SCORING SHOTS

You should attack the pin with your short irons. Here's how to do it with max control.

Even if you hit every fairway, you won't do your scores much good if you miss on your approach, especially from scoring range (any distance you can comfortably hit with a 7-iron or less). Here is where you have the easiest chance to knock the ball close. After all, these are short irons with lots of loft that give you more backspin and less sidespin (with fewer hooks and slices as a result). The trick is to build a short-iron swing that favors accuracy, not distance. If you need to hit the ball farther, switch to a longer club.

Swinging a short iron is no different than swinging your driver or fairway woods. But since your short clubs are shorter and sit on a steeper angle at address, you must make a more upright swing. In this section, the Top 100 Teachers share their secrets on how to get the job done right.

While a great short-iron swing doesn't guarantee more birdies, it certainly helps. You also must pick the right part of the green to hit to and learn how to adjust when caught at those tricky distances inside 100 yards. The Top 100 have plenty to say on that, too, so get ready to go low.

5 THINGS YOU'LL LEARN IN THIS SECTION

- *How to correctly swing your short irons and wedges.*
- *What to look for on the green so that you can choose the spot that will give you the easiest birdie putt.*
- *How to hit four distances with every wedge in your bag and add spin to make your short approaches bite.*
- *An easy trick to help you make pure contact in the center of the sweet spot and with a square clubface.*
- *When to attack the pin and when to play it safe.*

TIGHTEN UP YOUR WEAK LINKS

What area of your game would you like to improve the most? Here's what *Golf Magazine* readers had to say in a recent survey.

Here are your trouble spots:

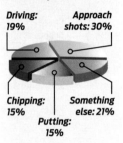

Driving: 19%
Approach shots: 30%
Chipping: 15%
Something else: 21%
Putting: 15%

● Don't be intimidated by the complexity of the golf swing—it's actually similar to some everyday tasks. Think of chopping wood or hammering, for example: You hold the implement with your hands and use your arms to apply the power. It's the same in golf. So as you swing, picture one of those activities. You won't think technique; you'll swing the club back with your hands and then forward with your arms as though it were one motion.
—Manuel de la Torre

THE SHORT-IRON SWING

From scoring range, use a swing that favors accuracy over distance

Make your normal swing at half speed.

Lead with the grip end of the club, not the clubhead.

Pure the Key Clubs

Get your left side and the club in line for better ballstriking

THE PROBLEM

It doesn't matter which iron you swing—at impact, it feels like you're hitting either a marshmallow or a cinder block. You're making impact anywhere but in the center of the clubface.

THE SOLUTION

You need to develop an impact position that has your hands, arms and club aligned with your left leg and hip at impact. This gives you the best chance to catch the ball in the center of the sweet spot. To do this, follow these simple steps.

1. Grip the club at the end of the handle and make your backswing [*left photo*]. You don't need a ball for this drill.
2. Swing back down at half speed. As you approach impact, check that the grip of the club is leading the clubhead [*middle photo*].

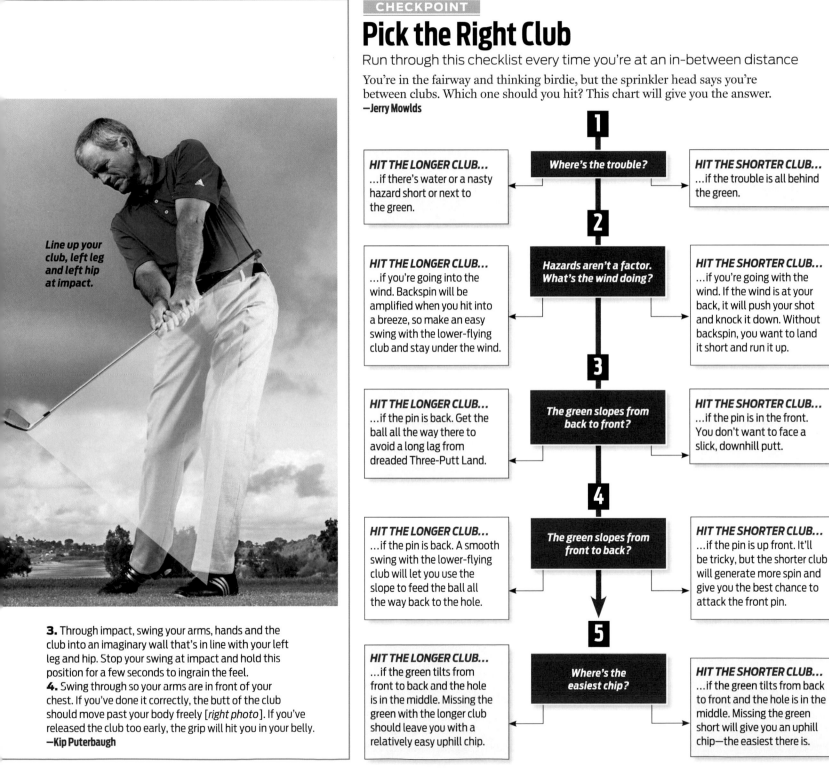

Line up your club, left leg and left hip at impact.

3. Through impact, swing your arms, hands and the club into an imaginary wall that's in line with your left leg and hip. Stop your swing at impact and hold this position for a few seconds to ingrain the feel.
4. Swing through so your arms are in front of your chest. If you've done it correctly, the butt of the club should move past your body freely [*right photo*]. If you've released the club too early, the grip will hit you in your belly.
—Kip Puterbaugh

CHECKPOINT

Pick the Right Club

Run through this checklist every time you're at an in-between distance

You're in the fairway and thinking birdie, but the sprinkler head says you're between clubs. Which one should you hit? This chart will give you the answer.
—Jerry Mowlds

1

HIT THE LONGER CLUB...
...if there's water or a nasty hazard short or next to the green.

Where's the trouble?

HIT THE SHORTER CLUB...
...if the trouble is all behind the green.

2

HIT THE LONGER CLUB...
...if you're going into the wind. Backspin will be amplified when you hit into a breeze, so make an easy swing with the lower-flying club and stay under the wind.

Hazards aren't a factor. What's the wind doing?

HIT THE SHORTER CLUB...
...if you're going with the wind. If the wind is at your back, it will push your shot and knock it down. Without backspin, you want to land it short and run it up.

3

HIT THE LONGER CLUB...
...if the pin is back. Get the ball all the way there to avoid a long lag from dreaded Three-Putt Land.

The green slopes from back to front?

HIT THE SHORTER CLUB...
...if the pin is in the front. You don't want to face a slick, downhill putt.

4

HIT THE LONGER CLUB...
...if the pin is back. A smooth swing with the lower-flying club will let you use the slope to feed the ball all the way back to the hole.

The green slopes from front to back?

HIT THE SHORTER CLUB...
...if the pin is up front. It'll be tricky, but the shorter club will generate more spin and give you the best chance to attack the front pin.

5

HIT THE LONGER CLUB...
...if the green tilts from front to back and the hole is in the middle. Missing the green with the longer club should leave you with a relatively easy uphill chip.

Where's the easiest chip?

HIT THE SHORTER CLUB...
...if the green tilts from back to front and the hole is in the middle. Missing the green short will give you an uphill chip—the easiest there is.

DRILL

How to Stop Missing the Sweet Spot

Practice cross-handed to groove solid contact

THE PROBLEM
You thought you had your swing grooved, but a rash of poor shots proves otherwise.

THE SOLUTION
Using a 7-iron on the practice tee, switch the position of your hands on the grip (left below right) and swing cross-handed. It will feel awkward at first, but if you stick with it you'll ingrain the following three swing keys that are difficult to perfect using a normal grip.
—John Elliott, Jr.

NEEDED HINGE
Since your right hand is on top, your right wrist will hinge sooner in your backswing and establish an extra lever for power.

1

PROPER ARM POSITIONING
The cross-handed grip forces your right arm to follow the lead of your left in your backswing—it will fold correctly as your left arm remains straight.

2

THE POWER APPROACH
You'll also feel a bent right elbow and an extended left arm deep into your downswing—both are vital to compress the ball and add power.

3

Never Hit a Short Iron Full

A longer club and a smoother swing does the trick

Most players make the mistake of taking full swings with their wedges and short irons. Honestly, if I use a full swing with a short club one time a round, it's a lot. I can move a 9-iron 150 yards if I have to, but I'm more likely to swing an 8-iron with an 80 percent pace and a choked grip. **I can't tell you how much swinging within yourself helps with short approaches.** It allows you to swing a longer club smoother and shorter, and is also brilliant at giving you extra control.

—PGA Tour player Graeme McDowell

10 YARDS LESS

5 YARDS LESS

GRIP SWITCH
I'll grip it all the way down to the steel if I need to take 10 yards off a short approach. This allows me to swing a longer club smoother, instead of hoping for that rare perfect all-out swing with a shorter club.

Stop Fats & Thins

Try this drill to catch it clean every time

STEP 1: Choke up several inches on a short iron.
STEP 2: Make some practice swings by taking the club halfway back with your right hand (stop at hip height) and then pulling your belt loop toward the target with your left hand.
STEP 3: Hold the club softly as your body turns—you should feel the clubhead lag behind your hand as it swings down.
STEP 4: Strike some balls softly with this same motion, being sure to lead the clubhead into the ball with your right hand. Don't hit at it with your right arm—let the rotation of your body drive your right arm and club.
STEP 5: Try it with both hands on the handle, then build up to your regular full swing, making sure to allow the rotation of your hips to drive the club through impact.
—David Glenz

1 Take the club halfway back with your right hand only.

2 Pull your belt loop counterclockwise with your left hand to encourage a stronger turn.

3 The extra turn should help you keep your hands ahead of the clubhead—an iron-contact must.

PLANNING YOUR APPROACH
How to be aggressive while avoiding costly mistakes

INSTRUCTION

How to Attack When the Pin Is Back
Here's your plan to get it close

THE SITUATION
You're on the tee of a 125-yard par 3 with the pin cut in the middle of the third tier on a green that slopes back to front. A stiff 20-mph wind is in your face.

THE TOP 100 SAY

48%—Play for the back tier with a punch/knockdown shot

38%—Play a safe low shot to the middle of the green and let your putter do the rest.

14%—When's the last time you practiced a punch? Make your regular swing and play to the middle of the green—always the smartest play.

20-mph wind

IF YOU'RE AN AGGRESSIVE PLAYER...
Hit a knockdown to the pin

Club Selection: If the card says the hole is 125 yards and the pin is back, figure you have 135 to the hole. The general rule for playing into the wind is one more club for every 10 mph. So if you normally hit a 9-iron from 135 yards, you should drop down to a 7-iron here. But since you're going to play a knockdown, drop down one more club to a 6-iron.
Swing Tip: Trust that you have enough club and make a three-quarter swing. Lead the club into impact with the shaft leaning toward the target.
Target: Aim at the middle of the second tier. Your knockdown shot should skip forward to the third tier before it grabs.

"Ben Hogan said, 'Never hit a high ball to a back pin.' That's great advice."
—Charlie Sorrell

IF YOU'RE NOT CONFIDENT WITH THE KNOCKDOWN...
Hit a regular full shot to the middle tier

Club Selection: Drop down two clubs for the wind. If you pure it you might reach the back tier. If you don't, you'll still have a good chance for a two-putt par.
Swing Tip: Forget the wind and make a relaxed swing. Don't try to "power" the ball or juice up your tempo, because even if you pure it you'll just create more backspin and the ball will fly higher (and shorter) into the wind.
Target: Even though you're planning to land your ball on the middle tier of the green, you should still aim for the top of the pin.

"How many clubs is a 20-mph wind worth to you? Most golfers come up short even without wind. Ask yourself: Can you hit the club you select over the green? If not, then you aren't swinging enough club."
—Shawn Humphries

IF YOU TEND TO SLICE OR HOOK YOUR IRONS...

Play a low shot to the middle tier, because low shots spin less.

You need to keep spin to a minimum because wind exacerbates backspin, and if you hit your normal shot you'll end up short.

Club Selection: Plus two for the wind.
Swing Tip: You don't need a pure knockdown—just something slightly lower to keep the ball under the wind. Think of hitting a long chip—play the ball back of center and think of squaring the clubface with your body, not your hands. That means rotating your hips and shoulders to the left of your target from the top of your backswing to well past impact.
Target: Center of the green.

"If you tend to cut or hook the ball, wind can spell disaster, especially on a tee shot on a par 3. A headwind magnifies any curving ball flight, so controlling the shot shape is a critical factor. An intentional punch is ideal in this situation because it's easier to control both the distance and direction and it keeps spin to a minimum."
—Keith Lyford

Use Your Head to Hit Better Scoring Zone Shots

A little forward thinking can pay huge dividends

The best thing you can do for your scoring game is to study the yardage book well ahead of time and take a good hard look at the pin sheet before you tee off. **Look for danger flags—the ones that if you go for and miss could lead to a double-bogey.** When you're on the course, remember that the odds of hitting the ball close decrease as your distance to the green increases. If you're swinging anything longer than a 7-iron, I recommend aiming for the fat part of the green.
—PGA Tour player Graeme McDowell

HOW TO PLAN A PERFECT APPROACH

DANGER SIGNS
Judge each possible pin location as a "green," "amber" or "red-light" situation. Green-light flags are the ones where even if you miss outside your normal dispersion pattern, you'll still be putting for your next shot. Red-light pins are those where you feel you have to hit an absolutely perfect shot or it'll be disaster. Remember, the farther you are from the green, the more those amber-light flags become red.

RED   AMBER   GREEN

PIN UP
If the pin is in the front of the green, add at least five yards to the overall distance and club up accordingly. The bad miss here is short, where your ensuing chip will leave you with little green to work with. Go beyond the pin and make sure you get on.

PIN BACK
Think in reverse if the pin is in the back of the green. If your yardage is 175 yards to a back pin, treat the shot like it's 170. Play short and ensure that you get on. The last thing you want is to fly the green and leave yourself with a downhill comeback chip.

NAIL YOUR YARDAGES

You won't always get a perfect lie at your favorite short-iron distance. Here's how to adjust for slope and hit the ball close to the target from anywhere inside 100 yards.

INSTRUCTION

How to Nail Every Distance

My distance-reduction system gives you the power to automatically subtract yards from your club without changing your swing

THE SITUATION
You're in no-man's-land—57 yards from the pin. Or maybe you're at 77 yards, or even 46. In other words, you're stuck hard between two wedges and don't know what to do.

THE SOLUTION
Good players know how to remove yards from each of their wedges in very specific increments, making it easy to hit the ball almost every distance from 125 yards and in. In the past, the only way to do this was to change the length of your swing. Now, all you need to do is tweak your setup and put your best swing on the ball. Follow the steps at right.
—Mike Adams

TOP 100 TEACHER POLL

Q When stuck between clubs, should you swing harder with the shorter club or smoother with the longer club?

More club, smoother swing —72%

Less club, harder swing—28%

"Swinging smooth with a longer club never goes out of style, but sometimes this causes you to decelerate. Swinging a shorter club harder makes sure this never happens."
—Keith Lyford

KNOCK DOWN THE PIN
Changing your setup takes yards off your shots without you having to think about it.

HOW IT WORKS

Take your sand wedge and your lob wedge to the range. Hit ten balls with each club, and calculate your average distance with each. Take the difference between these two numbers and divide it by the difference in loft. For example, if your average sand wedge distance is 12 yards longer than your average lob wedge distance, and your lob wedge has four degrees more loft than your sand wedge, divide 12 by 4. This gives you the number 3, which is how many yards you subtract off the distance you hit any of your wedges when you make any of the setup changes at right. Call it your **Distance Reduction Unit.**

EXAMPLE

Let's work with a Distance Reduction Unit of 3 yards using the example above (yours could be different). If you normally hit your sand wedge 75 yards and you're 66 yards from the pin, this means you need to change your setup to knock 9 yards off your swing. You can do this by making each of the three setup changes in the far left column, or one of these changes plus another from the middle column (or you can just use the setup in the third column, which reduces your yardage by three units). The trick is to mix and match the adjustments to get both the right distance and a good feel when you set up at address.

WHY IT WORKS

Each of the different setup changes effectively shortens your swing without you having to think about it. All you have to do is put what you feel is your best full swing on the ball, and your setup does the rest.

TO SUBTRACT 1 DISTANCE UNIT

Move your left foot back so that the toe is even with the ball of your right foot.

Narrow your stance by two clubhead widths.

Drop your hands to the middle of the grip.

TO SUBTRACT 2 DISTANCE UNITS

Move your left foot back so that the toe is even with the instep on your right foot.

Narrow your stance by three clubhead widths.

Drop your hands to the bottom of the grip.

TO SUBTRACT 3 DISTANCE UNITS

Move your left foot back so that the toe is even with the heel on your right foot.

> *Combining these various setup changes gives you dozens of address position options and allows you take anywhere from approximately 2 to 36 yards off each of your wedges.*

MAKE YOUR MARK (BUT DON'T LEAVE IT BEHIND)

Q: Most of the golfers at my course don't bother to fix their ballmarks. I'm tired of putting on pocked surfaces. Can you explain how to repair marks? I'll post the answer in the locker room.

Fixing ballmarks makes the world a smoother, prettier place, but a lot of golfers didn't learn how the right way. It's basic etiquette to do this— something every golfer should learn early on. When marks aren't repaired, the damaged grass grows back slowly, causing burn marks. To fix a mark the right way, follow these simple steps:

Take a tee, key or pronged repair tool and insert it at the edge of the mark, not in the middle.

Twist the edges gently toward the center, trying not to tear the grass. Don't lift the center.

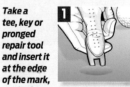

Use your putter to tamp down the surface so it's flat again. And remember, you should be happy to fix your ballmark because it means you've hit a good shot.

Even the best players on Tour miss five to six greens a round. Unlike you, however, they rarely make five or six bogeys. A solid short game turns potential disaster holes into easy pars.

SECTION 6

YOUR SHORT GAME

Whether it's an approach to a par 5 or a greenside chip, here's how to get it close

Some days your full-swing shots just can't miss; other times you can't hit greens even from a perfect lie with your favorite club in your hands. That's when your short game shows what an important role it plays in keeping your scores down. Those mild-mannered chips, pitches and lobs make up for poor shots in a hurry, taking you from parts unknown to a comfortable spot next to the pin, all with swings that rarely go above knee height.

There are thousands of ways to get the ball close from short range, but instead of confusing you with a multitude of setup and swing options, this section breaks down your short game into five simple shots: bump-and-run chips; high, medium and low pitches; and lob shots. Mastering these basic short-game plays arms you with enough shotmaking options to tackle anything the course throws at you during your round. Plus, by the time you have these short shots down pat, you'll understand the adjustments you need to make when facing more difficult short-game situations.

Short swings are easy to learn. So if you struggle to get the ball close, pay attention to the Top 100's advice and prepare to see an instant improvement in your scores.

5 THINGS YOU'LL LEARN IN THIS SECTION

- *The right way to set up for a chip so that your club automatically catches the ball clean.*
- *How to vary your club selection to produce the correct amount of carry and roll for any situation.*
- *How to pitch the ball close to the pin from the fairway— and even add spin if you want it.*
- *How to pitch higher or lower so you can attack the pin regardless of what's between you and the hole.*
- *The essential keys for pulling off flops and lob shots.*

Learn more about the short shots you need to save par at **golf.com/short game**

TOP 100 SAY

STICK WITH YOUR BUMP-AND-RUN

Q: Is the average player better off hitting bump-and-run chips, or learning to chip with a wedge and varying the trajectory?

62%
Change clubs and keep the ball low to the ground at all times

38%
Become a wedge master and vary your trajectory

● It's better to use a wedge and change the trajectory by leaning forward and moving the ball position back to hit it lower. If all you know is a bump-and-run, you're limiting yourself.
—Brady Riggs

● Most players have better distance control chipping with a 7- or 8-iron. Stick with your bump-and-run.
—Mike LaBauve

CHIP IT CLOSER

Here's how to make those tough little shots from off the green a piece of cake and get up and down every time

INSTRUCTION

How to Hit the Perfect Chip

Borrow from your putting stroke to create solid short shots

As with most shots, you'll hit better chips if your setup position is correct. The goal of your chipping address position is to situate your body, arms, hands and club to create a descending blow, without chunking the clubhead into the ground or striking the ball with the leading edge of the clubface. Your setup and technique are correct if your impact features the following five positions.
—Todd Sones

KEY MOVE

CLUBHEAD LOW
Compare the height of the ball with the height of the clubhead: The ball is high and the clubhead is still very low to the ground. This proves that a downward strike—not an upward flip—gets the ball rolling up the clubface and into the air.

TOE CLOSED
Although your hands should be passive and your left wrist straight, they do need to rotate so that the club turns over on its heel through impact. Try to smoothly rotate the toe of the club toward your target (don't jerk it) as you swing through the impact area.

SHOULDER DOWN
An easy way to create the desired descending blow is to keep your left shoulder down through impact. Don't raise your left shoulder—keep it low and square to your target line.

WRIST FLAT
You won't chip well if you flip your hands through impact or bend your wrists. Your left wrist should be as flat as possible. If you have trouble keeping your left wrist from breaking down, try using your putting grip.

WEIGHT FORWARD
At address, distribute the majority of your weight over your left foot and, more importantly, keep it there throughout your stroke. If you hang back on your right side, your swing will bottom out before the ball and you'll catch the ball thin.

INSTRUCTION

How to Set Up for Solid Chips

Get the heel of the club up and the handle forward for a solid, consistent chip stroke

STEP 1
Aim the clubface at your target and then raise the club slightly on its toe. This gives you a more upright lie, which makes your chip swing more of a putting stroke. A putting stroke is easier to control because it moves straight back and through. A flatter lie demands you swing the club on an arc.

Raise your wedge on its toe so it sits like a putter.

STEP 2
Move the handle of your club two inches farther toward the target than the front edge of the ball. This de-lofts the clubhead and promotes the downward strike that you're looking for. You can use any wedge with this technique, and even your 8- or 9-iron will work.

STEP 3
The butt of your club should point a couple of inches left of the center of your body. Make sure that your shoulders are square to the target line and your weight is over your left foot, and then play the ball off your right big toe.

STEP 4
Move the club with your arms and shoulders while keeping your hands and wrists quiet and your weight on your left side. As you swing through the hitting zone, you should feel as though you're striking down on the ball while gently closing the clubface.
—Todd Sones

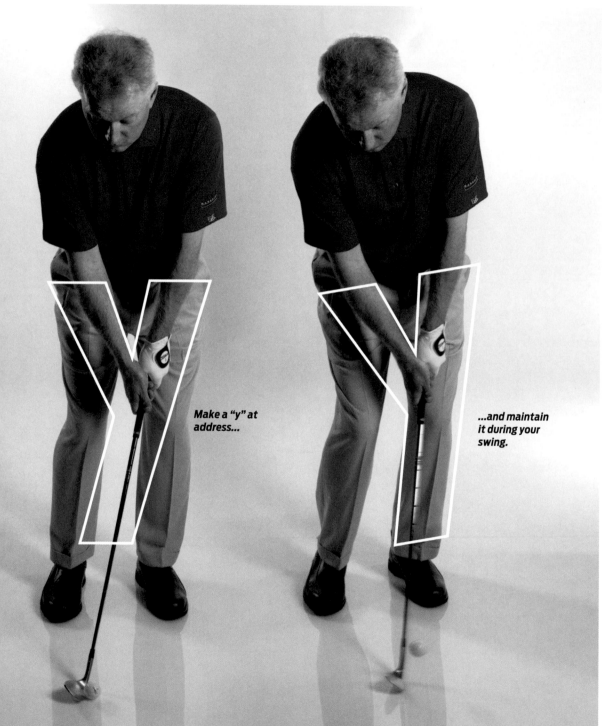

Make a "y" to Chip It Close

You'll catch the ball clean with the handle forward

FAULT

You hit your chips fat so they never get close to the flag, or you blade them over the green.

FIX

As you take your address, make sure you set most of your weight over your left foot and move the handle of the club forward. Notice that when you do this, your arms and clubshaft form a lower case "y."

Establishing this "y" and keeping it intact during your chipping motion will allow you to come down sharply on the ball and catch it clean before your clubhead makes contact with the turf. Try to trap the ball between your clubface and the ground at impact. This will keep your hands forward of the ball and ensure proper contact.
—Steve Bosdosh

Make a "y" at address...

...and maintain it during your swing.

DRILL

How to Chip From Every Lie

Let your backswing do the work for you

THE PROBLEM

You assume that one swing will get the job done for every chipping situation. In reality, however, you need at least two: one for lies in the rough and another for tight lies. Here's how to match your ball swing to the situation and leave your chips closer to the hole.

—Brian Mogg

DRILL

HOW TO FIND THE RIGHT CHIP PLANE

Spread some balls around a chipping green, making sure you're left with many different lies. Then vary your technique to match each shot. If it's available, place a mirror behind you and check that your backswing works to the inside on normal chips and outside on chips from the rough. If you're still struggling, exaggerate each move until you get the results you want.

—Brian Mogg

SWING INSIDE FROM A TIGHT LIE

Your goal is to sweep the ball off the turf with a rounded swing. Imagine a shaft stuck in the ground behind your ball and on your target line. **Take the clubhead away to the inside of the shaft with very little wrist hinge,** as though you were attempting a long putt. Do the same on your forward swing, and release the clubhead toward the target while keeping your hands at thigh height.

Keep your hands low.

TIP: Since this is a shallow swing, expect minimal spin and more roll once the ball hits the turf.

SWING OUTSIDE FROM THE ROUGH

When your ball is sitting down, **swing your clubhead outside the shaft on your backswing and hinge your wrists aggressively to get the club up.** (Think "low hands, high clubhead.") On your downswing, drop your arms toward the ground and across the ball (left of the target) without releasing your hands. This allows you to dig deep and pop the ball up without fear of catching it thin.

Quickly hinge the club up.

TIP: You'll generate extra loft using this technique, so plan to fly the ball at least three quarters of the distance to the flagstick.

Hit chips with your body turn, rather than with your hands and arms. You'll enjoy more consistent contact and better results.

Start here...

...and end here.

DRILL

How to Chip with Precision

Swing with your body to master short-range distance control

THE FAULT

Like a lot of players, you struggle with scoring shots, particularly those tricky, in-between wedge shots that call for a swing that's less than full. You don't make solid contact much of the time, and when you do, you're unable to control your distances. You need to solidify your technique in order to be more proficient around the greens.

THE DRILL

Follow these simple steps and you should quickly get the feeling of releasing the club with your body rather than flipping it with your hands. Repeat the drill regularly until you're able to make clean contact with the ball on all of your short-game shots.

STEP 1: Grip your wedge halfway down the shaft and get into your address position, placing the handle on your left hip.

STEP 2: Move the club away by rotating your right forearm—the toe of the club should move up while the handle moves down. Stop when the shaft is parallel with your target line.

STEP 3: Rotate the club back around your body toward impact, but do it by rotating your arms and chest together, not by flipping your hands.

STEP 4: Move your weight to your front side as you bring the club through the impact zone—if the handle of the club hits your left side, you've released the club too much with your hands. If it doesn't touch your side, you've successfully released the club with your body.
—Brad Brewer

INSTRUCTION

Brush, Look and Hit

How to stop freezing and pull the trigger on delicate chips

Contrary to popular belief, taking additional time over a delicate chip or pitch shot won't help the outcome. The more time you spend analyzing a shot, the more likely you are to tense up and either chunk or blade it over the green. **You'll enjoy much greater success if you keep your pre-shot routine short and simple.** The following "brush, look, and hit" routine does just that. When you arrive at your ball, examine the lie, the slope of the green and how much green you have to work with, and determine the shot you want to play. Picture the shot's trajectory, where it lands, and the amount of roll. This is the only time you should be deliberate. Next, take a few practice swings off to the side of the ball (from a similar lie), "brushing" the grass at the point in your stance where you play the ball. "Look" at the target while envisioning the shot, look back at the ball, and then without any hesitation, "hit." If you follow this simple three-step process, you won't have time to let any distracting thoughts in, and you should be in a relaxed frame of mind. This will help you establish a smooth, easy rhythm and make solid contact.

Take a few practice swings off to the side of the ball, "brushing" the grass.

Take one final "look" at the target and envision your shot, then hit away without hesitation.

QUICK TIP
Leave the flagstick in when chipping. Even if you don't hit the pin dead center, it will keep more of your shots in the hole.

INSTRUCTION

Make Ball-First Contact

Use your setup to chip it crisp

Good chips happen when you make ball-first contact with your hands ahead of the clubhead at impact. Adjust your setup to make it happen naturally. Here's how:
1. Find your center of gravity by hanging a golf club from the center of your chest.
2. Place the ball slightly behind your center of gravity to encourage a descending strike and a shaft that's leaning toward the target.
—Brad Brewer

Get on Your Left Side to Chip It Stiff

A proper weight shift will guarantee better contact from tight lies

THE PROBLEM
When you face a chip from a tight lie you fear skulling it, so you hit it fat.

THE SOLUTION
Pretend you're balanced on a small seesaw. At address, the seesaw should tilt to the left. This means your weight is perfectly positioned so you can hit down on the ball and catch it clean.

HOW TO PRACTICE IT
Hit chips with an empty plastic water bottle under your right foot. Play the ball slightly back of center, and use the bottle to remind you to shift your weight over to your left leg. Shifting your weight forward and keeping it there during your stroke correctly positions the bottom of your swing arc at the back of the ball—you won't be able to hit the ground behind the ball if you try.
—Bill Forrest

WRONG!

Simply shifting your hips to the left won't get your weight on your left side where it needs to be for clean contact.

RIGHT!

Practice chipping with a plastic bottle under your right foot to remind you to set your weight forward and keep it there.

If you chipped while standing on a seesaw, the right side would be up.

DRILL

How to Catch Every Chip Clean

Use this simple drill to play perfect little shots

FAULT
You try to lift the ball into the air and end up blading it across the green. Solid chips are the result of hitting down into the back of the ball, not trying to lift it up.

FIX
Here's a drill that will produce the kind of chips you dream about—unless they're the blue corn variety. You'll need to hit the snack aisle for those.

Balance a club on the top of a water bottle as shown (it's easier than it looks), and place the ball 12 inches behind the middle of the grip. Make your chip stroke without knocking the shaft off the bottle *[photo, right]*. You'll need to descend into the ball and keep your clubhead low to the ground after impact. If you try to scoop the ball or allow the club to pass your hands *[inset photo]*, you'll send the club and the bottle flying.
—Glenn Deck

Swing down, not up, to avoid a game of pickup sticks.

DRILL

How to Chip Without Yipping

Be aggressive without hitting it too hard

The next time you face a chip shot, think about your stroke being "SAD"—Short, Aggressive and Down. The enemies of good chipping are "LPU": Long, Passive and Up. Do any of those and you'll "CSC"—Chunk, Skull or Chili. So here's how you can be SAD about your chipping game in 10 minutes.

Pull the clubhead down to the ball with your left hand.

STEP 1: Take your pitching wedge or 9-iron. Set up with a narrow stance and play the ball about midway between your heels. Lay a second club on the ground one inch outside your right foot as shown. The idea is to swing over this club on the way back and down to the ball.

STEP 2: Swing back until your hands are about even with your right pocket. This is all you need—any longer and you'll decelerate on the downswing to compensate.

STEP 3: Pull the club aggressively down to impact with your left hand. Your wrists and hands should feel firm—that's how you know you didn't try to scoop the ball. You'll make a short follow-through and see your ball track to the hole.
—John Elliott, Jr.

Feel a firm left wrist at impact.

PITCH LIKE A PRO

*You hit 20- to 50-yard shots more than you think—
here's how to pull them off with razor-sharp precision*

INSTRUCTION

How to Pitch It Close

Keep your hands low and in to hit laser-like wedges from the fairway

THE SITUATION
You have a medium-length pitch of 50 yards from a tight, slightly downhill fairway lie.

THE USUAL MISTAKE
Flipping the clubhead underneath the ball in an attempt to create more loft. The result is often a thin, bladed shot or a chili-dip.

Keep your hands tight to your body as you swing through impact.

HOW TO GET THE TECHNIQUE

Like you've read, you should lead with the handle of the club, not the head. More importantly, keep your clubhead low and tight to your body as you rotate through the shot [*photo, below left*]. **The closer the handle is to your body, the easier it is to hold your wrist angles through impact.**

The key to avoiding the flip is to use the opposite end of the club from what seems natural—that is, the grip instead of the clubhead. By pulling the butt of the handle in and up to your left, you will turn to square the clubface and drop the clubhead down to the ball. Turn your body—not your hands—and just let the ball get in the way of your rotation.
—Rick McCord

Pull the handle in toward your body [left], not away [right].

WRONG!

DRILL

Knuckles to the Ground

As you swing through, you should feel as though you're trying to scrape your knuckles along the ground. This sensation will lower the shaft and bring your hands inside, making it nearly impossible to scoop. You can practice this by hitting half-shots, starting with your hands at thigh height. Think about maintaining the relationship between your hands and the clubhead as you swing forward, keeping your hands close to the ground. Pull—don't push—and you'll hit the ball solidly every time. —**Rick McCord**

Point your knuckles down...

...and scrape them against the ground.

30 MINUTES TO PERFECT PITCHING

Take three practice balls to a practice green. Set up and execute three each of the following shots:

1. Standard 15-yard pitch (10 yards of carry) with a lob wedge.

2. Open-faced lofted pitch over an obstacle (like a bunker) to a tight pin 15 yards away.

3. Low-running 15-yard pitch (five yards of carry) with a sand wedge.

On each shot, make practice swings in this order: 1) a "way too short" practice swing for the length of the shot; 2) a "way too long" swing; and 3) the swing you feel is appropriate. Repeat this third practice swing until you can visually imagine and kinesthetically feel that the motion you're making matches the shot trajectory, carry distance and roll you want to achieve. Then execute the shot using the same swing as your last practice swing.

Hit each shot with three balls before moving on to the next shot location. It should only take you 30 minutes, but the expertise you gain will last a lifetime.
—**Dave Pelz**

INSTRUCTION

Pitch It High or Low

Here are three shots that travel the same distance on three different trajectories

Not all pitches are equal—sometimes you need more loft to carry an obstacle or to fly the ball onto an upper tier, while other situations require you to hit a low runner so you can use the contour of the green to snuggle your ball up to the hole. So to get it as close as possible on any pitch shot, you must know how to alter the trajectory of the ball. All you need to do is alter your setup and swing length to produce the desired height. Follow the chart below to become an instant shotmaker from 20 yards, and you'll knock it tight regardless of what the course throws at you.
—Bill Moretti

LOW TRAJECTORY
Take the clubhead back to knee height and follow-through to your waist.

Swing along your shoulder line, which will point right of your target due to your closed stance.

Strengthen your grip by rotating your hands to the right.

QUICK TIP
For a smoother pitch swing, use a weak grip, with the Vs formed by your thumb and forefinger pointed at your chin.

PITCHING ADJUSTMENTS (20-YARD SHOT)

	LOW SHOT	MEDIUM SHOT	HIGH SHOT
Grip	Stronger (hands rotated to the right)	Standard	Weak (hands rotated to the left)
Stance	Closed shoulders; ball back of center	Square shoulders; ball middle of stance	Open shoulders; ball forward of center
Shaft lean	Butt end of club at middle of left thigh; hands 4 to 6 inches in front of ball	Butt end of club at middle of left thigh; hands slightly forward of ball	Butt end of club at navel; hands 1 to 3 inches behind the ball
Swing length	Knee-high to waist-high	Waist-high to waist-high	Chest-high to waist-high
Swing path	Along shoulder line (right of target due to closed stance)	Along shoulder line	Along shoulder line (left of target due to open stance)

Align the lead edge of your wedge just below the equator of the ball so you can reach for the ball and catch it crisp.

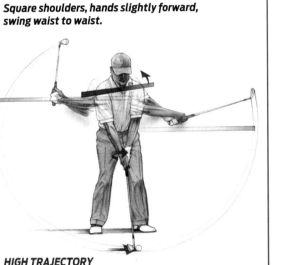

MEDIUM TRAJECTORY
Square shoulders, hands slightly forward, swing waist to waist.

HIGH TRAJECTORY
Weaken grip, open shoulders, swing chest-high to waist-high.

Reach for It!

Try this trick to stop blading your chips

Address the ball in a taller posture and align the leading edge of your club just below the equator of the ball [*photo, left*]. On your forward-stroke, stay loose and allow your arms to lengthen. If you do, your club will bottom out in front of the ball like it should. "Under-reaching" like this at address gives you a better margin for error to create crisp contact.
—Tim Mahoney

4 Steps to Perfect Pitching

This easy method gives you solid contact

THE PROBLEM
You don't make solid contact on your pitch shots, so you never have much luck controlling distance and direction. The two most common errors are locking the arms and becoming too rigid, or making a backswing that's much too long.

THE SOLUTION
The 4-step technique below eliminates these problems in an instant, and it will help you pitch the ball closer to the hole more often.
—Tim Mahoney

SETUP
Assume your normal setup, but make sure your hands are close to your thighs. Feel like your arms and club are connected to your body.

HINGE
Hinge your wrists back without rotating your body or turning your shoulders. Just hinge (more for longer shots, less for shorter shots).

TURN
Now simply turn your body forward. This should drop the clubhead directly down onto the ball, giving you crisp, ball-first contact.

HOLD ON
Don't re-hinge your wrists. Allow your arms to straighten so that the clubshaft is in line with your left arm. This guards against flipping.

Soften Up Your Pitches

How to hit it higher and land it softer

THE SITUATION

You're faced with a tricky pitch with an obstacle between you and the pin. You need loft and pinpoint distance control or you won't get up and down.

THE STANDARD PLAY

Hit a high, floating lob shot with your 60-degree wedge or a lower pitch with tons of spin to get your ball to stop after a single hop. Problem is, the lob shot is a high-risk alternative and most recreational players can't generate the spin needed to stop the ball on a dime.

THE BETTER PLAY

The Super Soft Pitch—a simple shot that adds extra loft to your everyday pitching motion. You'll get a high shot that stops near where it lands without having to make the perfect lob.

—Donald Crawley

HOW TO PLAY THE SUPER SOFT PITCH

The key to hitting the Super Soft Pitch is to preset your body in the correct impact position at address. This helps you strike the ball with the right amount of loft. In the past, you've pitched the ball either too low or too high because your poor impact position either added or subtracted loft from your clubface.

SETUP

Sole either your 56- or 60-degree wedge on the turf with the face square and pointing directly at your target. (There's no need to open it—that only creates extra bounce and increases the potential for thin contact.)

SHOULDERS

Make sure your shoulders are level and that your arms hang straight down. Ease up your grip pressure—the Super Soft Pitch requires soft hands.

BALL POSITION

Play the ball just slightly back of center and lean your shaft forward. (Be careful not to close the clubface.) Your grip should line up with your sternum about an inch in front of the ball, with your weight favoring your front foot.

SWING

Make your backswing by swinging your arms and chest away from the ball using soft hands and an easy hinge of your wrists. Your swing path should feel pretty straight, but with a slight turn so that the toe of the club points straight up once your hands reach knee height.

DOWNSWING

Stop your backswing just as your hands pass your right knee. On your downswing, turn toward the target and unhinge your wrists so that you return the club and your weight to the same positions they held at address. When you do this correctly, your club will contact the ball with the right amount of loft.

To execute the Super Soft Pitch to perfection, it's imperative that you rotate your chest through impact.

KEY MOVE

1

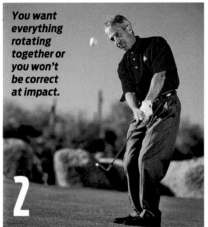

You want everything rotating together or you won't be correct at impact.

2

Finish your swing with your hands low and directly in front of your chest.

3

How to Make Your Pitches Bite

Accelerate, then stop to get the check, please

If your pitch shots fly straight, but they land on the green without any spin and run past the hole, use the keys below to help your pitches land on your target and then grab the green harder than a miner's handshake.

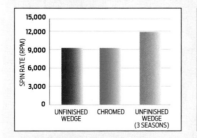

STEP 1
On your backswing, point your thumbs at the sky and the butt of the club at the ground.

STEP 2
Come down sharply into the ball, which will get it rolling up the clubface.

STEP 3
Once you feel impact, stop your hands abruptly at waist height and keep them and your club low.

CHECKPOINT

For Sale: Extra Spin

The right gear makes for easy checkups

Three tests by Golf Laboratories show that a rusty wedge and a clean, high-spin ball can give you thousands of extra revolutions of spin (**www.golflabs.com**).

(Chart 1 — SPIN RATE (RPM), vertical axis 0 to 15,000; categories: UNFINISHED WEDGE, CHROMED, UNFINISHED WEDGE (3 SEASONS))

(Chart 2 — SPIN RATE (RPM), vertical axis 0 to 15,000; categories: TITLEIST PRO V1, TOP-FLITE EXTREME DISTANCE)

(Chart 3 — SPIN RATE (RPM), vertical axis 0 to 15,000; categories: NORMAL CONDITIONS, MUDDY BALL, WET CONDITIONS)

UNFINISHED BUSINESS
New chromed and unfinished 56-degree sand wedges (same make and model) produced similar rpms, but the same unfinished wedge used over three seasons sent spin rates off the charts.

SPIN BALL WIZARDS
Does a true high-spin ball (like the Titleist Pro V1) spin more than a pure distance model (like the Top-Flite Extreme Distance) off the same wedge? The results speak for themselves.

CLEAN UP YOUR ACT
Mud on the ball reduced spin by 33%, and water (simulated by dunking the club and ball) cut the spin rate by 49%. So if you play under the lift, clean and place rule, take advantage of it!

SPECIALTY SHOTS

Sometimes you need more than a standard chip or pitch to get the ball close. These savvy plans can help you get up and down from anywhere.

Flip the club past your hands to lob the ball high from rough.

INSTRUCTION

Get Wristy to Lob It From Rough

On this shot, it's okay to make an early release

THE MISTAKE YOU SHOULD MAKE

On most shots, wristy impact is a recipe for disaster. However, when you have to pop the ball high and soft, you actually want to flip your wrists.

HOW TO COMMIT IT

Set up with a slightly open stance and play the ball slightly back of center. Take your regular pitch backswing, but as you come back down, slow your arms and hips (something you do anyway if you often muff pitch shots) and **quickly break your wrists through impact.** Don't allow your arms to pass your body. If it helps to think of folding your left wrist or bowing your right, do it. At the finish, your right hand should hide your left. While this is the opposite of traditional short-game advice, it's exactly what you need in this situation.

WHY IT WORKS

Flipping the club past your hands increases the effective loft of the clubface. So you get extra height on the shot that you normally wouldn't get if you adhered to the standard advice of keeping your hands ahead of the club at impact. Plus, deceleration is common on short swings, so you don't even have to practice this shot.

The technique works with any of your wedges, but to hit the ball extra high and help it land soft (don't expect much spin with this technique), use your lob wedge.
—Eden Foster

DON'T TRY IT WHEN...

Your lie is tight. The wrist-break flop shot requires perfect timing and has zero margin of error from a tight lie, so unless you have a fluffy lie in greenside rough, don't attempt this shot.

1 With your most lofted wedge, make your normal backswing and fully hinge your wrists.

2 As you approach impact, apply the brakes to your arms and step on the gas with your wrists.

3 Use your wrists to flip the clubhead under the ball and past your hands.

INSTRUCTION

How to Hit a Flop

My secret: Keep your hands behind your zipper until after impact

THE FAULT
When you try to hit high, soft lob shots, you either slam the clubhead down into the turf or blade the ball across the green. You also tend to place your hands well forward at address, thinking that it'll help you slide under the ball, but all it does is make it nearly impossible to execute the shot you want.

THE FIX
Set up with more weight on your front foot and your hands positioned behind the clubhead so that the grip points slightly behind your zipper. This will hinge your left wrist away from the target and lean the grip of the club in the same direction. Although setting up with the grip of the club leaning away from the target might seem counterintuitive, it makes it much easier to let the clubhead pass your hands through impact, which is critical for creating a high, lofted shot. Make sure you don't slide your body past the ball as you swing into impact.
—Jim Murphy

1 Set your hands and the butt of the club behind your zipper at address.

2 Allow the clubhead to pass your hands as you swing through impact, so that the grip again points behind your zipper.

INSTRUCTION

How to Pitch Clean From a Downslope

Success depends on how you set up

TRY THIS!

The key to pulling off this shot is to change your setup. Instead of an orthodox position, you should place your feet relatively close together and aim your toes down the slope at a 45-degree angle to your target line. Position the ball off your right heel (yep, your heel) and set your hands well in front of the clubhead. Once you have this setup all you have to do is cock your wrists and bring the club up so it's parallel to the ground and then swing down with the handle of the club leading the clubhead all the way. Don't allow the clubhead to pass your hands—this will cause the club to bottom out before the ball.

—Tom Stickney

Nose slightly ahead of the ball.

Hands well ahead of the clubhead.

Keep the clubhead behind your hands.

Stop your backswing when the club is parallel to the ground.

Ball positioned opposite your right heel.

Toes pointed 45 degrees to your target line.

Uphill Pitches Made Simple

Match your shoulders to the slope for an extra-crisp result

If you set up with your shoulders level to the ground, it's very easy to bury the club in the turf, which will keep you from making ball-first contact and ruin any chance you might have of following through properly. **So make sure to angle your shoulders so that they mirror the slope of the hill.** You should have an easier time catching the ball first and making a full follow-through, and this setup will provide you with a bigger margin for error should your contact be a little heavy or thin.

The key to hitting a shot from an uphill lie is to make sure that the angle of your shoulders matches the angle of the slope.

An uphill slope automatically adds loft to your shot, so take one more club (i.e., an 8-iron instead of a 9-iron) for every 4 or 5 degrees of slope.

Wedge It from the Collar

Here's a simple trick for a tricky situation

THE SITUATION
Your ball has come to rest just off the green against the first cut of rough. Time for what some players refer to as a "belly wedge," or intentional skull. This technique creates a tight, end-over-end roll and is pretty easy to execute.
1. Grab your pitching or sand wedge and take your grip where the handle meets the shaft using your regular putting grip.
2. Set the ball off your right foot and lean toward the target. Set the leading edge of your wedge even with the top of the ball.
3. Using your putting stroke, strike the top half of the ball with the leading edge while minimizing contact with the grass. Apply the same force you'd use to putt the ball the same distance. If you catch it right, you'll get a smooth roll out toward the cup.
—Dr. Jim Suttie

When you're up against the collar, your goal is to strike the top half of the ball with the leading edge of your wedge.

Make a long backswing...

...and then stop your through-swing abruptly.

...allow your downswing to accelerate the club...

INSTRUCTION

A New Way to Pitch

Swing long to short for smoother club acceleration

THE OLD PROBLEM

You struggle with pitching the ball, particularly when you're feeling some pressure. You typically make a short backswing and a strongly accelerating through-swing, which leads to inconsistent contact and poor distance control.

THE NEW FIX

Forget your short-to-long pitching swing and start doing the opposite. By trying to over-accelerate the clubhead through impact, you're relying too much on the muscles in your hands and arms, which doesn't work well under pressure. Instead, take a nice long backswing and then let the momentum of the downswing accelerate the clubhead through the ball. Once you pass through impact, stop the clubhead rather abruptly. Think "long to short" and you'll get the idea. This technique will take the jerkiness out of your pitching swing and help you make crisper, more consistent contact. You'll also produce more shot-stopping spin with this technique.
—Mitchell Spearman

> "Let the momentum of the downswing accelerate the clubhead through the ball."
> **—Mitchell Spearman**

Roll Your Hybrid for an Easy Save

You'll hit it closer by keeping the ball closer to the ground

THE PROBLEM
You're not sure if you should try to hit a hard putt or a long chip when you're just off the green.

THE SOLUTION
The good news is that the shot you're going to learn is one of the easiest in golf. To pull it off, forget your putter and your wedge and pick one of your hybrids instead. These amazing clubs are fantastic from the fairway and tee, but they're also terrific for short-game shots because they're so easy to hit and almost never dig into the turf. Follow the setup guides below and the technique guides at right and you'll learn to roll it close in just a few practice attempts.
—Tom Patri

PLAN YOUR PATH
Pick a path where you want the ball to roll, just as you would a putt. Consider the break on the green and before it. Also consider how hard you'll need to hit the ball to get it up onto the green and close to the flag.

CHOKE IT
Choke down a significant amount on the grip to help control the clubhead and make a comfortable, shoulder-driven chipping swing, concentrating on ball-first contact.

HANDS AHEAD
Your hands are ahead of the ball at address. Maintain this arrangement all the way through impact.

STAY LOOSE
Focus on rocking your shoulders, but also make sure you pivot your hips as though you're making a miniature swing.

HAND POSITION
Slightly ahead of the ball.

WEIGHT
Balanced evenly over both feet— don't lean too much weight toward the target.

BALL POSITION
In the middle of your stance.

The Skull-Proof Chip Shot

Save strokes by using your flatstick

When you miss a green and the ball sits on a tight lie in the fairway, chipping area, or anywhere else that makes using a wedge difficult, you need to start using your putter instead of your wedges. It's a higher-percentage play that takes the question of solid contact out of the equation. Here's how to do it.

STEP 1: Set up with the ball in the middle of your stance and the handle of the putter just ahead of your zipper. You don't want a lot of forward press here—just enough to ensure that you strike the ball solidly.

STEP 2: Pick a target that accounts for both the slope and the break, just as you would for a normal putt. Let your eyes gauge the distance and form a picture of the ball rolling over the grass and onto the green before you make your stroke.

STEP 3: Stroke the ball with confidence while keeping your head down as you swing. You'll be tempted to look up, but keep your eyes focused on impact until the ball is well on its way (at the very least, stay in your posture). Solid contact is an absolute must here.
—Tom Patri

EASY RIDER
Using your putter instead of a wedge eliminates the chance of mis-hits.

Getting out of bunkers is very easy if you have the right mind-set and use the proper techniques.

SECTION 7

ESCAPING THE SAND

Bunker shots come in many shapes, lies and levels of difficulty. Here's how to play 'em all.

There's a big gap between the bunker skills seen on Tour and those on display at your local muni. Most recreational golfers approach a sandy lie like the ball is covered in Kryptonite. Pros, on the other hand, thrive in sand, and would rather hit out of a bunker than chip from the rough. Tour players prefer bunker shots compared to other alternatives when they miss the green because (1) it's an easy shot, and (2) it's something they practice regularly. Unless the lie is very difficult, you can expect a top-tier player to get up and down from a bunker two-thirds of the time.

The goal of this section is to close this gap and help you become more familiar with sand shots and the relatively simple technique needed to get the ball out and onto the green. How simple? It's the only shot where it's okay for you to miss the ball. Plus, the club you use most often from sand comes with a special design trait—bounce—that makes blasting out just that much easier.

The instruction on the following pages will help you conquer any bunker lie imaginable, including the ones that typically send your scores through the roof. Soon, you'll look forward to hitting from the sand—just like the pros do.

Learn more about escaping every type of bunker lie at **golf.com/sand**

5 THINGS YOU'LL LEARN IN THIS SECTION

- *How to escape greenside bunkers on your first swing.*
- *Adjustments you need to make for different lies and conditions to blast the ball close.*
- *How to take the right amount of sand and correctly use the bounce on your wedges.*
- *How to add height and spin to stop your sand shots from short distances.*
- *Setup and swing keys to handle the most nasty and terrifying bunker situations.*

THE MOST DIFFICULT SHOT IN GOLF

In a recent *Golf Magazine* survey, we asked you what shot gives you the most trouble.

40-yard bunker shot: 33%

Approach shot over water: 22%

Other: 26%

Half-wedge shot: 19%

Even the Tour pros don't fare well from the sand when they're 40 yards from the pin, only getting up and down less than a third of the time. By comparison, the 2006 PGA Tour average for getting up and down from a greenside bunker was 55 percent.

● On long bunker shots, drop down to an 9- or 8-iron and make a U-shaped swing (instead of the V-shaped swing you make in greenside bunkers). Hit the sand about an inch behind the ball and follow through. Your ball will still ride out on a cushion of sand, but the less-lofted club and rounder swing will fly the ball to the green. —Dr. Jim Suttie

BUNKER-SHOT BASICS

Proven techniques for getting out of sand traps on the first try—every time

How to Blast It Close from the Sand

Follow these three easy steps for foolproof escapes from normal lies

12:00

Keep your legs wide and quiet

Attack from the inside.

STEP 1: With the flagstick representing 12:00 on a clock face, open up your stance just slightly, so your feet, hips and shoulders are pointing to 11:30. Aim the leading edge of your sand wedge at the flag.

STEP 2: Spread your feet two inches wider than normal. A wider stance helps quiet your legs so you can correctly swing more with your arms. Plus, a wider stance makes it easier to repeat your swing and control your clubhead.

STEP 3: These adjustments will help you attack the ball from the inside with the clubface square to the target, so not only will you get out of the bunker, the ball will fly at your target.
—**Scott Sackett**

How to Stop Leaving the Ball in the Bunker

Make a steep swing and a round follow-through to guarantee that your next shot is a putt

THE PROBLEM

You hit a lot of your bunker shots too fat, and many of them stay in the bunker.

WHY IT'S HAPPENING

Your swing is too shallow, causing your wrists to uncock too early. This forces you to hit too far behind the ball and chunk the shot.
—Martin Hall

Take a steep backswing...

Hit the sand here.

...and make a round follow-through.

Your swing should bottom out directly below the ball.

FIX 1: ALIGN LEFT AND MAKE A STEEPER SWING

Position your feet a little left of the target line and take the club straight up and down, contacting the sand just behind the ball. This vertical motion will prevent your wrists from uncocking prematurely on the way back down.

FIX 2: FOLLOW THROUGH TO YOUR LEFT

After impact, swing your club around your body, left of the target line. Following this path will encourage you to use your body more during your downswing so your hands won't take over and shut down the face.

HOW TO GET THE RIGHT DEPTH

Stick a tee in the sand so that you can see only the top, then place a ball on it. Now play a shot. If you make a steep enough swing, you'll hit the tee around its midpoint down in the sand. You'll know you've done it right if the tee flies out of the sand and your ball floats toward your target.
—Martin Hall

A big turn both back and through is key to hitting long bunker shots.

QUICK TIP
If the course has bunkers with fluffy sand, use a wedge with at least 10 degrees of bounce (less bounce if the sand is hard).

INSTRUCTION

INSTRUCTION

Big Turn for Big Blasts

Plenty of rotation and a straight right arm are key

THE PROBLEM
You're basically okay when you have to pop the ball out of a greenside bunker, but you always come up well short on long sand shots. This happens because your technique doesn't create enough clubhead speed to get the ball releasing all the way to the flagstick.

THE SOLUTION
To create enough clubhead speed to get the ball all the way to the hole, you need to add two critical moves to your technique:

KEY MOVE 1: Make a full turn so your left shoulder is under your chin and your back is to the target. I see a ton of players making short backswings on these shots and trying to muscle the club through the sand, which actually slows down the clubhead.

KEY MOVE 2: Straighten your right arm fully as you pass through the hitting zone. A common mistake is holding onto the club too much and never releasing the clubhead. Concentrate on making your right elbow go from bent to straight through impact and you'll have all the clubhead speed you need.
—Jason Carbone

Wind up like you would for any big hit...

...and then straighten your right arm through impact.

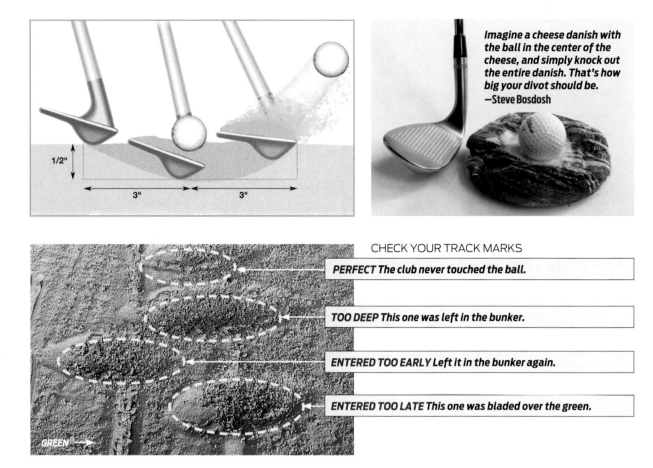

Is Your Divot in the Right Place?

This simple drill gives you the answer

A perfect bunker swing enters the sand about two to three inches behind the ball, skims a half-inch to an inch under the surface, then emerges about three inches in front of where the ball rested. **The clubhead never touches the ball itself. The sand carries the ball up and out.**

To see if you're doing it correctly, draw parallel lines in the sand about six inches apart, drop a ball between them and make your swing. Check the guide at right to see if you're entering the sand too early, entering the sand too late, or taking too large of a divot.
—Paul Marchand

Imagine a cheese danish with the ball in the center of the cheese, and simply knock out the entire danish. That's how big your divot should be.
—Steve Bosdosh

1/2"

3"   3"

CHECK YOUR TRACK MARKS

PERFECT *The club never touched the ball.*

TOO DEEP *This one was left in the bunker.*

ENTERED TOO EARLY *Left it in the bunker again.*

ENTERED TOO LATE *This one was bladed over the green.*

GREEN →

How to Use Your Wedge's Bounce

That chunk of metal on the bottom of your wedge is the key to hitting great bunker shots

THE PROBLEM

Most weekend golfers consider it an accomplishment just to escape a greenside bunker in one shot. If you take the time to learn how to utilize the club's bounce, however, you won't have to settle for such mediocre results. Bounce, which is defined as the angle between the clubhead's leading edge and sole's trailing edge, allows the head to glide through the sand without digging. Use it correctly and you'll not only overcome your fear of burying bunker shots, you'll make a few more up-and-downs too.

THE SOLUTION

Rotate the clubface open (about 45 degrees for a shot of 10 yards, and half that for one of 20 yards) so it's pointing right of the flagstick. Align your feet, knees, hips and shoulders several yards left of the flagstick, in proportion to how much you open the face. Your stance line (the line across the front of your toes) and the line bisecting the face should now form a letter "V." This exposes the max amount of bounce on your sand wedge, which should help you glide through the bunker more easily.

Open the clubface about 45 degrees for a 10-yard shot, and progressively less as the shot gets longer.

45°

After you open the face, your stance line and a line bisecting the face should form a "V."

EXTREME SAND ESCAPES

What to do when you're facing something other than the garden-variety greenside-bunker lie

EYE ON THE PRIZE
Keep your head back to further encourage a swing that travels with the slope.

LOW RIDER
At address, set your right shoulder lower than your left to create a shoulder angle that matches the slope. Keep that angle through impact and the club won't stick in the sand.

INSTRUCTION

How to Make an Uphill Escape

Keep your weight back when your ball sticks on the upslope

THE SITUATION
Your ball has settled on the upslope in a bunker, and you lack confidence in your ability to get the ball out of the bunker.

THE SOLUTION
This is one of the easiest shots in golf, not the hardest, because the slope automatically provides the loft you need to carry the lip. If you've struggled from similar lies in the past, it's because you've swung the club into the slope rather than up the slope.

SUPPORT COLUMN
Since your body is angled to match the slope, your right foot should support most of your weight. As you swing through the ball, push off the sand with your right foot and drive your hips to the target.

All you need to do to hit a perfect bunker shot (one that settles near the flag and rolls very little) is angle your hips and shoulders to match the slope and make your everyday bunker swing. It's the same principle as hitting from an upslope in the fairway or rough.

—Brian Mogg

Set your body parallel to the slope.

STEP 1

Play the ball in the center and dig your right foot in deep to anchor your swing. Unlike a standard bunker shot where you open the clubface, address the ball with the face square. The slope will give the ball ample lift. Tilt your body so that your shoulders are angled the same as the slope you're standing on. (Lay a club across your chest to check if you're angled correctly.)

Keep your weight back.

STEP 2

Pick a spot two inches behind the ball and try to hit the sand at that exact spot. Swing your arms and club up the slope and on the same angle that your hips and shoulders are on. This produces an ascending path through impact. It's easy to do if you keep your shoulders tilted and your weight back. You should feel most of your weight on the ball of your right foot as you blast through the sand.

FACE SQUARE
You don't need to manipulate your clubface. Set up with the lead edge square and keep it square throughout your motion—the slope will provide more than enough loft on the shot.

MISS THE BALL
Pick a spot a few inches behind the ball and bring your club into the sand at that point. Your goal is to hit the sand, not the ball. The explosion carries the ball out of the bunker.

"You should feel most of your weight on the ball of your right foot as you blast through the sand."
—Brian Mogg

The club will dig with your normal setup.

WRONG!

DON'T DO THIS

From this lie, your typical bunker setup—shoulders level with the flat part of the bunker—will cause the club to dig in rather than glide through the sand, and your ball will stay in the hazard.

Bury Your Club From Buried Lies

For nasty buried lies, your best bet is to go pound sand!

THE SITUATION

Your ball is three-quarters buried in loose sand toward the upper part of a steep bunker lip. Even taking a stance won't be easy. You'll have no trouble swinging the club back, but deep sand and the overhanging lip will severely limit your follow-through.

THE SOLUTION

Realistically, you can't do much more to the ball than dislodge it. But guess what? That's about all you have to do! In fact, you're free to commit the most common bunker error of all time: You can quit on the shot. More good news? You get to make a violent, no-finish swing and pound that stupid bunker!

HOW TO DO IT

STEP 1: Use whichever of your wedges has the most bounce and open the blade just a bit at address. As you finish settling into your posture, dig your back foot deeper into the sand than your front.

STEP 2: Make a full backswing, then slam the club powerfully into the sand an inch or two behind the ball, as though you're trying to bury the clubhead.

STEP 3: Don't expect any follow-through, just a soft rebound effect as your club emerges lazily from the sand. Meanwhile your ball and a half cup of sand are already crossing the bunker lip on their way to the green.

WHY IT WORKS

The difference between this shot and one where you quit on it unintentionally is that, in this instance, you're accelerating the clubhead, not decelerating it. As a result, you can still displace enough sand to get the ball up and out of the bunker on an almost vertical trajectory. **—Eden Foster**

Be sure to keep most of your weight on your left side.

Anchor your back foot by digging it deeper into the sand than your front foot.

There's no need to turn your right arm over your left after impact because any follow-through will be minimal.

Your clubhead should literally burrow into the sand beneath the ball.

QUICK TIP
If the ball is only half-buried, use the same technique, but close the face and don't slam the club into the sand as hard.

The ball can plug, but it can't hide.

LOW BLOW
You'll get a lower trajectory on a long blast, so don't try to help the ball into the air.

The No. 1 Bunker Key

Soften your left elbow to make easy work of every bunker lie

TRY THIS!
I know you've been told to hit two or three inches behind the ball when playing from sand, but this bit of advice usually does more harm than good because it makes it easy to take too much sand behind the ball. The better advice is to simply swing under the ball and forget about where your club enters the bunker. The key is to displace the sand the ball is sitting on and use it to carry the ball up and out, and the best way to do it is to make your normal swing but allow your left wrist to cup through impact so that the clubhead passes your hands. **The trick is to soften your left elbow through impact, so that it folds as your left wrist breaks down.** It may sound strange, but it works.
—Krista Dunton

How to Hit a 40-Yard Sand Shot

Make long bunker shots look easy with my five rules for a pro-style escape

THE SITUATION
You're facing what's considered the toughest shot in golf: the 40-yard bunker blast. Or it could be 30, or even 50 yards—whatever. You're in a tough spot. When I teach this shot, I ask my students to follow five simple rules [*right*]. Once you've read them, give this shot a go a few times at the range. The long blast is rarely practiced, and experience will go a long way when you attempt this shot during your round.

RULE NO. 1: LEAVE YOUR SAND WEDGE IN THE BAG
With only 56 degrees of loft, your trusty sand iron can't get you all the way home. Opt for at least your gap wedge, and if the bunker isn't very deep, use your pitching wedge.

RULE NO. 2: OPEN THE CLUBFACE
I know this takes distance off the shot, but with a GW or PW you have plenty of club, and opening the face gives you more bounce to work with and makes it less likely that the club will dig into the sand and cause the ball to come up short.

RULE NO. 3: GO BACK TO BASICS
Hit behind the ball as you would for any sand shot around the green. Your goal is to catch the sand, not the ball (never try to pick this shot clean).

RULE NO. 4: DON'T TRY TO LIFT IT
I know that your worst fear is skulling the ball, but try to avoid helping the ball up by flicking your hands and wrists. Picture a lower trajectory during your pre-shot routine and get comfortable with it. Seeing this lower ballflight will help you move your body through the shot without hanging back.

RULE NO. 5: GO FOR IT!
Kick your fear to the curb and swing away. Be both confident and aggressive—give the shot more speed than normal and apply the same body rotation you'd use when hitting a full shot from the fairway or a drive from the tee box. This will make it easier to power through the bunker and create enough force for the sand to propel your ball toward the green.
—Brady Riggs

EASY OUT
Allowing your left wrist to cup and softening your left elbow after impact leads to easy escapes.

What to Do When You're Up Against the Lip

This bunker buster will do the trick

THE SITUATION
Your ball has stopped in the sand a foot or so below the lip.

THE SOLUTION
Because the ball is sitting on such an extreme upslope, don't feel as though you need to use the most lofted club in your bag—your sand wedge, pitching wedge or even your 9-iron will work just fine. And since the ball is too low on the face for you to keep both feet out of the bunker, you're going to have to get dirty.

Start by stepping down into the bunker so that your back foot is as far below the ball as the ball is below the lip. This will effectively put the ball in the center of your stance. Open the clubface, aim right of your target, and lower your right shoulder to get your shoulders more even with the slope. Then take the club back on a steep, V-shaped path and bring it down hard into the sand just below the ball, driving the heel of the club into the hill.

There's no need to make a conscious follow-through—the concussion of the club hitting the sand is what drives the ball out and onto the green.
—Jason Carbone

Drive the heel of your club into the sand to get the ball out.

Plant your right foot as far below the ball as the ball is below the lip.

Drop your right shoulder so your shoulders are even with the slope.

How to Stop It Quick From the Sand

No green? No problem!

THE SITUATION

You have a good lie in a greenside bunker, but you've short-sided yourself and have just a few paces of green between you and the flag. You need a high, soft sand shot that stops on a dime.

THE SOLUTION

Here are four easy steps to make the ball sit:
—Todd Sones

Use your most-lofted wedge and a lot of wrist action to hit the ball high from short distance.

STEP 1: Select your most-lofted wedge. Position the ball slightly forward in your stance and move the handle of the club in-line with your right thigh to add extra loft to the clubface.

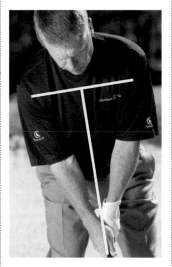

STEP 3: Make sure your shoulder line and shaft line form an angled "T." Your job is to recreate the "T" at impact so that your club enters the sand with the same amount of loft you established at address. Swing your club more with your arms and your wrists, using minimum shoulder movement.

STEP 2: Spread your stance by taking a step out with your right foot, and then dig both feet into the sand a half inch for balance. Your shaft should now point just left of the center of your torso.

STEP 4: Keep your chest pointed down and swing your arms and hands underneath your body. Move onto your left hip through impact to keep the club from releasing past your hands. Try to keep your hands and clubhead low in your follow-through so the clubface stays open through impact.

A LAST RESORT: THE DROP SHOT

Taking your allowable drop might be a better bet than trying to pull off a miracle escape

According to Rule 28 of the *USGA Rules of Golf,* a player "may deem his ball unplayable at any place on the course except when the ball is in a water hazard." In this case, you have three options, all of which carry a one-stroke penalty:

(a) Play a ball as near as possible to the spot from which the original ball was last played.

(b) Drop a ball behind the point where the original ball lay, keeping that point directly between the hole and the spot on which the ball is dropped.

(c) Drop a ball within two club-lengths of the spot where the original ball lay, but not nearer the hole. If you choose b or c, you must drop the ball within the bunker.

How to Hit a High Blast

Copy these moves when you need to carry a high lip

THE PROBLEM

You're scared of bunker shots because your technique makes them nearly impossible to play successfully. This is especially true when the bunker is deep and lofting a high shot isn't your speciality.

THE SOLUTION

To get enough loft on your bunker shots to clear a high lip, you need to do a few simple things or you'll risk leaving the ball in the bunker. The first is to select the highest-lofted club in your bag—don't immediately pull your sand wedge just because it's the one you use for most bunker shots. A lob wedge should easily do the trick. The second is to copy the setup and swing adjustments pictured here so that you can make a more vertical backswing and downswing.

HOW TO DO IT

1. Set up so that your feet are farther apart than the width of your shoulders. Hold your hands lower than normal (i.e., flatten the shaft).
2. Keep your stance square to your target with the clubface just slightly open.
3. Point the grip away from the target (it should be just behind the ball).
4. Make a short backswing with the clubshaft pointing toward the sky. This is critical to providing the proper angle of attack.
5. Swing along the line of your stance, not across it. As soon as you power through the sand, pull your hands and the club in tight to your chest. This ensures that your swing is sufficiently steep on both sides of the ball.
—Scott Sackett

The deeper you stand, the steeper you swing.

Take an extra-wide stance and set your hands low.

Point the clubhead at the sky as soon as possible in your backswing.

Pull your hands and the club in close immediately after impact.

If there's no lip or high grass between you and the hole, try putting from the sand.

A putter is a safer alternative than a sand wedge in the right situation.

56

WHAT TO DO IN HARD OR WET SAND

WHEN THE SAND IS WET...
Add more clubhead speed

● Your brain tells you thick wet sand should be more difficult to deal with—you'll get the club stuck in the sand or skull it trying to pick the ball clean. In fact, there's only one adjustment you need to make: swing harder! The sand hasn't changed—it's just heavier, so you need more clubhead speed to displace it. Other than that, keep your technique exactly the same.
—**Paul Marchand**

WHEN THE SAND IS HARD...
Lose your bounce

● Hard sand requires two things: (1) a wedge designed with minimal bounce, and (2) the clubface must be wide open when it hits the sand. Less bounce and an open face should allow your club to slide under the ball. When the sand is so shallow that even these adjustments won't work, chip the shot cleanly (ball-first contact). Clean contact requires practice, but it's a good shot to have.
—**Dave Pelz**

INSTRUCTION

Putt from the Bunker

When the lips is low, try this alternative method

It's rare for a greenside bunker to have no lip, but if it doesn't, and there's only a few feet of grass or fringe standing between you and the green, try your putter. **The flatstick is a much safer option than the wedge, especially if the green is sloping away from you and there's trouble lurking behind the hole.** Make a confident, rhythmic stroke, making sure to keep your head still; don't worry about coming up short of the hole because that's much better than blading a wedge into the water.

Your scores drop when
your putts do likewise.

SECTION 8

HOLING OUT

It all comes down to the most important part of the game—putting. Here's how to get the ball in the hole in far fewer strokes.

In the end, the object of the game is to get the ball into the hole. While holing a shot isn't your objective on every swing, it is when you're on the green. Here, the cup becomes your true target for the first time on that hole, so pressure builds. If you miss your landing spot in the fairway by a few yards or hit your approach to a section of the green other than the one you planned on hitting, it's just a miss. Do the same while putting and that miss turns into a stroke lost forever.

The demands of putting are severe, which is ironic since they involve the simplest move you'll make on the course other than getting out of your golf cart. It boils down to that tiny target and the slips, slides, turns, breaks and bumps between it and where your ball lies. There's a lot to overcome, and a lot of questions to be answered. How fast will it go? How hard should I putt it? Is it downhill or flat? Will it go straight or curve left?

There's a school of thought that says it takes years of experience to answer these questions correctly. The Top 100 Teachers disagree, and over the next several pages they'll sufficiently arm you with everything you need to putt the lights out from any distance. You know what the target is—here are the skills to find it.

5 THINGS YOU'LL LEARN IN THIS SECTION

- *How to align your body and aim your putter so your putts start out on the right line.*
- *How to find an alternative grip that can compensate for errors in your stroke so your putts still find the hole.*
- *How to study and read greens like a Tour caddie to get the right line and speed.*
- *How to practice and improve your stroke—without getting bored—using the Top 100's best drills.*
- *How to lag putts close so you'll never three-putt again.*

Learn more about rolling the ball close and holing the short ones at **golf.com/putting**

TOP 100 SAY

HOW DO YOU STACK UP AGAINST THE PROS?

If you think you already have the magic touch on the greens, try sizing up your game against the true bosses of the moss—you'll see that you have some work to do. If your putting stats can get even close to these PGA Tour levels, you'll see that solid putting makes up for bad swings from the fairway or the tee box in a hurry.

29.3
Putts per round

0.55
Three-putts per round

87%
Putts made within 10 feet of the hole

6.6
One-putts per round

2'4"
Proximity to hole following first putt

Average numbers for 2011 PGA Tour. Stats courtesy of ShotLink.

SETUP AND STROKE BASICS

How to grip your putter, aim it and swing it so that you turn knee-knockers and lags into tap-ins

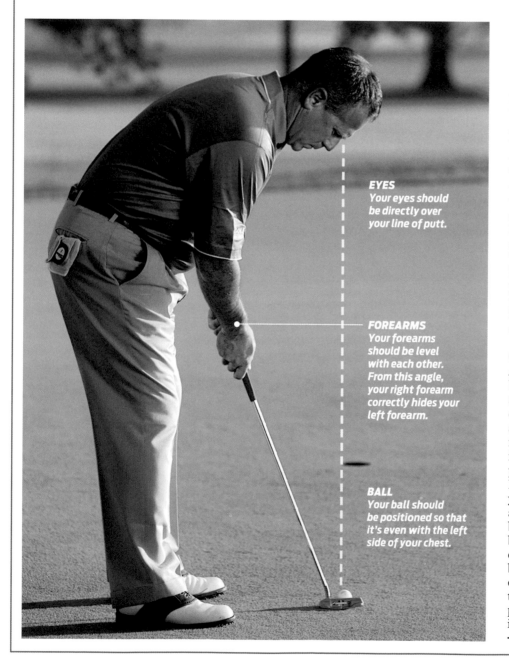

EYES
Your eyes should be directly over your line of putt.

FOREARMS
Your forearms should be level with each other. From this angle, your right forearm correctly hides your left forearm.

BALL
Your ball should be positioned so that it's even with the left side of your chest.

INSTRUCTION

How to Nail Your Alignment

A great putting setup needs eyes and arms

Use the following quick, two-part check to build a solid putting foundation every time.

CHECK 1: FOREARMS

Your forearms should be level with each other at address. There are two ways to check this. If there's someone else on the putting green, have him stand behind you along the line of your putt at address and look at your forearms. Your right forearm should hide your left forearm. If you're alone, take your address position and look down at your forearms—if they're level with each other, you're good to go.

CHECK 2: EYES

At address, your eyes should be directly over your ball and your line of putt. This is crucial—even if your forearms are correct, if your eyes are too far outside the ball or too far inside the ball, a consistent path will be almost impossible. If you're not sure whether your eyes are over the line at address, check their position by dropping a ball from the bridge of your nose. If your eyes are too far forward, the ball will land outside your ball on the ground. If your eyes are too far inside the line of your putt, the dropped ball will land inside the ball on the ground.
—Tom Patri

NO! Your arms are uneven and closed to the line of the putt.

NO! Your arms are uneven and open to the line of the putt.

NO! Your eyes are inside the line of putt.

NO! Your eyes are outside the line of putt.

DRILL

Get Your Putts on the Right Track

Use a CD to make sure your eyes are over the ball

Use an old CD to see where your eyes sit at address. Eyes inside or outside the ball decrease the likelihood of hitting the putt on your intended line.

FAULT: You consistently pull or push putts because your eyes are either too far inside the ball at address (causing a push) or too far outside the ball at address (causing a pull).

FIX: Position a ball in the little hole in the middle of an old music CD, shiny side up. Address the ball as though you were going to putt it and check where your eyes reflect on the CD. If your eyes are inside the ball, bend slightly forward from your hips until they move over the middle of the CD. If your eyes are outside the ball, bend slightly back from your hips. Positioning your eyes over the ball gives you the best view of the line and stops pull and push strokes in their tracks.

—Scott Sackett

DRILL

Point the Face Straight

How to nail it every time

1. *Draw a straight line lengthwise across the top of a triangular framing plate (available at your local DIY) and set it about two feet from the hole, making sure that the line points straight at the cup.*
2. *Place a ball on the line at the base of the plate. Next, make a gate with two tees about 10 inches in front of the ball. The gate should run perpendicular to the line on the plate and be just wide enough to allow the ball to pass through.*
3. *Use the edge at the base of the connector to guide you into a perfectly square putterface position at address. This is important—one of the reasons golfers putt off line is that they don't know what a square putterface at address looks like. Now try to stroke the putt through the gate without allowing the ball to touch the tees. This helps you control your motion so that you don't manipulate the face during your stroke, even after you set it square at address.*
—Brian Mogg

Use the straight edge at the base of a framing plate to practice setting the face perfectly square.

How to Putt with Consistency

Taking the same stance width is key

THE PROBLEM
You don't set up to the ball with a consistent stance width. In fact, you never think about your stance width when you putt. This is a problem, because now you don't have a baseline to control the length of your stroke. Taking your putter back to your big toe, for example, will produce entirely different speeds if your toe is never in the same place.

THE SOLUTION
Take a consistent stance width so that you can accurately monitor the length of your strokes—right foot for your backstrokes, left foot for your through-strokes. This will make it much easier for you to calibrate your ball speed.

The easiest way to **ensure that your stance width is the same every time** is to use the grip of your putter and a ball. Lay your putter on the ground so that the bottom end of the grip is on the inside of your left toe and then place a ball at the other end. Once you have this arranged, place your right toe next to the ball. This is the stance width I recommend— do it every single time you practice, and you should quickly get it locked in.
—Tour putting coach Marius Filmalter

Same stance width every time.

How to Make a Money Stroke

One thin dime can change you from a hitter to a stroker

FAULT: You stab at the ball with your putter rather than making a smooth stroke, giving you zero speed control.

FIX: Place a dime on the back of your putter as shown and make your normal stroke. If you're stroking your putts using a pure pendulum motion, the dime will stay on the putter, no matter how far back and through you take the putter. If you're stabbing the ball, however, the dime will slide off the back of your club as soon as you transition from the backstroke to the forward stroke. You may not be able to tell if you're decelerating, but a dime will pick it up instantly.
—Dr. Jim Suttie

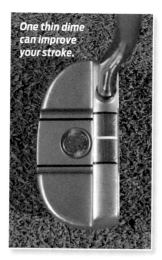

One thin dime can improve your stroke.

Deceleration will knock the dime off your putter here... ...while a smooth pendulum stroke will make sure it's on here.

Add Smooth to Your Stroke

Swing from low to high to generate a purer roll

To generate true roll with minimal bouncing or skidding, you must swing the putter slightly upward through impact. Set most of your weight over your right foot and you'll discover that your putter will naturally—and correctly—swing back lower and finish higher. If you address the ball with most of your weight over your left foot, you'll make a descending strike that presses the ball into the turf and causes it to hop off line.
—Eddie Merrins

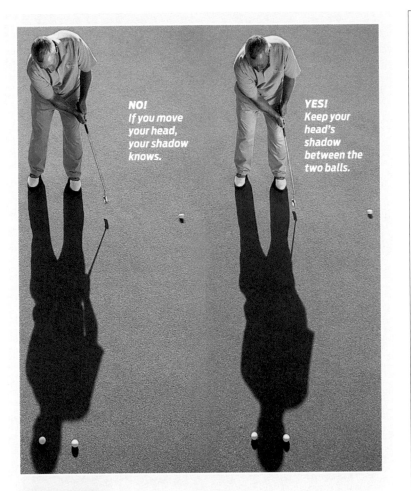

NO!
*If you move
your head,
your shadow
knows.*

*YES!
Keep your
head's
shadow
between the
two balls.*

Keep Your Head Still

Your shadow will show you how

YOUR GOAL
Contact in the center of the putterface so the ball starts on the line you've chosen.

HOW TO ACHIEVE IT
One trait all good putters share is that they keep their head still. You can't keep your putter on line if you move your head, nor can you keep your head still if you move the putter on the wrong path. **A steady head allows your hands, arms and shoulders**

to move the putter correctly. On a sunny day, set up to the ball with your shadow directly in front of you. Place two balls on the green about a foot apart and address another one so that your head's shadow is between the two balls. Make your putting stroke, hold your finish and check your shadow to see if your head moved. If you have difficulty keeping your head still, use more arms and hands in your stroke and less shoulder movement.
—Paul Trittler

Beat the Green Freeze

Free your stroke—NOW!

FAULT: Remember when Sergio Garcia couldn't stop gripping and regripping his club? I once counted 23 regrips! This is the ultimate example of freezing over the ball, but it's actually more common on putts. If this sounds like you, your problem is that you don't know how to start your stroke. You need a specific cycle or pattern to free it up. You also need to stop worrying about the outcome.

THE DRILL THAT FIXES IT
STEP 1: Line up nine balls on the green, as shown below.
STEP 2: Step into the first one, look at the hole, and hit the putt.
STEP 3: As soon as the ball is on its way, step to the next ball and, without looking at the cup, make your stroke.
STEP 4: Repeat this method until all nine balls are gone. Don't worry about where the

next ball is going each time, just continuously step to the next ball and smoothly make your putting stroke.
STEP 5: After a couple of turns with this drill, perform the entire cycle (step, look, putt) with each ball, individually. Once you feel this cycle is ingrained, take it to the course and putt with confidence.
—Tour putting coach Marius Filmalter

*REPEAT AFTER ME
Step in, look
at the target,
then immediately
start your stroke.*

DRILL

Push Your Putter With Your Palm

The right grip and technique will help more of your putts find the center of the cup

The shortcut to saving strokes is in the palm of your hand. When you set the putter grip in the palm of your right hand, it gives you a stable, repeatable stroke that will do more for your game than beating balls on the driving range. Here's how to palm your way to better putting.

STEP 1: LET YOUR PALM BE THE PILOT

Set your putter behind the ball and position the grip in your right palm before placing your left hand on the club. The grip should be in line with your forearm [*below, right*], and the putter should feel like an extension of your arm. Avoid the fault of gripping the putter in your right fingers [*below, left*].

STEP 2: PUT THE PUSH ON

If your alignment is correct, your right palm will face the target, which is where you want it at impact. Your through-stroke should feel like you're pushing the ball down the target line with your right palm. This stroke will point the clubface at the hole and make it easier for you to release the putterhead for a more consistent roll.

—Dr. David Wright

Push the ball toward the hole with your right palm

WRONG!

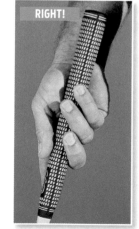

RIGHT!

A finger hold makes it easy for your stroke to break down; a palm grip gives you extra control.

How to Putt with Perfect Pace

Find your personal putting tempo and roll it smooth every time

THE FACTS

Every player has his own unique pace—a tempo fingerprint. You can't avoid it because (1) your personal pace is a strong part of who you are, and (2) if you do try to avoid it, you'll be forced to make compensations in your stroke—compensations that are difficult to time and that almost always result in bad misses.

HOW TO PUT THEM TO GOOD USE

The secret to putting well is to find this personal rhythm and then work it into your motion. Follow these steps:

STEP 1: FIND YOUR PERSONAL TEMPO

The pace at which you should swing your putter is the tempo that's wired into your system—it's the personal pace at which you go about most of the motor actions you execute in a day. The easy way to find it is to find a flat section of ground and walk around. Have a friend time you for 45 seconds and count the number of steps you take during that time. At the end of 45 seconds, tally the steps and repeat. Do this five times, then compute your average pace count. That number is a concrete representation of your tempo.

STEP 2: BUILD YOUR PERSONAL TEMPO INTO YOUR STROKE

Set your personal tempo number on a metronome (there are a number of very good apps for this that you can download and use on your smart phone). Next, anchor two blocks of wood to the green with some tees, setting one outside your right foot and the other where you play the ball in your stance [*photos, right*]. Take your stance and swing your putter back and forth, striking each block on successive beeps from the metronome. It helps to count "1-2, 1-2" in your head as you strike the blocks in time with the metronome. After a while, move the block on your right closer to the impact block, and then even farther away. Regardless of the stroke length you're practicing, try to maintain the same "tick-tock" pace for all putts.
—Mike Adams

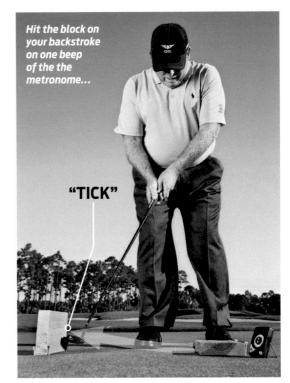

Hit the block on your backstroke on one beep of the the metronome...

"TICK"

Your normal walking pace is the rhythm you should use to stroke putts.

...and the other block in your through-stroke on the next beep.

"TOCK"

JUDGE LINE, SPEED & BREAK

The best stroke in the world won't get the ball into the hole unless you know how the putt will react to the green once it gets rolling. Try these time-honored techniques for picking the right line.

A physical representation of your line can be very helpful.

How to Stay on Your Line

A five-step plan to get your putts tracking from the start

It's critical to build a setup that gives you the best chance to get your ball rolling in the right direction, because a ball that starts off line stays off line. Here's a five-step plan to correctly position your body and putter on the line you've chosen.
—Donald Crawley

STEP 1: FIND YOUR LINE
On the practice green, stand behind your ball and imagine how it will roll. Run a raised string along the starting point of the line and burn the image of what your starting line looks like into your brain. This physical representation of your putt line will give you an idea of what a straight line actually looks like.

STEP 2: ALIGN YOUR BALL
Draw a straight line across the logo on your ball. Use this mark to align your ball along the intended line of the putt by placing it underneath and parallel to the static line. Now you have a reference point to get your putterface pointed in the right direction.

STEP 3: AIM YOUR PUTTER
Remove the string and sole your putterhead on the ground. Align the face so that the top edge makes a perpendicular angle with the mark on your ball. This will ensure that your putter starts the ball on the correct line after contact, as long as you don't dramatically open or close the face during your stroke.

STEP 4: SET YOUR EYES
Set your eyes over the ball and parallel to your intended line. If you set your eyes to the inside of the ball your stroke will have a tendency to move inside and push your putts; set your eyes outside and you'll likely pull your putts. Either way, you'll miss the putt.

"If you know what to look for, you'll know what to do even before you get behind your ball." —Todd Sones

CHECKPOINT

Be a Green-Reading Detective

All the clues to the break are out in the open

While a course designer will do his best to challenge your green-reading abilities, he'll also leave obvious clues about how the ball will roll on different areas of the green. If you know what to look for, you'll know what to do even before you get behind your ball. —Todd Sones

CLUE 1: PUTTS BREAK AWAY FROM HILLS
Don't forget the obvious. Putts will break away from greenside bumps, hills and rises, especially if they're close to the line of your putt.

CLUE 2: PUTTS BREAK AWAY FROM THE CLUBHOUSE
While not always true, clubhouses are normally built on the highest point on the course, usually for drainage purposes. Look for home, and you'll get a good idea of the general lay of the land—information that can come in handy when you can't tell exactly which way a putt falls.

CLUE 3: PUTTS BREAK TOWARD WATER
For obvious drainage reasons, greens will slope toward the nearest body of water. On oceanside courses, don't underestimate the natural roll of terrain toward the sea—putts break especially hard toward the agua here.

CLUE 6: PUTTS BREAK TOWARD COLLECTION AREAS
Those funny, tightly mown greenside spots that your ball finds when you short-side the green are always below the level of the putting surface, and they usually house a drain at the lowest point. If you're putting near one of these collection areas, the break will favor that direction.

CLUE 5: PUTTS BREAK AWAY FROM BUNKERS
The last thing a course designer—and especially the superintendent—wants is water draining into a bunker. More often than not, the green slopes away from the sand to avoid extra bunker maintenance.

CLUE 4: PUTTS BREAK TOWARD THE SUN
The grass on the green grows all day long, following the path of the sun. In the late afternoon, when the blades are at their longest, greens feature a serious grain toward the setting sun. Your putts will break with the grain. This clue is especially important when playing on long-blade Bermuda grass.

STEP 5: ALIGN YOUR BODY
Allow your arms to hang straight down from your shoulders, and then place your hands on the grip. Loose, free-hanging arms are needed to create the tension-free stroke that you need to be a consistent putter.

GREEN READING

Here's how to become an expert planner on the greens and get the right line every time

Find the Spine

The first step to reading the green

You've probably heard TV announcers refer to the "fall line" when talking about a certain putt. What they're referring to is the road map to a particular hole position. The "spine" or fall line influences nearly every putt. Think of it as the Rosetta Stone to figuring out your line. Once you identify it, you're on your way to fully understanding the putt you face.
—**AimPoint founder Mark Sweeney**

See the Slope

Watch were the water goes

Every green has built-in drainage points, low spots where water can run off. Knowing where they are is the key to finding the spine. Determine the highest point above the hole and walk to that spot. Imagine you have a hose and you're streaming water in the direction of the hole. The water will funnel toward the hole and follow a certain line as it drains off the green. That line is the spine.
—**Fred Griffin**

SHARP CURVES
The farther the ball is from the spine, the more it will break. Maximum break occurs when you're putting at 90 degrees to the spine, and at the farthest point away from the spine. Depending on the slope—putting downhill will increase the amount of break— you may be playing as much as 5 to 10 feet of break.

A RIVER RUNS THROUGH IT
There are multiple spines to every green (as indicated by the blue lines here), but only one spine per hole location. The spine runs through the hole—not the ball—its path dictated by how the green drains. *(See left to learn how to find the spine.)*

THE SPINE LINE · · · · · · · · · ·
The green doesn't have just one. Each hole position does.

THE BREAK LINE ━━━━━━
Your ball's position in relation to the spine determines the big breaks.

LEFT TO RIGHT
Putting uphill, any ball to the left of the spine will break from left to right. The closer the ball is to the spine, the straighter the putt.

RIGHT TO LEFT
A ball right of the spine will break from right to left.

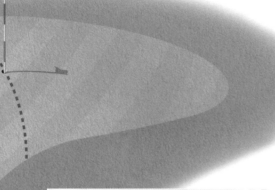

Be Your Own Stimpmeter

Try this to get the right speed

Find a flat spot on the practice green of your home course, take a stance that's about 12 inches wide, and position the ball just inside your left heel. Swing your putter back so it goes directly in front of the big toe on your right foot. Hit five putts this way and note how far the ball rolls. Do the same thing when you're playing a different course. If the stroke that produces an eight-foot roll on your home course produces a 12-foot roll on the unfamiliar one, you'll know the greens are that much faster and that you should plan on more break.
—**Fred Griffin**

TOP 100 SAY

Read Greens Like a Caddie

Six things the experts look for when judging slope

1 The faster the putting surface, the more break you have to allow for. This is because you'll be hitting the ball much more softly and it will take more time to reach the hole. The more uphill it is, the less it will break because a firmer putt takes less time to reach the hole.

2 If the grass looks shiny along the line of your putt and darker when you look at the ball from behind the hole, you're putting down grain (that is, the grass is bending toward the sun). Expect a quicker putt and more break.

3 If the grass looks dark along the line of your putt, but shiny from behind the hole, you're putting against the grain. The putt will be slower and break less.

4 Feel the ground with your feet as you walk on the putting surface. Does the green feel firm (faster) or spongy (slower)? Do your leg muscles feel as if they are walking uphill toward the hole (slower) or downhill (faster)?

5 Watch the ball of everyone who putts before you. You'll get a sense what the ball will do near the hole and where it's most sensitive to break. Also note what any ball does when it goes beyond the hole. This gives you the perfect read and speed for any comeback putt.

6 Make your first read from behind the ball, looking toward the hole. Crouch down as low as you can to get a better view of the contours. Also, take note of water and drainage areas (putts often break toward these features), or mountains (putts break away from hills). If you're still unsure about your read, walk behind the hole to get a different perspective.

Your putter doesn't care how you set up, only that your forearms are square.

Set Up on Your Line

How to get the ball started on whatever line you see

THE PROBLEM
You consistently miss on the low side of the hole.

THE SOLUTION
Because your right hand is lower than your left on the handle, your right forearm naturally sits farther away from your body and misaligned from your left. **Good putters offset this by bringing their right elbow in close to the right side of their torso at address.** Notice as you do this how your right shoulder drops and magically lines up your forearms. You'll know you're doing it correctly when you feel your spine tilt ever so slightly away from the target.
—**Tour putting coach Marius Filmalter**

THE RIGHT PUTTER FOR YOU

Choosing from the hundreds of putter models on the market is a daunting task. The following gear tips will help you find a new favorite flatstick.

INSTRUCTION

How to Make a Model Stroke

The secret is in the design of your putter

THE MYTH
Depending on your preference, swing your putterhead straight back and through or on a slight arc.

THE TRUTH
The design of your putter—not your preferred putting style—determines the type of path you should trace. Toe-weighted putters are engineered to open and close during your stroke and travel on an arc, while face-balanced models (ones that feature a centered shaft connection or a double-bend shaft) are engineered to remain square and travel on a straight line.

WHAT TO DO
Match your stroke to your putter, or buy a model that's designed to complement your putting style.
—**Mike Adams**

IF YOUR PUTTER IS FACE-BALANCED...
Take it back and through on a straight line, keeping the face square all the way.

Allow your arms to hang directly underneath your shoulders.

Bend from your hips more to get your eyes over the target line.

Play the ball slightly forward of center with the putterhead directly below your nose.

FACE-BALANCED STROKE
Move the putter straight back and through by **rocking your shoulders like a teeter-totter.** To ingrain the feel of this stroke, place a club across your chest as shown and secure it underneath your armpits. Hit some putts by pointing the triangle formed by the club and your arms away from the target and then to the target.

IF YOUR PUTTER IS TOE-WEIGHTED...
Take it away to the inside of your target line, return it square and finish back on the inside.

Play the ball off your left armpit.

Stand erect, with your eyes inside the target line.

Position your hands in front of your shoulder line.

TOE-WEIGHTED STROKE
Since your hands are outside your arms, you'll naturally move the putter to the inside. The key is to maintain a free-flowing motion so you don't disturb the integrity of the arc. **Practice putting with your left arm only to develop a free-swinging motion.** Think of how a gate swings open and shut on its hinges—that's the feeling you're after.

CHECKPOINT

Is Your Putter Ruining Your Stroke?

If the shaft is too long or short for you, the answer is yes

YOUR PUTTER IS TOO SHORT...

If you have zero elbow bend

When the handle is so low that your have to straighten your arms to take your grip, it forces you to tip your shoulders up and down to make your stroke. You'll have distance-control problems because you'll make contact with a different amount of loft on every stroke.

YOUR PUTTER IS TOO LONG...

If your arms are jammed into your sides at address

When you grip an overly long putter, you're forced to bend your elbows too much, and when you swing your putter your body will get in the way. Choking down will only alter your putter's swingweight and send your tempo out of whack.

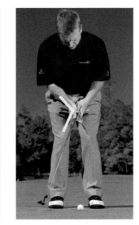

YOUR PUTTER IS JUST RIGHT...

If your arms hang under your shoulders when you grip the top of the handle

Look for elbows just under your rib cage with a slight amount of flex, which allows your arms and shoulders to swing the putter under your body without excess wrist and head motion.

—Todd Sones

Choose the Right Hosel

Make sure it benefits your setup and stroke

If you pull more putts than you push, you'll fare better with a shaft/hosel-in-the-heel design (such as the flare-tip), which will hold off the rotation of the face. If you push putts, try a center-shafted putter (such as the straight-in), which gives you more direct control of the face position through impact.

If your stroke is of the "straight-back-and-straight-through" variety, you'll putt more consistently with a face-balanced putter, or one with a shaft/hosel attachment closer to the center of the head. Most face-balanced putters come with a double-bend shaft, so keep your eyes out for those. On the other hand, If you're more of a "Crenshaw" putter, and like to gently roll the putter on an "inside-to-square-to-inside" stroke, you'll be better off with a hosel/shaft attachment that favors the heel.

Plumber-neck hosels increase your ability to see how your putter is aligned at address. But they also impact your hand position. If you strive to keep your hands ahead of the putter at impact, which many good putters do, a hosel/shaft offset like a plumber-neck will benefit your stroke.

Flare-tip

Straight-in

Double-bend

Slant-neck

Plumber-neck

THE NEW WAYS TO PUTT

Tried-and-true techniques never go out of style—unless the ball isn't going into the hole. Then it's time to try something new.

INSTRUCTION

How to Roll With the Right Speed

This drill will give you the right pace for short putts

FAULT: You leave short putts short, or they lose their line due to a lack of speed.

FIX: Secure a scorecard pencil between two sets of tees in front of the hole as shown at right. Putt a few balls from anywhere from three to five feet from the hole. **The idea is to hit these putts with enough force that the ball pops over the pencil and then into the hole.** You'll quickly learn that to sink your putts with the proper amount of speed; you can't baby the ball to the hole, nor can you rocket it because too much speed will pop the ball over both the pencil and the hole.

Once you get to the point where you can consistently pop eight out of 10 putts over the pencil and into the hole, remove the pencil and try to sink your putts with the same velocity through the two tees—these putts should always hit somewhere on the back of the cup. Then remove the tees and work on maintaining the same speed and line.
—Dr. Gary Wiren

The speed that will pop the ball over a pencil and into the cup is perfect for short putts.

CHECKPOINT

Apply the Right Type of Force

Here's an easy thought to help you hone your distance control from short range

The key to making short putts is getting the ball started on the right line and rolling it with the correct amount of pace. The amount of force you need to generate the correct speed is the same amount of force you'd use to toss a penny to the hole from the same distance. Thinking of the simple image of flipping a penny to the target tells you exactly how hard or soft to stroke your putt, allowing you to shift more of your focus to the hole.
—Eddie Merrins

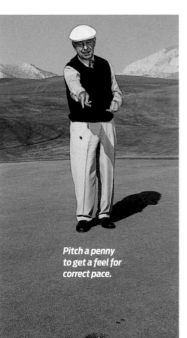

Pitch a penny to get a feel for correct pace.

INSTRUCTION

How to Putt Under Pressure

Use this drill to turn knee-knockers into kick-ins

On short pressure-packed putts, it's vital to keep your head and body still. If you lift your head to watch the ball you'll pull your shoulders and the putterhead off line, causing the putt to miss to the left. To stay still, try pinching your knees inward, like Arnold Palmer used to do. As you stroke, let your ears be your eyes: Listen for the ball to hit the bottom of the hole.

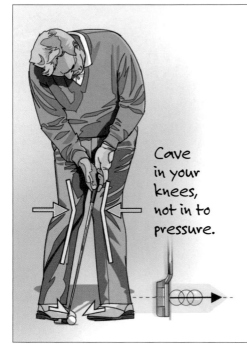

Cave in your knees, not in to pressure.

INSTRUCTION

How to Be a Clutch Putter

Brain-wave analysis proves the less you think, the more you'll make

MISSED PUTT
This is a 10-second snapshot of a golfer's brain activity as he addressed, hit and missed a five-foot putt.

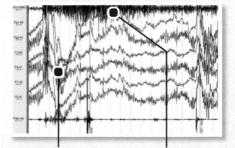

These jagged lines show a spike in brain activity before contact, as if he were thinking, "Don't miss!"

This line shows the movement of the golfer's facial muscles, also suggesting major tension.

MADE PUTT
This reading was taken over a similar putt that the same golfer made. The quiet readings below reveal a relaxed mind.

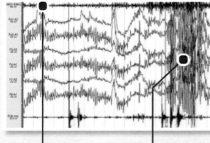

The inner line indicates that the golfer's face was relaxed, while the quiet readings below reveal a relaxed mind.

No, there wasn't an earthquake. The sensors detected the golfer's mental delight as the putt dropped in the hole.

This is your brain on golf
Red numbers are good, but as this MRI of a golf-stressed brain shows, if your head is red, you're dead.

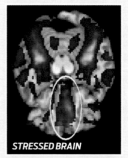

STRESSED BRAIN

CLUTCH BRAIN

CODE RED!
The red shows intense electrical activation in the ventral medial frontal cortex. That's the part of your brain that recognizes danger and forces your heart rate to increase and muscles to tense up, helping you to survive threatening situations. But tension and a racing heart don't help much on the course. When a nervous golfer stands over a tough shot, this is literally what his fear looks like.

PRAISIN' THE BLUES
The blue means less brain activity. This is typically a good thing in golf—it means you're not overthinking the shot. You don't want your ventral medial cortex activated when you're putting. An MRI of a Tour player's brain would likely show more blue than a Picasso!
—Analysis provided by Dr. Richard Keefe, associate professor of sports medicine at Duke University

Learn the Pop-Piston Stroke

This unique putting method makes long lags seem like tap-ins

THE PROBLEM

On long putts, you have difficulty getting the ball to the hole with your Tour-style, back-and-forth pendulum stroke.

THE SOLUTION

A "pop-piston" stroke will help you get long putts to the hole with ease.

HOW TO DO IT

Position the ball toward your left toe. Open your stance slightly to accommodate the forward ball position, and keep your eyes over the line of putt. Place your thumbs on the top of the grip, with your left index finger on top of your right fingers on the target side of the shaft. Anchor your right elbow against your right hip. Push the putterhead straight back with your left index finger, and keep your right elbow fixed to your right hip. This will ensure that the putterhead stays on line. At the end of your backstroke, your right wrist should be bent back while your left wrist should remain unhinged and in line with your left forearm.

To start the club forward, use your right palm as a piston and shove everything (hands, arms and putterhead) forward. Your right elbow should straighten as it pushes the putter, but no other part of the assembly should move. Straightening your right elbow is a key element of the "piston" forward stroke. It's a natural movement that makes it much easier to gauge distance—especially on long lag putts.
—Dr. T.J. Tomasi

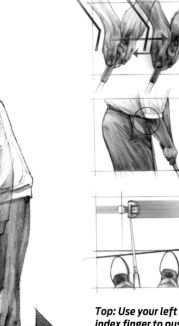

Top: Use your left index finger to push the club back and your right palm to move it forward.

Center: Anchor your right elbow against your right hip.

Bottom: Open your stance and position the ball off your left toe.

"Pop" your putterhead back by hinging your wrists, and use your right arm as a piston to maintain acceleration and centered contact.

TOUR TIP

How to Nail Your Path Like a Tour Pro

This drill helped me, and it'll work for you, too

TRY THIS!

My coach developed this drill to help me make sure my putterface is square at impact and that my stroke path is correct so I can consistently start the ball on line. We find a straight putt and set up a gate for my putterhead to pass through about 6 feet from the hole, and a second gate a foot from the hole [*photo, right*]. Once we have the tees set up **I simply stroke putts through the gates and into the cup, making sure my putterhead doesn't touch the tees.**

An addition we sometimes make is to place a tee behind the left side of the ball and another in front of the gate on the right side. This prevents me from taking the putter too far inside-out during my stroke—my typical mistake. If you have the opposite problem and struggle with swinging too much outside-in, just reverse the position of the additional tees.
—PGA Tour player Lucas Glover

Add tees [circled] to keep you from swinging too much inside-out.

INSTRUCTION

Learn the Pro Way to Stroke Putts

The Tour path is from the inside and then down the line

CHECK THIS!

The two most commonly taught stroke types (straight-back-straight-through and arcing) have merit, but they fall short of perfection. It's impossible to take the putterhead straight back without lifting it off the ground or letting your right elbow fly. Test it by putting against a wall and watch how the putterhead must rise in order for you to keep the toe in contact with the baseboard. Lifting the putter in your backstroke is bad because it results in a downward angle of attack—the exact opposite of what you need to create proper roll. So yes, your backstroke—and subsequent path back to the ball—must arc. But what about impact? While it's true that your putter will eventually arc back to the inside at some point in your through-stroke, **it's critical that you work straight down the line for at least the first 4 inches past the ball.** This straight-line impact—paired with an inside delivery—ensures that you won't cut across the ball and promotes a full release of the putterhead.
—Tour putting coach Marius Filmalter

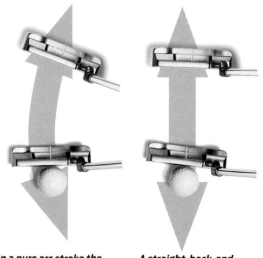

DON'T DO THIS!

In a pure arc stroke the face points at the target for a very brief instant, leaving you with very little margin for error.

A straight-back-and-through stroke sounds good, but you can't make one without lifting your putter off the ground.

The best putters in the world arc going back, but then putt straight down the line through the impact zone.

INSTRUCTION

Lag Putts Made Easy

There are few things more demoralizing than reaching a long par 4 or par 5 in two, only to three-putt a possible birdie away from 30-plus feet. It's the kind of mistake that lingers with you for a few holes and, in many cases, even longer. To take full advantage of your length, you must learn to become an exceptional lag putter, and that means hitting your first putt tight enough to the hole so that you have no worse than a 3-footer coming back. Here are a few keys to get you rolling.

DRILL 1: STAND, GRIP TALLER
Try to stand taller at address, as though you were preparing to hit a chip shot, and **grip about a half-inch higher on the putter.** These two minor adjustments will allow you to extend your arms and create more wrist hinge during the stroke, which in turn will produce more power so your first putt travels a sufficient distance. If you're too bent over—as you might be on a short, six-foot putt—your arms will be too tight and rigid, making it more difficult to swing the putterhead freely with the necessary momentum.

On long putts, stand taller and grip the shaft higher at address.

DRILL 2:
HOOK YOUR PUTTS

Swing the putterhead on an arc, as though you were trying to hook or draw the putt toward the hole. The head should swing back to the inside and release to the inside after impact, creating plenty of momentum to get the ball to the cup. Much like a pitching swing, **you want the backstroke and through-stroke to be roughly the same length,** so that the putterhead is accelerating smoothly through impact. Many amateurs take too short a backstroke and, as a result, are forced to swing longer and overaccelerate on the through-stroke. This leads to a jerky stroke and poor contact. As with the short putts, you want the putterhead to travel on the same pace both back and through.

Let the putterhead swing back to the inside and then release to the inside.

DRILL 3: FOCUS ON THE END

Consider how the ball will stop as it's approaching the hole. Putts break most around the cup, since that's when they're moving the slowest; therefore, **make sure to look at the green around the hole to see how much slope there is.** Also pay attention to the line the ball takes after it runs by the hole, as this will show you the line for your next putt.

Watch the last few feet of the putt, which can clue you in on your next attempt.

INSTRUCTION

How to Roll It the Right Length

Build an inventory of three strokes to take the guesswork out of distance control

STEP 1: ROLL IT 40 FEET

Hit the practice green with a small bucket of balls. Get into your regular stance, and roll a few putts by taking your hands back to just outside your right thigh and then motoring through at your best putting-stroke pace. Notice how this stroke rolls the ball about 40 feet (you may roll it longer or shorter depending on your stance width and tempo).

STEP 2: ROLL IT 20 FEET

Do the same thing, but this time stop your hands when they reach the middle of your right thigh in your backstroke. This stroke should roll the ball about 20 feet.

STEP 3: ROLL IT 10 FEET

Repeat the drill, but this time stop your stroke when your hands swing back to the inside of your right thigh. These should roll about 10 feet.

Voilà! Three strokes that you can count on to roll the ball three common distances, which is probably three more than you have right now. Make this drill a regular part of your practice (you should be able to create three nice clusters of putts once you get good at it). If you need to roll the ball longer or shorter, simply widen your stance (for longer putts) or bring your feet closer together (for shorter putts), but continue to apply the same stroke lengths: Outside thigh, middle thigh, inside thigh.
—**Tour putting coach Marius Filmalter**

40-foot Putt   20-foot Putt   10-foot Putt

A Better Way to Putt

After analyzing nearly 3,000 putts, our research reveals there's a better way to get the ball into the hole

THE CONVENTIONAL WISDOM
You should look at the ball for the duration of your putting stroke, and keep your eyes on that spot until well after the ball has been struck.

THE UNCONVENTIONAL THEORY
You should look at the hole–not the ball–from the moment you set the club behind the ball until you complete your putting stroke.

THE STUDY
We divided 40 players ranging in handicap from eight to 36 into two 20-person groups, with each group balanced in terms of handicap, age and gender. One was the experimental group. The other was the control group, which used the conventional method of looking at the ball.

THE EXPERIMENT
Using the conventional method of looking at the ball, both groups putted nine balls to holes ranging from three feet to 43 feet away. The results were statistically equal.
Next, the control group putted one ball to each of nine targets in random order. The experimental group did the same but with one huge change: They were instructed to go through their normal pre-putt routine, but rather than looking at the ball as they made their stroke, they were told to look at the hole. Then we compared the two groups. How did looking at the hole measure up? The results [*right*] will surprise you.

THE NEW WAY TO PUTT

1 Address the ball and place your putter behind it.

2 Start looking at the hole, and don't look back at the ball. (We promise it's still there.)

3 Hit your putt, and keep looking at the hole until you complete your stroke.

Rather than looking at the ball as they made their stroke [left], the subjects were told to look at the hole the entire time [right].

THE SHOCKING RESULTS!

● **Long putts end up significantly closer to the hole when you look at the hole while making your stroke.** On average, after all was said and done, on putts between 28 feet and 43 feet in length, the experimental group (those who looked at the hole) had slightly less than 28 inches remaining to the hole. By comparison, on the same long putts, the control group (those who looked at the ball) left themselves nearly 37 inches remaining to the hole. That means the experimental group was 24 percent closer, nine inches that could be the difference between a two-putt and a three-putt.

● **Looking at the hole may be more effective on short putts, too.** On putts between three feet and eight feet, the experimental group left an average of just under nine inches to the hole. On the same putts, the control group ended up with leaves that averaged 12.5 inches. Strictly speaking, that's not statistically significant, but those inches might be the difference between a routine tap-in and the occasional short miss.

> "On average, after all was said and done, on putts between 28 feet and 43 feet in length, the experimental group (those who looked at the hole) had slightly less than 28 inches remaining to the hole."
> —Eric Alpenfels

MORE RESULTS:
Two other facts of note from our research: From 13 to 23 feet, both methods produced similar results. Neither method produced more holed putts from any distance.

PUTTS END UP CLOSER WHEN YOU LOOK AT THE HOLE

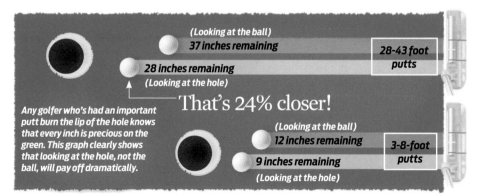

(Looking at the ball)
37 inches remaining

28 inches remaining
(Looking at the hole)

28-43 foot putts

Any golfer who's had an important putt burn the lip of the hole knows that every inch is precious on the green. This graph clearly shows that looking at the hole, not the ball, will pay off dramatically.

That's 24% closer!

(Looking at the ball)
12 inches remaining

9 inches remaining
(Looking at the hole)

3-8-foot putts

Why it works

There are three main reasons why the new method improves on your old one:

1 You're using both eyes to to see your target, giving you highly accurate depth perception.

2 Maybe it was a fear of whiffing the putt, but testers who looked at the hole maintained their posture like statues.

3 Testers who looked at the hole didn't decelerate through the ball. In other words, they established natural speed control.
—Eric Alpenfels

Are You a Candidate?

Should you look at the hole instead of the ball when you putt?

Take this test and find out:

Q: Do you typically three-putt more than twice per round?
Yes ❑   No ❑

Q: Do you consistently leave yourself a putt of more than five feet after hitting a 25-footer?
Yes ❑   No ❑

Q: Do you take longer than two seconds to pull the trigger after your last look at the hole?
Yes ❑   No ❑

Q: Do you second-guess yourself after you've addressed the ball more than twice per round?
Yes ❑   No ❑

Q: Do you find it hard to strike putts aggressively and avoid decelerating?
Yes ❑   No ❑

Score: If you answered "yes" this many times...
0: We still need a partner for the member-guest, but you're probably too busy playing in the U.S. Open.
1-2: You might think it sounds quirky, but it could be all that's standing between you and breaking your next scoring barrier.
3 or more: You've got nothing to lose.

You're going to find trouble every time you play. The trick isn't avoiding it— it's learning to get out of it.

SECTION 9

TROUBLE SHOTS

Even the best-made plans sometimes go awry. Here's how to get out of any predicament on the course.

Face facts: You'll never play a round in which you hit every shot off tightly mown grass with a level lie. Bad shots happen, and even good ones end up in trouble via bad bounces, strange kicks and other "rub of the green" effects that defy explanation but are nonetheless a very real part of the game.

A trouble situation is any one that prohibits you from making your regular swing. Most often it takes the form of an obstacle between you and your target. Other times it's the lie itself, like when your ball comes to rest in ankle-deep rough or in a sand-filled divot. When you think of how many times you alter your technique to accommodate anything but a perfect lie, you realize just how often trouble shots pop up during the normal course of play.

The point is, finding trouble is something every golfer does. The trick is getting out of it. And while finding trouble is bad enough, taking two or three swings to get back on the fairway or green is much, much worse. It would be difficult to tackle every possible trouble situation is a section this size—there are just too many. Instead, the Top 100 Teachers describe how to overcome the most common forms. Learn and perfect these escapes and you'll be sitting pretty—even when your ball isn't.

5 THINGS YOU'LL LEARN IN THIS SECTION

- *How to hit under and around trees that block the path to your target.*
- *Three plays to find the fairway on windy days.*
- *How to escape rough with three different clubs.*
- *The secret to setting up on a sidehill lie and adjusting your swing to make clean contact.*
- *How to hit two chips from difficult situations around the green with two unlikely clubs.*

Learn more about escaping tough situations around the course at **golf.com/trouble**

HOW TO MAKE A TOUGH COURSE EASY

Step one is discovering where it can do the most damage to your game

The key to playing well is to have no surprises during your round. That's why I recommend taking a hard look at the courses you play most with an eye toward two things: (1) the kind of shots you can expect to face when you drive off the fairways, and (2) whether the course features large, super-fast greens (which can lead to 3-putts), or small, well-guarded greens with deep bunkers (which will test your short game). Then determine your three biggest weaknesses. Ask several of your closest golf buddies (you'll want multiple opinions) to honestly describe what shots they see costing you strokes, and then commit to improving them. By knowing where and where not to miss, and improving the shots you're least likely to pull off, you'll avoid danger and situations that in the past have caused big numbers on your scorecard.
—**Dave Pelz**

HOW TO GET OUT OF TROUBLE

Each situation is unique. The key is to get creative and stay confident.

How to Hit Out of Trees

Choke down to keep it low

THE SITUATION

You've missed the fairway, and though your lie is good and you're only 100 yards from the green, a low-hanging branch prevents you from playing a wedge shot.

THE STRATEGY

STEP 1: Stay aggressive—never let a tree or its limbs come between you and a chance for birdie.

STEP 2: Determine which is the highest-lofted club in your bag that will keep the ball under the branch.

STEP 3: Mix and match your grip (how much you choke down on the handle) and backswing length to produce the appropriate distance.

HOW TO DO IT

For the shot depicted here, a 6-iron is the highest loft that will keep the ball under the limb. Let's say you normally hit a 6-iron 160 yards. Here's the trick to hitting it the 100 yards you need.
—Dr. Gary Wiren

KEY MOVE
This technique only works if you swing to a full finish. The ball will fly low enough to avoid the trouble and travel far enough to stop safely on the green.

160 YDS
Take your normal grip on the end of the handle.

150 YDS
Now choke down to the middle of the grip. This takes 10 yards off the shot.

140 YDS
If you choke all the way down to the bottom, that subtracts 10 more yards.

140 YDS
With a full swing you'll still produce 140 yards—that's still too much.

OPTION-MINDED
Mixing and matching the three choke distances with the three different backswing lengths allows you to produce seven distances with each one of your irons.

120 YDS
Shorten your backswing by 10 inches (hands at chest high) to hit it 20 yards less.

100 YDS
Shorten your backswing another 10 inches (hands at hip height) to take off another 20 yards.

INSTRUCTION

Another Way to Keep It Low

Cut your finish to keep the ball from rising

TRY THIS!

There are several basics you need to know to successfully hit the ball low and with enough power to get back to the fairway or onto the green. First, select your lowest-lofted iron (or hybrid, though they tend to hit the ball too high) and choke down on the grip about an inch. This will help you deliver the clubhead to the ball more accurately and also take a bit of loft off the club.

Once you have your grip, take some abbreviated practice swings. **You don't want a big backswing or follow-through on this shot—you only need to swing about hip high.** Now address the ball but place more weight forward in your stance. This adjustment will steepen your swing a bit and help you strike down through the rough. When you feel you have these adjustments made, simply focus on the target you've chosen and make a solid, aggressive swing through the ball.
—**Michael Breed**

Make a half backswing and a steep, abbreviated downswing.

INSTRUCTION

Avoid Trouble with Your Grip

Altering your hold gives you the shotmaking power to curve the ball away from danger

Your tee shot stops on the left edge of the fairway, but you find your approach to the green blocked by a large tree. This would be the perfect time to hit a draw, which you can do quite easily by simply adjusting your setup and grip pressure. A change in pressure will allow you to hit all different types of finesse shots, from a draw to a fade to a lob shot.

For a standard shot, your grip pressure should be somewhere between very soft and firm, with both hands providing equal amounts of pressure via the last three fingers of your left hand and middle two fingers of your right. To hit a draw, firm up the pressure in your right hand while relaxing the left. This will encourage the right forearm to rotate over the left through impact, turning the face over and imparting right-to-left spin on the ball. For a fade, it's the opposite: You want to grip the club lightly with your right hand and firmly with the left to hold off the release of the clubface, which imparts left-to-right spin to help you attack those tough-to-reach right-side hole locations.

With both shots, **make sure to aim the clubface at your target (where you want the ball to finish) and your body where you want the ball to start**, and then swing along your body line with the appropriate amount of grip pressure in each hand.

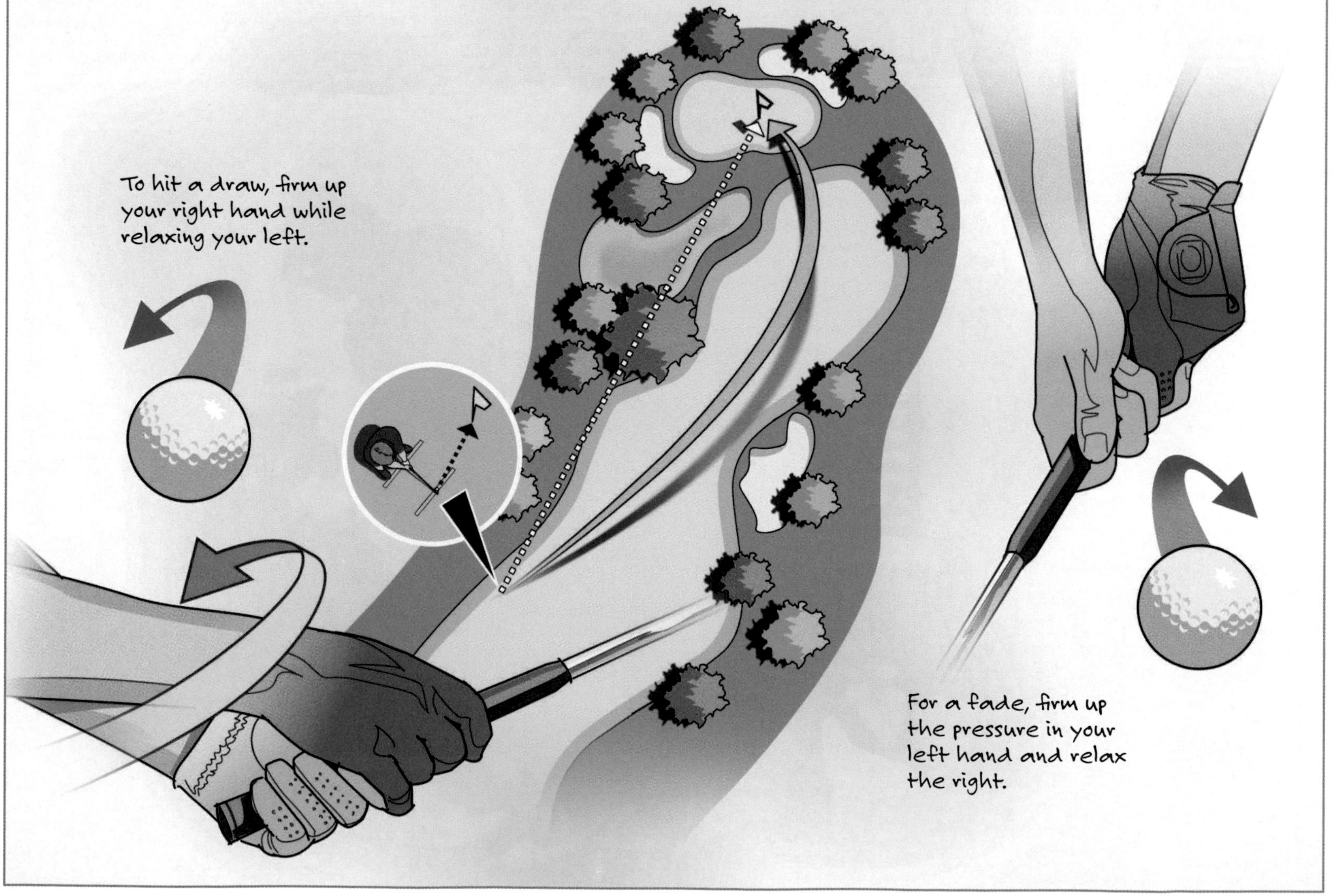

To hit a draw, firm up your right hand while relaxing your left.

For a fade, firm up the pressure in your left hand and relax the right.

The Secret To Hitting Off a Sidehill

When the ball's above your feet, use your hand to find the target

THE PROBLEM
You're not sure how to aim your club when the ball is above your feet.

THE SOLUTION
When you address a ball that's sitting above your feet, the leading edge of your club may appear to be facing your target, but that doesn't mean the clubface is looking there as well. Luckily there's an easy way to gauge the true direction in which you're aiming from an uneven lie.
Dr. Gary Wiren

HOW TO LINE UP ON TARGET FROM A SIDEHILL LIE

STEP 1
Hold the club you're going to use in your left hand, and then match the loft of the clubhead with your right hand.

STEP 2
Cock your right elbow so that your right forearm is perfectly horizontal, then hinge your right hand up until it matches the angle of the hill.

STEP 3
Place the clubshaft between the ring and middle finger of your right hand so that the shaft forms a right angle with your palm. The butt end of the club will point to exactly where your clubface is actually facing—in this case, left of your target.

STEP 4
With the shaft still between your fingers, turn your body until your club points at your target. Your body will face right of the target, but the clubface will point at the target. Sole your club and swing along your toe line.

Make a Back-Handed Escape

Here's what to do when an obstacle interferes with your stance

Choose one of your wedges, since these have the largest faces. Because you won't be looking at the ball during contact, you'll benefit from the broader hitting area.

STEP 1: Turn your back to the target, stand about a half-foot to the right of the ball and grip your wedge in the middle of the handle. Flip your club around so that the face points at your target with the club resting on its toe.

STEP 2: Cock your club up by bending your right elbow (keep your upper arm still). Add just a touch of wrist hinge.

STEP 3: Straighten your arm and slap your clubhead into the back of the ball.

This is a trick shot that's actually very easy to pull off with a little practice. Make sure you accelerate all the way to the ball so the club doesn't flip past your hands and hit the ball thin.
—**Tom Stickney**

How to Attack Doglegs on Windy Days

Play to your strengths to find the fairway

WIND DIRECTION

THE SITUATION

You're on the tee of a 400-yard par 4 that doglegs to the left, and the pin is cut on the far left side of the green. There's tree trouble to the left of the fairway, water up the right side, and a stiff wind blowing from left to right.

THE TOP 100 SAY

45%: *Play your fade and ride the wind*

22%: *Fight the wind and play a draw*

19%: *Hit into the wind and let it blow your ball back*

14%: *Other (long-iron, hybrids, low shots)*

BEST SPOT

IF YOU CAN WORK THE BALL...

PLAY A HOLD-UP DRAW
SETUP: Middle of tee box
AIM: Center of fairway
SWING: Play your everyday draw with a 3-wood (it's easier to shape than a driver). The left-to-right wind and right-to-left shot shape should even out, putting you in the middle.
PRO: Takes water out of play.
CON: Overcook it and you'll be in the trees; undercook it and you're in the drink.

"Always err on the opposite side of a dogleg. You can still make par even if you hit into the water off the tee. If you hit into trees, you still need to waste a shot to get out of them."
—Mike Adams

IF YOU FEAR SHAPING SHOTS...

PLAY INTO THE WIND
SETUP: Toward right tee marker
AIM: Left side of fairway
SWING: Don't make any setup or swing adjustments. Make your regular swing with either your driver or 3-wood and hit toward the left edge of the fairway. The wind should blow the ball back to the center.
PRO: No need to make any setup or swing adjustments.
CON: Slight loss of distance.

"Most of a hole's yardage occurs before the dogleg—hit only what you need to get past the bend and in the fairway, even if it's an iron."
—Dr. T.J. Tomasi

IF YOU'RE A FADER...

RIDE THE WIND
SETUP: Toward right tee marker
AIM: Up the left side
SWING: Hit your driver and start the ball up the edge of the treeline. The combined effects of the left-to-right wind and left-to-right spin should put you in the right side of the fairway.
PRO: Takes the trees out of play
CON: None, unless you really slice it.

"With the pin cut left, position A is the right side of the fairway because it gives you the clearest view of your target. Distance is never as important as hitting to the correct side. If you don't have to hit driver, then don't."
—Jim Murphy

INSTRUCTION

How to Blast from an Upslope

Lean into the hill to make sure you don't catch it fat or come up short

THE SITUATION

You have a good lie but you're on an uphill slope, with your right foot noticeably below your left when you take your address.

THE COMMON ADVICE

Tilt your spine to the right to set your shoulders even with the slope, so you can swing up the hill and catch the ball cleanly

WHY IT DOESN'T ALWAYS WORK

Tilting your spine and setting your shoulders even with the slope tends to cause you to hang back on the shot. The common result is that the ball launches too high and lands short of your target (and you tumble back down the hill). You could use a longer club, but then you'd run the risk of jamming the ball into the slope in front of you.

THE BETTER PLAY

Buck convention on an uphill lie and actually lean into the slope a little as you execute this shot. At address, try setting your weight over your front foot and your shoulders parallel to the horizon—not the slope—as you would on any normal shot from a level lie. As you swing into the ball, get your weight moving left and try to extend your arms down the line and "chase" the ball up the slope. **Feel like you're leaning into the hill at impact, not falling or hanging back.** Not only will you catch the ball cleaner, you'll have a better chance to carry the ball all the way to the target. This technique is especially useful if you're playing into the wind (where the ball tends to balloon up into the air anyway), or if you like to keep the ball lower for extra control.
—Tom Stickney

NO! Shoulders parallel to the slope can cause you to come up short.

YES! Set your shoulders even with each other.

Lean into an upslope to get the most yards out of the club in your hands.

INSTRUCTION

Beat a Downslope

Match your body—and swing—to the slope to stick shots from downhill lies

THE SITUATION

It seems like anytime you're faced with a downhill lie in the fairway, you tend to either make thin, slicing contact or chop down behind the ball, hitting it fat. Your setup is faulty and it's preventing you from properly executing these challenging shots.

THE FIX

The good news is that mastering downhill lies is actually pretty simple. All you have to do is make three basic changes to your technique and you'll quickly lose your fear of these shots for good. Here's what I want you to do:

STEP 1: Lay your club across your shoulders and tilt your spine until the shaft matches the angle of the slope. This easy trick will help you get your shoulders and swing on the same plane as the hill you're standing on—a must.
STEP 2: Play the ball in the middle of your stance to promote ball-first contact, and shift 75 percent of your weight to your front foot. It's important not to hang back on these shots, so you need to feel like your body is ready to move in the direction of the slope.
STEP 3: As you swing through impact, extend your arms fully so the clubhead travels along the slope. By tracing the slope with the clubhead like this, you'll ensure solid contact and a solid result.
—Tom Stickney

Extend your arms for ball-first contact on all downhill lies.

Escape Rough With Your Worst Swing

Fix your slice for straighter drives, but keep it in your pocket to save par from nasty lies

THE SITUATION

On the tee, you hoist your driver like you're trying to squish a bug on a 10-foot ceiling. On the way back down, you make a severe cut and leave a sizable divot on the tee box. There's no "around" to your swing—it's all up-and-down. The result: a 165-yard slice that lands in a patch of nasty, thick rough.

THE SILVER LINING

You're now faced with 200+ yards to the green. You need some distance on your second shot so you can play your third shot close to the pin. The good news: with a mid-iron and that ugly, steep, cut swing you made on the tee, you'll be in business.

The steep cut swing associated with slicing limits contact with the grass for extra-long escapes from the rough.

HOW TO SLICE IT FROM THE ROUGH

1
The slice swing starts by taking the club up vertically so that your hands are way above your shoulders.

2
From the top, come down steeply and allow your clubhead to move outside your hands.

3
Swing to the left of the target to complete the over-the-top move and escape the rough with power.

WHY IT WORKS

The major problem with rough is that it gets between your ball and the clubface. You'll always suffer a loss of distance as a result. Plus, the long grass tends to grab the hosel through impact and close the face, making it impossible to control the ball. A steep cut swing solves both of these problems. **With your club approaching the ball on a steeper angle of attack, there's less contact time between the clubface and the grass, so your shots will fly nearly full distance.** And since your clubface is open (a natural by-product of a cut path), the shutdown from the grass will make everything flush at contact.
—Eden Foster

Beat Buried Lies in the Rough

Set the club on its heel for an easy escape

THE SITUATION
You hit your share of wayward drives and approach shots, and your ball often winds up in the rough.

THE SMART PLAY
To get the ball out of thick grass, you need to get the club and your body set up properly so that you can maximize three important factors: 1) the hitting surface of the clubface, 2) the bounce of the sole (so the club doesn't dig into the rough) and 3) the loft on your wedge. The easiest way to accomplish this is to simply set your wedge down on its heel at address. Don't forward press or lay the clubface open, but rather set it up on the heel in a relatively square position. Once you've done that, choke down on the grip and open your stance a bit. This will force you to bend over, placing your wrists in more of a pre-cocked position, which will help you take the club up and down more steeply (go ahead and set the club earlier than usual in your backswing). The open stance will open the clubface, which you need to offset the fact that the club is resting on its heel. These simple adjustments make buried lies in the rough a breeze.
—Mike Adams

PRE-SET FOR SUCCESS
Bend over more and create a larger hinge in your wrists. These elements give you the chopping action you need to escape rough.

HEEL DOWN, FACE OPEN
Maximizes the strike area on the club.

You need to strike down on the ball to ensure solid contact.

Punch It From the Pines

As with most trouble lies, ball-first contact is key

THE SITUATION
You missed the fairway and your ball ended up in a bed of pine needles under a thick canopy of trees. You think a power swing will help, but this results in fat contact and a follow-up shot from an even worse situation.

THE SMART PLAY
Stop trying to swing so hard and instead concentrate on making ball-first contact. Here's how:
1. Set up with the ball back of center and more of your weight on your left side.
2. Make a three-quarter backswing with plenty of wrist hinge. You want the clubshaft pointing toward the sky at the top of your backswing.
3. Swing down to the ball with a quiet lower body and a smooth arm action. Concentrate on delivering the clubhead down onto the ball before you contact the pine straw.
—Mark Hackett

Working on your game won't stop you from never hitting a bad shot again, but it will stop you from hitting the same bad shot twice during play.

SECTION 10

FLAWS AND FIXES

How to make sure you don't make the same mistake twice when bad habits creep into your swing

It doesn't matter who you are, how long you've been playing or how low your handicap is—you're going to hit bad shots in every round. The key to turning poor rounds into good ones (and good ones into great ones) is to not hit the same bad shot more than once. Since bad shots always come in groups, you can save loads of strokes by stopping a negative trend before it builds momentum.

Owning the ability to quick-fix your game on the course is the hallmark of any great player. Granted, you need practice to completely eradicate flaws in your technique, but Band-Aid fixes can and do work, or at the very least can stop the bleeding during your bad rounds.

In this section, the Top 100 Teachers address the 12 most common swing flaws. Their fixes are simple—you can use them during play or as the foundation for a practice session dedicated to completely working out your kinks. That's the way to make sure your fixes stick. A dozen flaws may sound like a lot to you, but these are only the tip of the fault iceberg. Luckily, fixing these takes care of much of the rest. In fact, eliminating just half of these disaster shots will make your next round a nice, low number.

5 THINGS YOU'LL LEARN IN THIS SECTION

- *How to stop short-game errors like hitting your pitch shots thin and your chip shots fat.*
- *How to get a feel for distance and avoid three-putting.*
- *How to self-diagnose your bunker problems.*
- *How to swing on plane more consistently, along with three ways to fix your slice—and one to fix your hook.*
- *How to stop topping your drives and hit for more power off the tee.*

Learn more about fixing the most common swing fault there is at **golf.com/slicing**

YOUR GAME

WHAT MAKES YOUR SHOTS CURVE?

There are nine ways to approach a golf ball, and these result in nine possible ball flights. Here are the path/face combinations that cause them. Look for yours to discover what you should be working on.

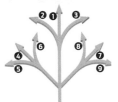

1 Straight: Swing path along target line, clubface square.

2 Hook: Path along line, face closed.

3 Slice: Path along line, face open.

4 Pull: Path out-to-in, face square to path.

5 Pull-hook: Path out-to-in, face closed to path.

6 Pull-slice: Path out-to-in, face open to path.

7 Push: Path in-to-out, face square to path.

8 Push-hook: Path in-to-out, face closed to path.

9 Push-slice: Path in-to-out, face open to path.

TOUR TIP

Stop Swing Errors Before You Start

My foolproof setup routine sets you up for a mistake-free swing

TRY THIS!

I'm a big believer in the notion that a solid setup is a cure-all for most in-swing mistakes and errors, especially when you're hitting driver. A great way to think about your setup is to see the club as an extension of your grip, and your grip as an extension of your left arm—a single lever that you swing back and through the ball. You want as few angles as possible at address, and getting a straight line from the tip of your left shoulder, down the clubshaft and through the clubface is a great way to eliminate any excess kinks in your setup. Perform the following steps the next time you practice to get a feel for this connected address and how it automatically sets you up to hit up on the ball with your driver, as you should.
—PGA Tour player Ernie Els

> "See the club as an extension of your grip, and your grip as an extension of your left arm."
> —Ernie Els

STEP 1
With the ball teed off your left heel, hold the clubhead out in front of you, lining up your left arm, your left-hand grip and the clubface.

STEP 2
With your right hand still off the grip, sole the clubhead behind the ball by dropping your left arm down while bending forward from your hips and flexing your knees. Everything— left arm, hand, shaft and club— should line up.

STEP 3
Set your right hand even with your left. Open your fingers so that your palm points through your left hand and toward the target.

STEP 4
Swing your right hand up and into the grip. Let your right shoulder drop down a little as you do this. This upward move gets you in a good frame of mind for when you swing the club for real. You don't ever want to hit down on the ball with a driver.

DRILL

Stop Three-Putting

This drill helps you find the elusive touch you need in just minutes

Can you feel it? Putt with your eyes closed to master the art of distance control.

THE FLAW

You lack an innate sense of feel for putting distance. While your eyes are great for sending signals to your brain that tell you how long or short a stroke to make for a given distance, there's more to it than trusting your peepers. Mastering the art of distance control is about trusting yourself and your stroke.

THE FIX

Place a ball 10 feet from the hole and put your glove in the cup (to take away sound). Survey the putt. Once you think you have a feel for the distance, turn your head away from your target and close your eyes.

Stroke the putt and continue looking away until you can estimate where your ball ended up. Look up to see how closely your estimate matched the actual distance. Your goal is to create a perfect match.

Make this drill part of your practice routine (varying the distance and break each time), and **you won't have to rely on mechanics to putt the ball a given distance**—your feel will do it for you.

—Pia Nilsson

FACE FIRST

A major key to consistently stroking putts the correct distance is making consistent contact in the center of your putterface. Contact out toward the toe or heel results in far less energy transfer, which also explains why you roll your ball way past the hole on one putt and then roll it way short the next, even with exactly the same stroke.

To improve your contact consistency, wrap two rubber bands around the left and right sides of your putter's sweet spot. Practicing with the bands on your putter instantly tells you when you fail to stroke the ball in the center of your face. You'll feel a "thud" rather than a "click," meaning you missed the center and hit one of the bands. For feel putters, it's either centered contact or bust.

—Lynn Marriott

Hitting the ball on the sweet spot is the key to distance control.

CHECKPOINT

Why Can't I Chip?

Whether you chunk 'em or skull 'em, here are four common chipping errors and four ways to get it close

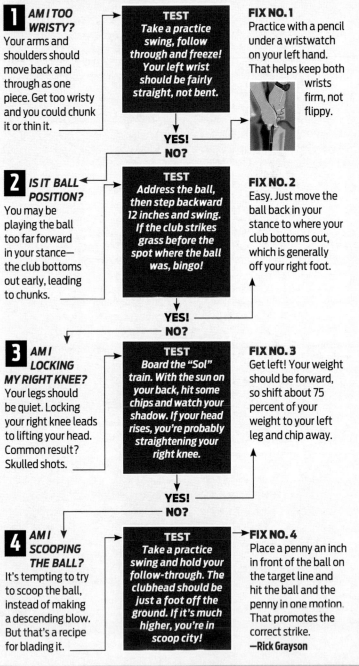

1 AM I TOO WRISTY?
Your arms and shoulders should move back and through as one piece. Get too wristy and you could chunk it or thin it.

TEST
Take a practice swing, follow through and freeze! Your left wrist should be fairly straight, not bent.

FIX NO. 1
Practice with a pencil under a wristwatch on your left hand. That helps keep both wrists firm, not flippy.

YES!
NO?

2 IS IT BALL POSITION?
You may be playing the ball too far forward in your stance— the club bottoms out early, leading to chunks.

TEST
Address the ball, then step backward 12 inches and swing. If the club strikes grass before the spot where the ball was, bingo!

FIX NO. 2
Easy. Just move the ball back in your stance to where your club bottoms out, which is generally off your right foot.

YES!
NO?

3 AM I LOCKING MY RIGHT KNEE?
Your legs should be quiet. Locking your right knee leads to lifting your head. Common result? Skulled shots.

TEST
Board the "Sol" train. With the sun on your back, hit some chips and watch your shadow. If your head rises, you're probably straightening your right knee.

FIX NO. 3
Get left! Your weight should be forward, so shift about 75 percent of your weight to your left leg and chip away.

YES!
NO?

4 AM I SCOOPING THE BALL?
It's tempting to try to scoop the ball, instead of making a descending blow. But that's a recipe for blading it.

TEST
Take a practice swing and hold your follow-through. The clubhead should be just a foot off the ground. If it's much higher, you're in scoop city!

FIX NO. 4
Place a penny an inch in front of the ball on the target line and hit the ball and the penny in one motion. That promotes the correct strike.

—Rick Grayson

Stop Pulling Your Shots

Maintain your forward bend to hit straighter shots

THE FLAW

You're losing your "power angle." Your power angle is the one formed between your upper and lower body at the top of your backswing with your spine—the top half of the angle—tilted 5 to 15 degrees away from your target. The only way to create your power angle is to take your club to the top while maintaining the forward bend in your hips from address.

THE FIX

Get into a powerful setup by bending at your hips so that your bottom rib feels like it's being pulled in closer to your belt buckle. **Maintain the distance from your bottom rib to your belt line as you turn and swing to the top.** You've done it right if your spine angles away from the target with your head behind the ball and your weight is set in your left hip. Make your first move down a turn of your left hip back toward the target. Feel as though your lower body is separating from your upper body and leading your downswing. A chain reaction should now occur from the ground up—lower body, torso, arms and then club whip through impact at max speed.

WHY IT WORKS

Keeping your forward bend intact not only creates solid posture at the top, it also allows you to start your downswing correctly by turning your hips without prematurely firing your upper body. Conversely, swinging hard from the top with your shoulders destroys your power angle. You've done it wrong if your head is even or ahead of the ball and your hips are as open as your shoulders. Expect pulls, tops and slices from this position.
—Dave Phillips

...and maintain it to explode through impact.

Create your power angle on your backswing...

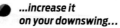

...increase it on your downswing...

`DRILL`

Stop Swinging Off Plane

Take this quick test to get your swing back on track

THE FLAW

Your inconsistent ballstriking is the result of never getting your club on the correct plane. For most golfers, this has been a difficult thing to gauge—until now.

THE FIX

Grip a mid-iron in just your left hand and, with your right hand, hold a second mid-iron by its hosel. Take your normal address and position the grip of the club in your right hand about six inches behind the clubhead of the one in your left [*photo, far right*]. Swing both clubs slowly to the top, doing your best to keep them exactly six inches apart all the way. If both of the shafts feel light in your hands and are still parallel (use a mirror or ask a friend to watch you), you found the correct plane [*photo, right*]. Ingrain that feel.

WHY IT WORKS

If you make the common mistake of swinging too much around your back (below the correct plane) rather than up around your shoulders, gravity will cause one or both clubs to feel heavy as they hang behind your back.
—**Brad Redding**

You're on plane if both clubs are parallel and feel light in your hands.

This drill will get you on plane in seconds.

`CHECKPOINT`

Why Can't I Hit a Fairway?

Here are three common causes of wild tee shots—and three ways to split the fairway

1 AM I SWINGING TOO HARD?
Don't swing so you almost fly out of your FootJoys. That throws you off-balance and your swing out of whack.

TEST
Swing! Then hold your finish for five seconds. If you need to take a step, you're off-balance.

NO? YES!

FIX NO. 1
Try this drill: Set up, then point your left foot at the target. This promotes a shorter, more controlled backswing, which leads to better balance.

2 AM I SLIDING MY HIPS?
With longer clubs, it can be tempting to slide your hips in your downswing, instead of rotating them. That throws the clubhead off its path.

TEST
Make a backswing and stop at the top. If you feel most of your weight on the right side of your right foot, you're sliding your hips.

NO? YES!

FIX NO. 2
Hit the range and bust some drives while keeping your feet together. This makes sliding impossible and forces you to rotate through impact.

3 IS THE SHAFT TOO LONG?
Probably. More than half of all everyday players use a shaft that's too long for them.

TEST
A push slice is the common result of a too-long driver. The longer shaft is harder to square at impact.

FIX NO. 3
Get fitted. In the meantime, choke down about a half-inch or so.
—**Rick Grayson**

Stop Topping Your Tee Shots

Use these three fixes to turn your dribblers into drives

THE FLAW

There's more than one way to top a drive. The big three are:

1. DROPKICK

You swing on a steep, inside-out plane and the sole of the club bounces off the ground well behind the ball.

2. NEAR WHIFF

You lift up at impact, and the sole of your driver contacts the top of the ball in a "near-miss" attempt. The ball barely topples forward off the tee.

3. THIN SKIM

You swing on a steep, outside-in plane, resulting in a glancing blow off the top of the ball that sends it scurrying along the ground.

FIX 1: DROPKICK
Your swing is steep and too inside-out

An inside-out swing plane in and of itself can be a good thing. It promotes a draw, which will help you add distance. It's when you overdo it that you create the dropkick. On your downswing, **strive to contact the inside lower quadrant of the ball,** but rotate your hands so that the club exits the hitting area on a line that parallels your target line. Try to "throw" the clubhead at your target.

Swing your club down the target line after impact.

WRONG!

Don't swing too far from the inside.

FIX 2: NEAR WHIFF
You raise up at impact

To ensure that you stay down and through the ball, keep your knees flexed but relaxed throughout your swing, and keep your right heel on the ground for as long as possible. Also, **resist the urge to "slap" at the ball,** and instead focus on swinging through it, with your right shoulder turning under your chin through the hitting area. You don't need to help the ball into the air—the club will do that for you.

FIX 3: THIN SKIM
Your swing is steep and too outside-in

To stop your right shoulder from pulling your clubhead across the line, address the ball with your right shoulder lower than your left, and **bend your right elbow so that it sits closer to your torso than your left.** These fixes will help you make the correct turn and will keep your shoulder movement in check, helping your club to remain on plane.
—**Laird Small**

Maintain your knee flex to keep from lifting up.

WRONG!

Don't raise up or straighten your right knee.

Set your right shoulder low to help keep your club on plane.

WRONG!

Don't pull your shoulders across the ball.

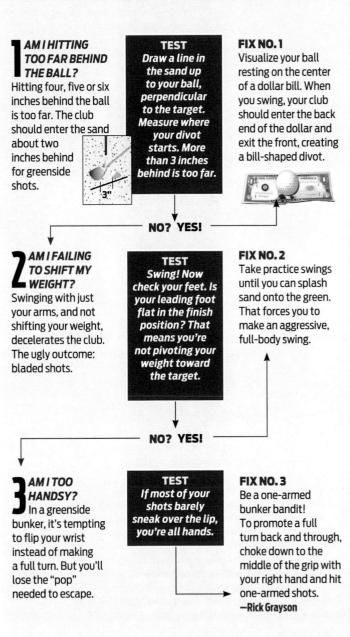

Why Can't I Escape the Sand?

Here are three common causes for bunker blues—and three easy ways to make a great escape

1 **AM I HITTING TOO FAR BEHIND THE BALL?**
Hitting four, five or six inches behind the ball is too far. The club should enter the sand about two inches behind for greenside shots.

TEST
Draw a line in the sand up to your ball, perpendicular to the target. Measure where your divot starts. More than 3 inches behind is too far.

3"

FIX NO. 1
Visualize your ball resting on the center of a dollar bill. When you swing, your club should enter the back end of the dollar and exit the front, creating a bill-shaped divot.

NO? YES!

2 **AM I FAILING TO SHIFT MY WEIGHT?**
Swinging with just your arms, and not shifting your weight, decelerates the club. The ugly outcome: bladed shots.

TEST
Swing! Now check your feet. Is your leading foot flat in the finish position? That means you're not pivoting your weight toward the target.

FIX NO. 2
Take practice swings until you can splash sand onto the green. That forces you to make an aggressive, full-body swing.

NO? YES!

3 **AM I TOO HANDSY?**
In a greenside bunker, it's tempting to flip your wrist instead of making a full turn. But you'll lose the "pop" needed to escape.

TEST
If most of your shots barely sneak over the lip, you're all hands.

FIX NO. 3
Be a one-armed bunker bandit! To promote a full turn back and through, choke down to the middle of the grip with your right hand and hit one-armed shots.
—**Rick Grayson**

Stop Slicing

Try these three drills to eliminate your banana ball for good

1. HOOD THE CLUBFACE

STEP 1: Assume your normal setup with a mid-iron and swing your hands back to hip height and stop.

STEP 2: Look at your hands. If you can clearly see the logo on your glove, you've fanned the face open [*photos, below left*]. Your right hand is under the grip and in position to hit a slice.

STEP 3: Go back to address and take the club away again to the same position and stop, but this time try to get the back of your right hand more on top of the grip [*photos, below right*].

STEP 4: Look at your hands. If the logo on your glove is hidden, you've made the right move with your right hand and hooded the clubface a bit (the strike area is facing the ground, not the sky). This is the position you want in order to promote right-to-left spin and put an end to your slice.

—**Michael Breed**

NO!
Right hand under the grip means you've fanned the face open.

YES!
Right hand on top of the grip means you've slightly hooded the face—an easy slice fix.

2. DRAG THE RIGHT PATH

Take your setup and drop a ball a solid foot and a half to the right of your right foot and in line with your right toe [*left photo*]. Sole your clubhead behind the ball and get into your swing posture. Notice how this ball position forces you to drop your right shoulder lower than your left. That's good, because that's the tilt you need to deliver the clubhead from the inside. Now, drag the ball forward along the ground [*middle photo*] and try to shoot it out to the left of your left foot after you reach the hitting zone [*right photo*]. If you're prone to leaving the clubface open, your clubhead may swing left but the ball will shoot out to the right. When you can get your clubhead as well as the ball left of your left foot, you'll start to ingrain the feeling of releasing the club fully and imparting right-to-left spin on the ball.

—**Mark Steinbauer**

If the ball shoots out to the right of your left foot, you left the face open.

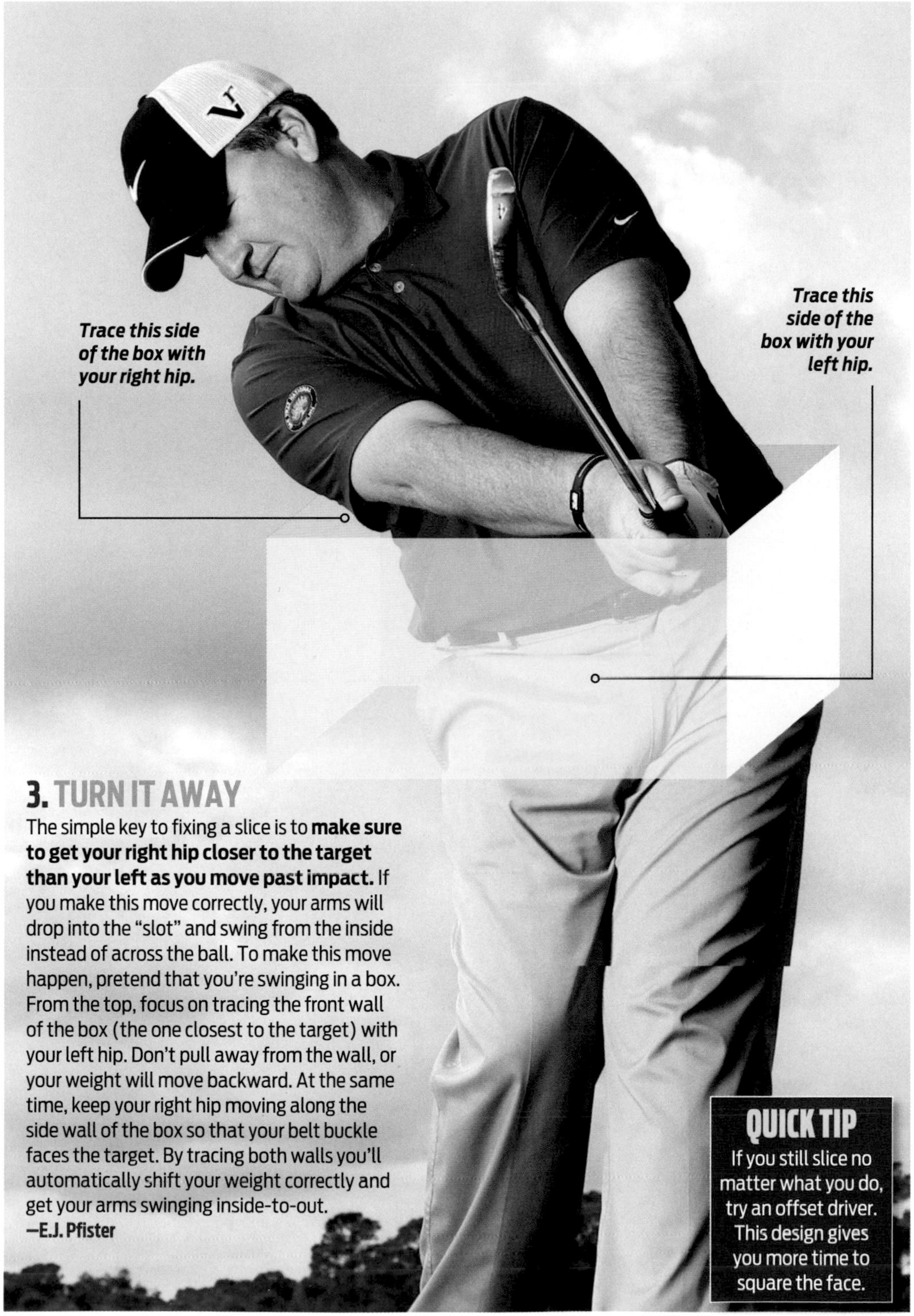

Trace this side of the box with your right hip.

Trace this side of the box with your left hip.

3. TURN IT AWAY

The simple key to fixing a slice is to **make sure to get your right hip closer to the target than your left as you move past impact.** If you make this move correctly, your arms will drop into the "slot" and swing from the inside instead of across the ball. To make this move happen, pretend that you're swinging in a box. From the top, focus on tracing the front wall of the box (the one closest to the target) with your left hip. Don't pull away from the wall, or your weight will move backward. At the same time, keep your right hip moving along the side wall of the box so that your belt buckle faces the target. By tracing both walls you'll automatically shift your weight correctly and get your arms swinging inside-to-out.
—E.J. Pfister

QUICK TIP
If you still slice no matter what you do, try an offset driver. This design gives you more time to square the face.

Stop Chunking Your Wedges
My easy drill gives you the contact to knock it close from short range

Even though you're longer than most of your playing partners, you're not going to reach every par 5 in two. But you can still make more birdies than pars if you have a strong, reliable wedge game. Solid contact is key: The more often you connect with the sweet spot on the clubface, the more dialed in your distances will be. Here's a drill from our Short Game Schools that will have you flushing your wedges every time.

Lay a two-by-four-inch board on the ground so that its long side is facing you. Place a ball about one inch from the board and swing. If the clubhead is coming in too steeply and hitting the top or side of the board, keep practicing until you can make crisp contact without touching the wood before or after impact. When you can do this consistently enough, you'll be making the proper inside-square-inside swing necessary to hit the sweet spot on the wedge.
—Dave Pelz

Avoid hitting the two-by-four to groove a perfect wedge swing.

How to Check If Your Stroke is Smooth

Knowing the answer can help you cure your yips for good

THE FLAW

You have a basic form of the yips—forcing the putterhead to speed up suddenly during your stroke. This makes it nearly impossible to control distance. You need to smooth out your stroke ASAP.

THE FIX

Grip your putter using only your thumbs and forefingers as shown. Place your left hand at the top of the handle and your right hand at the very bottom of the grip. Set up in your normal stance and make your stroke. If you have any accelerating yip in your stroke, the grip end of the shaft will tilt backward and the putterhead will flip past your hands [*left photo*]. The only way to keep the putter from "wobbling" is to maintain constant speed. This is a great drill because the finger hold removes your control of the putter and exposes even the slightest trace of the yips.

—**Tour putting coach Marius Filmalter**

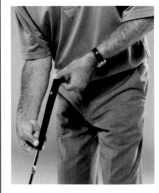

This thumb and forefinger grip will tell you if you yip or not.

NO!
Putterhead passing the hands indicates yips.

YES!
Constant speed makes you smooth.

DRILL

Never Hit It Fat Again

Get your downswing sequence right for better ballstriking

TRY THIS!
The best way to stop fat shots is to correct your sequence. In a good swing, the hips reach the ball first, then the hands, and then the clubhead. Unfortunately, many amateur players do the exact opposite. Follow this simple drill.

START: Set up three balls on an arc, one at impact, another two feet ahead, and a third one two feet ahead of the second ball. Set the arc so that the third ball is even with your left toes.
CHECK 1: Make a slow-motion swing. Try to get your hips to arrive at the ball first, with your hands and clubhead lagging behind [*photo, top right*].
CHECK 2: Your hands shouldn't reach the first ball until your hips (use your belt buckle as a guide) point toward the second ball [*middle*]. If your hands arrive early you won't get the contact you're searching for.
CHECK 3: When your hips start pointing at the third ball, your clubhead should finally reach impact [*bottom*]. This sequence is the telltale trait of solid ballstriking.
—Brian Manzella

HIPS FIRST
Near impact, the hips are still ahead of the hands and club.

HANDS SECOND
Your hands reach impact only after your hips clear.

CLUBHEAD LAST
The clubhead needs to lag behind your hips and hands.

DRILL

Fix Off-Center Contact

Practice with a bucket between your ankles to hit better irons

THE DRILL
To improve your iron contact you need to stop moving around during your swing. The good news is, it's not as difficult as you think. Practice this simple drill and your ballstriking should improve quickly:

STEP 1: Take an empty ball bucket and place it between your feet in your normal address position.
STEP 2: Place a ball in the middle of your stance—this will promote ball-first contact, which is key.
STEP 3: Make some practice swings to get the feel of maintaining contact with both the ground and the bucket throughout your full motion.
STEP 4: Hit some shots for real. If you maintain contact with both the bucket and the ground, you should feel more balanced and make much crisper contact.
—Mark Hackett

Through impact you want to feel connected to the ground and the bucket.

You don't need a complete swing overhaul to break your scoring barrier, just small improvements in 6 key areas of your game.

HOW TO BREAK 80

Your six-week plan to a lifetime of low scores

Your plan to finally break 80 requires you to do a number of things, the first of which is to accept that striking the ball like Ben Hogan and knocking down every flag is probably not going to happen. This is a common misconception among amateur golfers—that you need to be a shotmaking machine to shoot in the 70s. Not only is this not true, it's also an unrealistic goal for the vast majority of recreational players. Instead, you need to take an honest look at six parts of your game, each of which can gain or cost you strokes, and make a concerted effort to improve each.

The six critical areas are: 1) your scoring shots, 2) driving accuracy, 3) short game, 4) putting, 5) strategy, and 6) bunker play. Before you start working, however, realize that the final 10 or so strokes you need to save to break 80 aren't going to magically drop off by themselves. You're going to have to dedicate at least three hours a week to the process, and during those hours you're going to have to work in an organized fashion. But if you follow the plan outlined on these pages by Top 100 Teacher Brady Riggs (and the videos and worksheets available at golf.com/break80), we guarantee that your overall game—and your scores—will improve. Think of your game as the pieces of a puzzle. You need to get each one right to put them all together. Improving in the key areas just enough to cut one or two strokes per skill set is all you need to do.

5 THINGS YOU'LL LEARN IN THIS SECTION

- *Dial-in your scoring clubs to take advantage of birdie opportunities from short range.*
- *Develop a trustworthy go-to drive to stop wasting strokes from the tee box.*
- *Groove a can't-miss chip and pitch swing so you'll never score worse than par when you miss greens.*
- *Take the guesswork out of your putting stroke, bunker swing and shot planning to put your game on autopilot.*
- *Drills to improve each area week by week.*

Tools, worksheets and videos for your 6-week improvement plan at **golf.com/break80**

GO OUT AND LEARN!

Brady Riggs has breaking your main scoring barrier covered on the following pages, but the fact remains that too many golfers don't take lessons, and there's a reason for that: lame excuses. Consider our rebuttal to common cop-outs:

NOT ENOUGH CASH
Play one less round a month, and apply that money toward a lesson with a qualified PGA teaching pro. You can make up for the missed on-course experience by playing an imaginary round on the range.

I DON'T HAVE TIME
See above, or simply make time. Get up an hour earlier on your day off. This works on weekdays, too.

I JUST NEED A TUNE-UP
Fine. Your instructor can build a plan, or even a single lesson, to match your goals.

TOO EMBARRASSED
That's like saying your teeth are too rotten to go see a dentist.

HOME LIFE TOO BUSY
C'mon! Make your lesson a family event. You should be introducing your kids to the game anyway.

WEEK 1

DIAL IN YOUR SHORT CLUBS

Fill in your distance gaps at the bottom of your set to knock short shots closer

While it's always a good idea to get your clubs fitted, **the most important thing for scoring is to get your wedges and short irons dialed in.** First you need to be sure your distance gaps are correct. In many modern iron sets the lofts are jacked very strong to encourage more distance. Unfortunately, this can wreak havoc on your distance gaps and short-game scoring shots.

Basically, you want 4-degree gaps between each of your scoring clubs; I recommend having the lofts checked. Then, make sure you have the right collection of wedges to complement your short irons.

For example, if you have a 37-degree 8-iron and a 41-degree 9-iron (common in game-improvement iron sets), you need to make sure you have 50-, 54-, and 58- or 60-degree wedges to round out your arsenal. If you don't, you should invest in new ones, or have your existing wedges bent (be aware that if you strengthen your wedge lofts, you'll take away bounce, which isn't always a good thing).

THE STAT YOU NEED TO BEAT: *SCORING-SHOT CONTROL*

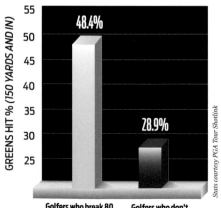

GREENS HIT % (150 YARDS AND IN)

48.4% — Golfers who break 80
28.9% — Golfers who don't

Stats courtesy PGA Tour Shotlink

---

*Good dispersion pattern
Bad dispersion pattern*

WEEK 1 DRILL: WEDGE ASSESSMENT

Get close and personal with scoring club distance

Once you have your wedges and scoring irons set up properly, you need to get out to the practice range and dial in your distances. To do so, **take your 8-iron through LW and hit 10 practice balls with each** (if possible, the balls you normally play, not range balls). Hit these shots from a good flat spot on the range. It's important to do this on a quiet day with little wind. It's also important to know your yardages as accurately as possible, so I recommend using a rangefinder.

Mark the average yardage you hit with each club. You should notice a 10- to 15-yard gap between the distance you hit successive clubs (for example: 60-yard LW, 75-yard SW, 90-yard GW, etc.). It may not be exact, but you should be close to this gap structure.

Now, the real test: Hit 10 solid shots with each club, paying close attention to your landing spot. Your goal here is to see how consistently you can hit each club based on the yardage you charted in Step 1. At the end of six weeks you should be able to consistently land about 70 percent of your shots with each of these clubs in a 10-yard radius. The other thing to figure out during this session is which scoring club is your favorite, or the most reliable. If you're going to cut those last few strokes and break 80, you'll need to have a go-to layup distance. **For more on this exercise, see my video at golf.com/break80.**

Use a rangefinder to map your scoring distances.

WEEK 2

DEVELOP A GO-TO DRIVE

Eliminate one side of the fairway to get more of your tee shots in play

Hitting fairways is a key to saving strokes, especially if you're currently shooting in the high 80s or low 90s. Every missed fairway is a chance to lose strokes, and if you want to reach your scoring goal, you're going to have to start putting the ball in play consistently. **I tell my students that they need to hit at least seven fairways per round if they hope to break 80,** so this should be your goal. To do so, you'll need to shore up your setup position and then develop a go-to shot shape [*see below*]. Forget about trying to bomb it every time—if you want to shoot a score, you have to think strategy, not ego.

BUILDING AN "ANTI-SHOT"

Eliminating one side of the fairway means building a swing that you know can only produce one of two "anti-shots": An anti-slice shape to avoid trouble on the right, or an anti-hook shape to avoid trouble on the left. This starts by changing your setup to naturally produce the shape you're looking for [*photos, below*]. The proper setup will help you "feel" the shot shape before you swing. For actual swing tips, see my video lesson at **golf.com/break80.**

THE STAT YOU NEED TO BEAT:
SCORING-SHOT CONTROL

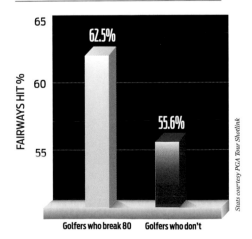

FAIRWAYS HIT %

- 62.5% — Golfers who break 80
- 55.6% — Golfers who don't

Stats courtesy PGA Tour Shotlink

Your goal is to curve the ball away from trouble and toward the center of the fairway.

If your go-to shot is anti-right, consider a drive that crosses over to the left side of the fairway a miss.

Work the ball toward the middle of the fairway without crossing over the centerline.

WEEK 2 DRILL: DON'T CROSS YOUR LINE

How to eliminate the "bad" side of the fairway

Once you've determined what shot shape you're going to use as your go-to drive, you need to **test yourself and improve your ability to play it under pressure.** To do so, find a practice fairway or area of the range with plenty of flat ground in front of you. Picture a centerline to your target and use that as your guide. If you're going to use an anti-right shot (draw) as your go-to drive, for example, your goal should be to start every drive right of the centerline and draw it back toward the line without crossing over it. If you want to fade the ball (anti-left), do the opposite. Take 10 balls and test yourself with the intention of getting at least 70 percent of the shots in the target area. If you can learn to do this, you'll be on your way to breaking 80.

ANTI-LEFT SETUP (FADE)

- Level shoulders
- Ball forward in stance
- Open stance

Key ingredient:
Right forearm above left.

ANTI-RIGHT SETUP (DRAW)

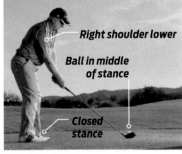

- Right shoulder lower
- Ball in middle of stance
- Closed stance

Key ingredient:
Right forearm below left.

WEEK 2 ACTION PLAN
(3 HOURS)

GOAL: 70% DRIVER ACCURACY

1. Find Your Go-To Drive
(60 mins.)
Decide if your "get it in play" drive will be a draw or fade. Shore up your setup for the shot you choose and spend some time working on hitting that shot on a consistent basis.

2. Cross-the-Line Drill
(60 mins.)
Perform the Week 2 drill. If at first you don't succeed, stick with it. Your goal at the end of six weeks is to hit 7 out of 10 drives in the correct area of the fairway.

3. Scoring Club Distance Practice *(60 mins.)*
Perform the wedge drill on the opposite page. At this point in the six-week plan you should be able to get at least 4 out of 10 balls into a 10-yard radius with each of your scoring clubs.

> "Every missed fairway is a chance to lose strokes."
> —Brady Riggs

CHIP AND PITCH IT CLOSER

It's a matter of judging carry versus roll and fine-tuning your technique

The key to becoming good around the greens is to take some of the variables out of the equation. I'm sure some of you like to use your LW for every short shot, carrying the ball as close to the pin as possible, while others like to use a pitching wedge and bump and run the ball. Instead of using this strategy, **I want you to start playing a neutral shot with the same swing every time, only changing the club you use to suit the situation.**

By simplifying your technique and not trying to play any extreme-spin shots, you'll be better able to predict the flight and roll of your ball. Also, by adopting a more standardized method, you'll be much more likely to make solid contact, which in turn will give you more confidence around the green. Instead of feeling like you're guessing every time you walk up to one of these short shots, you'll know that you have a solid approach and a good plan. It won't be long before you're knocking it tight consistently and saving strokes.

Creating consistent carry and roll ratios with each club is the easy way to land short shots close.

THE STAT YOU NEED TO BEAT:
SCRAMBLING ABILITY

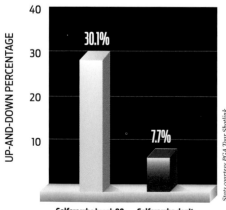

UP-AND-DOWN PERCENTAGE

40

30 — 30.1%

20

10 — 7.7%

Golfers who break 80   Golfers who don't

Stats courtesy PGA Tour Shotlink

STEP 1: GET THE TECHNIQUE

Keep it simple and consistent for good results

To make consistently solid contact on pitch and chip shots, position the ball in the middle of your stance with your feet together and your hands slightly ahead. Make sure you have your right wrist angled away from the target. In the backswing, allow your right wrist to hinge comfortably and let your hands lead the clubhead through impact. Turn your torso to the left to drive your swing and finish with your right arm and the clubshaft in line. Be sure to use this same technique every time.

STEP 2: DRILL

One swing, six clubs, six shots

To hone the proper technique, find a practice green with flags of varying distances and take all of your wedges and scoring irons (8- and 9-iron). You should hit 10 balls to each target with the goal of getting every shot within 5 feet of the pin. Remember to use the same basic swing every time but with a variety of clubs. To do this drill successfully, you'll have to pick your landing spots carefully and be conscious of how much roll you get from each of your short-game clubs.

5%

The make percentage for most golfers drops dramatically once they get outside 5 feet, meaning that it's critical to stop the ball within this distance.

STEP 3: CARRY V. ROLL

Know your distances

Becoming proficient around the greens depends largely on knowing how much carry and roll your shots produce with every club. To figure this out, experiment on a practice green with all of your short-game clubs. Pick a basic landing spot and see how much roll you get with each club after landing the ball in your spot. Learn to produce this same combination of carry vs. roll every time and you'll find it much easier to get the ball close to the pin consistently.
For more on this technique, see my video at golf.com/break80.

Figuring out how much carry and roll you get from each club is key.

CARRY DISTANCE   ROLL DISTANCE

WEEK 3 ACTION PLAN
(3 HOURS)

GOAL: EVERY CHIP TO 5 FEET

1. Pitch & Chip Practice
(60 mins.)
Make sure your setup is sound and that your stroke can produce solid, ball-first contact every time [*photos, below left*]. Practice with your pitch, sand and lob wedges until you feel confident.

2. Carry & Roll Practice
(60 mins.)
Go to a practice green with different-length pins, or set up some targets yourself that correspond with the distances you pitch each of your wedges using the same swing and the carry-to-roll ratio you built in Step 2. Your goal is to land five balls out of 10 within 5 feet of the pin or target with each wedge. (By the end of six weeks you should be able to get 70 percent of the balls within one-putt territory with each club.)

3. Cross-the-Line Drill
(30 mins.)
Work on the exercise on page 207).

4. Scoring Club Distance Practice *(30 mins.)*
Perform the wedge drill from page 206. At this point in the 6-week plan, you should be able to get at least five out of 10 balls in the 10-yard radius with each of your scoring clubs.

DOWNLOAD THE WEEK 3 WORKSHEET
golf.com/break80

Your assigment for Week 4: Roll 10 balls, each slightly longer than the previous, and all within a 10-foot radius.

WEEK 4
IMPROVE YOUR PUTTING

Shave strokes by developing better control and holing the short ones

To break 80, you have to do two things when it comes to putting: **make three-putts extremely infrequent, and make a very high percentage from inside 5 feet.** First things first: make sure your stroke and putter match each other. If you like to take the putter straight back and through, consider a face-balanced model. If you prefer to putt with a bit of an arc in your stroke, you'll be better off using a toe-weighted putter. By matching your stroke to the proper putter design, you'll make more short putts, since these are the ones most dependent on line.

SPEED IS KEY

Proper speed is critical for eliminating three-putts, because it's the key to good lag putting. To improve your distance control, pick a spot about 10 feet away on the practice green and try to roll a ball directly onto the spot. Once the ball comes to rest, try to roll another ball just past the first, but as close to it as you can. Don't come up short—if you do, you have to start over. Your goal is to get 10 balls into a 10-foot area, each one just a bit farther away than the previous ball. **For more on this drill, see my video at golf.com/break80.**

THE STAT YOU NEED TO BEAT:
SHORT PUTT SUCCESS

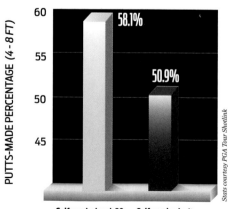

Stats courtesy PGA Tour Shotlink

Chart: PUTTS-MADE PERCENTAGE (4 - 8 FT)
- Golfers who break 80: 58.1%
- Golfers who don't: 50.9%

WEEK 4 DRILL: **PLAY A GAME**

Competition is key to improving performance

If you really want to become a better putter, you need some competition that mimics on-course pressure. My favorite is a one-on-one game called "Sinks." **Find a friend and play nine holes on the putting green, with each hole a par 2.** One-putts count for a point, two-putts are zero, and three-putts are negative one. Make winning this game important by letting the loser buy lunch and soon enough your lag putting, and short putting, will get a lot sharper—especially if you lose the first game or two.

KILL THOSE 5-FOOTERS!

NEWS FLASH: You have to make the knee-knockers if you're going to break 80, and this is where you're really going to have to do a bit of grinding. To begin, find a relatively flat putt and take 10 balls. From this length, I want you to make at least 8 out of 10, if not 9. Start putting with the goal of making 10 in a row. When you miss, start over. I assure you, the prospect of starting over will eventually sharpen your focus and make you a better short putter.

DEVISE A GAME PLAN

Create a safe and smart strategy for every hole on your home course

If you think the pros go out and shoot the scores they do without a specific plan for each hole, you're wrong. They play several practice rounds before a tournament, often on courses that they've played many times during their career. Although you might not have this luxury, you do need to have a strategy for every hole if you want to optimize your scoring. **Your basic approach, however, should be to avoid double-bogeys at all costs.** If you do, you can make seven bogeys and still break 80.

To devise your strategy, get a yardage book (or draw one if you have to) from your home course and go through every hole, paying extra attention to the par-3s and par-5s. Decide if and when you need to hit driver off the tee, and where you should try to land your tee shots. Mark areas you need to avoid both off fairways and around greens. Keep in mind as you go through every hole that your main goal is to avoid blowups. Think about how to avoid doubles more than how to make birdies.

THE STAT YOU NEED TO BEAT:
PAR-3 AND PAR-5 SCORING

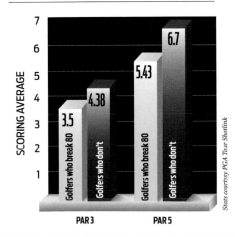

Stats courtesy PGA Tour Shotlink

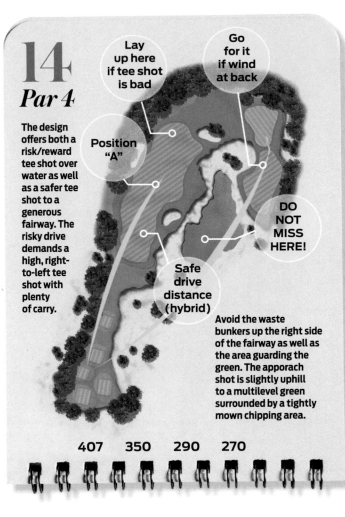

14
Par 4

Lay up here if tee shot is bad

Go for it if wind at back

Position "A"

The design offers both a risk/reward tee shot over water as well as a safer tee shot to a generous fairway. The risky drive demands a high, right-to-left tee shot with plenty of carry.

DO NOT MISS HERE!

Safe drive distance (hybrid)

Avoid the waste bunkers up the right side of the fairway as well as the area guarding the green. The approach shot is slightly uphill to a multilevel green surrounded by a tightly mown chipping area.

407   350   290   270

Par 3s
Par is birdie

The key for shaving strokes on par 3s is to think of them, especially the longer and harder ones, as par 3.5s. When you face a long par 3, take a good look at your possible miss areas, almost as you would when surveying a fairway from the tee. Your goal should be to find the least penal area to miss and aim for that part of the green. The worst thing you can do is to shoot at a flag that's surrounded by trouble and wind up making double- or triple-bogey. On these holes, be happy with a "4" and think of a "3" as a bonus. Forget about birdies here.

Par 5s
Bogey is double

First, you need to carefully consider whether or not you have a realistic chance to reach the green in two, even with your very best drive. If not, hit a more conservative club off the tee. Use the same thought process from the fairway: don't automatically assume you're going for the green in two. In fact, the only time you should go for the green is if you can reach the greenside bunkers with a comfortable shot with your longest club. If you can't, you're better off laying up to a nice wedge distance (use your go-to layup developed in Week 1).

WEEK 5 ACTION PLAN
(3 HOURS)

GOAL: TIGHTEN UP YOUR STRATEGY

1. Make a Plan *(30 mins.)*
Go through the yardage book or scorecard from your home course and devise a strategy for each hole. Pay particular attention to the par 3s and par 5s.

2. Lock in Your Speed *(30 mins.)*
Continue working on your lag putting with the Speed Drill on the opposite page. By the end of six weeks, you want to be able to lag at least eight balls in a row.

3. Make 10 5-Footers/ Play a Game *(30 mins.)*
Keep working on those key short putts and your compeitive edge via "Sinks" (opposite page).

4. Scoring-Club Distance Practice *(30 mins.)*
Perform the wedge drill from page 206. At this point in the six-week plan, you should be very close to the goal of getting at least 70 percent of your wedge shots into a 10-yard radius with each club.

5. Cross-the-Line Drill *(30 mins.)*
Continue working on your go-to drive (see page 207).

6. Pitch/Chip Drill *(30 mins.)*
Continue the drill from page 208.

DOWNLOAD THE WEEK 5 WORKSHEET
golf.com/break80

WEEK 6
GET OUT IN ONE SWING

Don't get cute—get out! Save a few strokes with a conservative approach

I know you've probably tried to do this before, but if you want to break 80 you have to learn how to get out of greenside and fairway bunkers on the first try, every time. I'm sure you can go back to numerous rounds and count up the number of strokes you left in the sand, simply because you either couldn't pop the ball out on the first try or you made a tactical error.

The first thing you need to change about your bunker play is your strategy. **When you land in a fairway bunker, forget about going for the green.** I know it's tempting at times, particularly when you have a good lie, but don't do it. Unless you're supremely confident and competent at these shots, you should simply lay the ball up to a comfortable distance and try to get up and down for par. In a greenside bunker, you should take the same approach. Don't worry about going at the flag— just get the ball out and somewhere on the green. Remember, one of your main goals is to avoid double-bogeys, and these situations are ones in which you are in danger.

THE STAT YOU NEED TO BEAT:
SAVING PAR FROM SAND

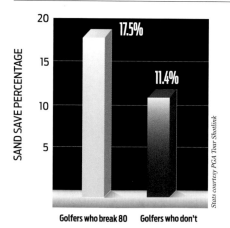

SAND SAVE PERCENTAGE

20 — 17.5%

15

11.4%

10

5

Golfers who break 80   Golfers who don't

Stats courtesy PGA Tour Shotlink

"Your fear of the sand disappears because you're not stressed over hitting it close."
—Brady Riggs

HOW TO BLAST IT OUT CONSISTENTLY
Before you begin practicing, you need to make sure you have a wedge with plenty of bounce and plenty of loft. This combination is critical. Then you need to learn to slap the sand out of the bunker. That's all you really have to do, and I recommend practicing with a broken tee or a pebble before you use a ball. Just work on slapping the sand, not digging in, and you'll get the hang of it soon enough. **For more on how to escape sand, see my video at golf.com/break80.**

Just slap the sand to get the ball out every time.

WEEK 6 DRILL: 10 BALLS OUT

Forget spin, distance and direction. Get it out!

Strategy is one thing, but you still have to hit the shot. Believe me, getting the ball out on one try is not very difficult if you put in a bit of practice using the blast techniques described on the opposite page.

I suggest finding a bunker at your practice range and starting with 10 balls. Line them up with the simple goal of popping each one out on the first try. Don't worry about distance, spin, or even direction. Work on this until you can get at least 8 out of 10 out on the first try. What you'll find is that your fear of the sand disappears because you're not stressed over hitting it close. You'll swing a bit more freely and relaxed. This will improve your results more than if you worked on trying to stick the pin every time.

WEEK 6 ACTION PLAN
(3 HOURS)

GOAL: 80% SAND SHOTS OUT

1. 10 Balls Out *(30 mins.)*
Find a practice bunker and drop 10 balls in the sand. Hit all 10 with the simple goal of getting each one out on the first try. When you leave one in the sand, start over until you can get all 10 out in a row.

2. Lock in Your Speed
(30 mins.)
Continue working on your lag-putting skills with the Speed Drill on page 210).

3. Scoring Club Distance Practice *(30 mins.)*
Perform the wedge drill from page 206. At this point in the six-week plan, you should have reached your goal of getting at least 70 percent of your wedge shots into a 10-yard radius with each club.

4. Cross-the-Line Drill
(30 mins.)
Continue working on your go-to drive (see page 207).

5. Pitch/Chip Drill
(30 mins.)
Continue the drill from page 209. Get all 10 balls close to the hole.

6. Performance Review
(30 mins.)
Use the worksheets to see how close you are to each of the goals associated with the five main drills.

DOWNLOAD THE WEEK 6 WORKSHEET
golf.com/break80

THE TOP 100 TEACHERS IN AMERICA

There are more than 36,000 PGA and LPGA of America members, and Golf Magazine uses only the 100 most elite among them to help you lower your scores, improve your swing, hammer the ball longer and putt the lights out

MIKE ADAMS
Facility: Hamilton Farm G.C., Gladstone, N.J.; The Medalist Club, Hobe Sound, Fla.
Website: mikeadamsgolf.com
Teaching since: 1977
Top 100 since: 1996

ROB AKINS
Facility: Spring Creek Ranch, Collierville, Tenn.
Website: robakinsgolf.com
Teaching since: 1987
Top 100 since: 2001

ERIC ALPENFELS
Facility: Pinehurst Resort, Pinehurst, N.C.
Website: pinehurst.com
Teaching since: 1984
Top 100 since: 2001

TODD ANDERSON
Facility: Sea Island Golf Learning Center, St. Simons Island, Ga.
Website: seaisland.com
Teaching since: 1984
Top 100 since: 2003
2010 PGA Teacher of the Year

ROBERT BAKER
Facility: Logical Golf, Miami Beach, Fla.
Website: logicalgolf.com
Teaching since: 1989
Top 100 since: 1999

JIMMY BALLARD
Facility: Ballard Swing Connection, Key Largo, Fla.
Website: jimmyballardgolf.com
Teaching since: 1960
Top 100 since: 1996

MIKE BENDER
Facility: Magnolia Plantation G.C., Lake Mary, Fla.
Website: mikebender.com
Teaching since: 1990
Top 100 since: 1996
2009 PGA Teacher of the Year

STEVE BOSDOSH
Facility: Members Club at Four Streams, Beallsville, Md.
Website: stevebosdoshgolf.com
Teaching since: 1983
Top 100 since: 2001

MICHAEL BREED
Facility: Sunningdale C.C., Scarsdale, N.Y.
Website: michaelbreed.com
Teaching since: 1986
Top 100 since: 2003

BRAD BREWER
Facility: Brad Brewer Golf Academy at Shingle Creek Resort, Orlando, Fla.
Website: bradbrewer.com
Teaching since: 1984
Top 100 since: 2007

HENRY BRUNTON
Facility: Henry Brunton Golf Academy, Maple, Ont.
Website: henrybrunton.com
Teaching since: 1985
Top 100 since: 2005

JASON CARBONE
Facility: Baltusrol G.C., Springfield, N.J.
Teaching since: 1993
Top 100 since: 2007

CHUCK COOK
Facility: Chuck Cook Golf Academy, Austin, Tex.
Website: chuckcookgolf.com
Teaching since: 1975
Top 100 since: 1996
1996 PGA Teacher of the Year

DONALD CRAWLEY
Facility: Boulders Golf Academy, Carefree, Ariz.
Website: golfsimplified.com
Teaching since: 1974
Top 100 since: 1999

MIKE DAVIS
Facility: Walters Golf Academy, Las Vegas, Nev.
Website: waltersgolf.com
Teaching since: 1970
Top 100 since: 2007

GLENN DECK
Facility: Pelican Hill Resort, Newport Coast, Calif.
Website: pelicanhill.com
Teaching since: 1983
Top 100 since: 2003

DOM DiJULIA
Facility: Dom DiJulia School of Golf, New Hope, Pa.
Website: dijuliagolf.com
Teaching since: 1990
Top 100 since: 2007

KRISTA DUNTON
Facility: Berkeley Hall, Bluffton, S.C.
Website: kristadunton.com
Teaching since: 1989
Top 100 since: 2011
2002 LPGA Teacher of the Year

JOHN ELLIOTT, JR.
Facility: Golden Ocala Golf and Equestrian Club, Ocala, Fla.
Website: jmegolf.com
Teaching since: 1970
Top 100 since: 1996

CHUCK EVANS
Facility: Gold Canyon Golf Resort, Gold Canyon, Ariz.
Website: medicusgolfinstitute.com
Teaching since: 1970
Top 100 since: 2009

BILL FORREST
Facility: Troon C.C., Scottsdale, Ariz.
Website: billforrestgolf.com
Teaching since: 1978
Top 100 since: 2007
2006 PGA Teacher of the Year

EDEN FOSTER
Facility: Maidstone Club, East Hampton, N.Y.
Teaching since: 1988
Top 100 since: 2003

BRYAN GATHRIGHT
Facility: Oak Hills C.C., San Antonio, Tex.
Teaching since: 1987
Top 100 since: 2001

DAVID GLENZ
Facility: David Glenz Golf Academy, Franklin, N.J.
Website: davidglenz.com
Teaching since: 1978
Top 100 since: 1996
1998 PGA Teacher of the Year

RICK GRAYSON
Facility: Rivercat G.C., Springfield, Mo.
Website: rickgraysongolf.com
Teaching since: 1976
Top 100 since: 1996

FRED GRIFFIN
Facility: Grand Cypress Academy of Golf, Orlando, Fla.
Website: grandcypress.com
Teaching since: 1980
Top 100 since: 1996

RON GRING
Facility: Gring Golf at Timber Creek G.C., Daphne, Ala.
Website: gringgolf.com
Teaching since: 1978
Top 100 since: 2003

LOU GUZZI
Facility: Lou Guzzi Golf Academy at Talamore C.C., Ambler, Pa.
Website: louguzzi.com
Teaching since: 1992
Top 100 since: 2011

MARK HACKETT
Facility: Old Palm G.C., Palm Beach Gardens, Fla.
Teaching since: 1988
Top 100 since: 2009

MARTIN HALL
Facility: Ibis Golf & C.C., West Palm Beach, Fla.
Teaching since: 1978
Top 100 since: 1996
2008 PGA Teacher of the Year

JOE HALLETT
Facility: Vanderbilt Legends Club, Franklin, Tenn.
Website: pgaguy.com
Teaching since: 1990
Top 100 since: 2011

HANK HANEY
Facility: Hank Haney Golf, McKinney, Tex.
Website: hankhaney.com
Teaching since: 1977
Top 100 since: 1996

JIM HARDY
Facility: Jim Hardy Golf, Houston, Tex.
Website: jimhardygolf.com
Teaching since: 1966
Top 100 since: 1996
2007 PGA Teacher of the Year

CLAUDE (BUTCH) HARMON, JR.
Facility: Butch Harmon School of Golf, Henderson, Nev.
Website: butchharmon.com
Teaching since: 1965
Top 100 since: 1996

CRAIG HARMON
Facility: Oak Hill C.C., Rochester, N.Y.
Teaching since: 1968
Top 100 since: 1996

MICHAEL HEBRON
Facility: Smithtown Landing G.C., Smithtown, N.Y.
Website: mikehebron.com
Teaching since: 1967
Top 100 since: 1996
1991 PGA Teacher of the Year

SHAWN HUMPHRIES
Facility: Cowboys G.C., Grapevine, Tex.
Website: shawnhumphries.com
Teaching since: 1988
Top 100 since: 2005

ED IBARGUEN
Facility: Duke University G.C., Durham, N.C.
Website: golf.duke.edu
Teaching since: 1979
Top 100 since: 2001

ERIC JOHNSON
Facility: Oakmont C.C., Oakmont, Pa.
Website: ericjohnsongolf.com
Teaching since: 1991
Top 100 since: 2011

HANK JOHNSON
Facility: Greystone G.C., Birmingham, Ala.
Teaching since: 1970
Top 100 since: 1999
2004 PGA Teacher of the Year

CHARLIE KING
Facility: Reynolds Golf Academy at Reynolds Plantation, Greensboro, Ga.
Website: reynoldsgolfacademy.com
Teaching since: 1989
Top 100 since: 2003

JERRY KING
Facility: Kapalua Golf Academy, Lahaina, Maui, Hi.
Website: jerrykinggolf.com
Teaching since: 1992
Top 100 since: 2009

PETER KOSTIS
Facility: Kostis/McCord Learning Center, Scottsdale, Ariz.
Website: kostismccordlearning.com
Teaching since: 1971
Top 100 since: 1996

PETER KRAUSE
Facility: Hank Haney Academy, Lewisville, Tex.
Website: peterkrausegolf.com
Teaching since: 1981
Top 100 since: 1999
2005 PGA Teacher of the Year

MIKE LABAUVE
Facility: Westin Kierland Resort, Scottsdale, Ariz.
Website: kierlandresort.com
Teaching since: 1980
Top 100 since: 1996

ROD LIDENBERG
Facility: Prestwick G.C., Woodbury, Minn.
Website: pgamasterpro.com
Teaching since: 1972
Top 100 since: 2007

JACK LUMPKIN
Facility: Sea Island Golf Learning Center, St. Simons Island, Ga.
Website: seaisland.com
Teaching since: 1958
Top 100 since: 1996
1995 PGA Teacher of the Year

KEITH LYFORD
Facility: Golf Academy at Old Greenwood, Truckee, Calif.
Website: lyfordgolf.net
Teaching since: 1982
Top 100 since: 1999

TIM MAHONEY
Facility: Talking Stick G.C., Scottsdale, Ariz.
Website: timmahoneygolf.com
Teaching since: 1980
Top 100 since: 1996

MIKE MALASKA
Facility: Superstition Mountain G.C., Apache Junction, Ariz.
Website: malaskagolf.com
Teaching since: 1982
Top 100 since: 1996
2011 PGA Teacher of the Year

BRIAN MANZELLA
Facility: English Turn Golf & C.C.
Website: brianmanzella.com
Teaching since: 1984
Top 100 since: 2011

PAUL MARCHAND
Facility: Shadowhawk G.C., Richmond, Tex.
Teaching since: 1981
Top 100 since: 1996

LYNN MARRIOTT
Facility: Legacy Golf Resort, Phoenix, Ariz.
Website: vision54.com
Teaching since: 1982
Top 100 since: 1996
1992 LPGA Teacher of the Year

RICK McCORD
Facility: McCord Golf Academy, Orange Lake C.C., Orlando, Fla.
Website: themccordgolfacademy.com
Teaching since: 1973
Top 100 since: 1996

MIKE McGETRICK
Facility: Colorado G.C., Parker, Colo.
Website: coloradogolfclub.com
Teaching since: 1983
Top 100 since: 1996
1999 PGA Teacher of the Year

JIM McLEAN
Facility: Jim McLean Golf School, Miami, Fla.
Website: jimmclean.com
Teaching since: 1975
Top 100 since: 1996
1994 PGA Teacher of the Year

BRIAN MOGG
Facility: Waldorf Astoria G.C., Orlando, Fla.
Website: moggperformance.com
Teaching since: 1992
Top 100 since: 2005

CONTRIBUTORS

BILL MORETTI
Facility: Moretti Golf, Austin, Tex.
Website: morettigolf.com
Teaching since: 1979
Top 100 since: 1996

JERRY MOWLDS
Facility: Pumpkin Ridge G.C., North Plains, Ore.
Teaching since: 1970
Top 100 since: 1996

SCOTT MUNROE
Facility: Nantucket G.C., Siasconset, Mass.
Website: moneygolf.net
Teaching since: 1978
Top 100 since: 2009

JIM MURPHY
Facility: Jim Murphy Golf at Sugar Creek C.C., Sugar Land, Tex.
Website: jimmurphygolf.com
Teaching since: 1984
Top 100 since: 2003

TOM NESS
Facility: Reunion G.C., Hoschton, Ga.
Website: affinitigolfacademy.com
Teaching since: 1972
Top 100 since: 2007

PIA NILSSON
Facility: Legacy Golf Resort, Phoenix, Ariz.
Website: vision54.com
Teaching since: 1987
Top 100 since: 2001

DAN PASQUARIELLO
Facility: Pebble Beach Golf Academy, Pebble Beach, Calif.
Website: pebblebeach.com
Teaching since: 1970
Top 100 since: 2007

TOM PATRI
Facility: Friar's Head G.C., Riverhead, N.Y.
Website: tompatri.com
Teaching since: 1981
Top 100 since: 2001

BRUCE PATTERSON
Facility: Butler National G.C., Oak Brook, Ill.
Teaching since: 1980
Top 100 since: 2005

DAVE PELZ
Facility: Pelz Golf, Austin, Tex.
Website: pelzgolf.com
Teaching since: 1976
Top 100 since: 1996

MIKE PERPICH
Facility: RiverPines Golf, Alpharetta, Ga.
Website: mikeperpich.com
Teaching since: 1976
Top 100 since: 2001

GALE PETERSON
Facility: Sea Island Golf Learning Center, St. Simons Island, Ga.
Website: seaisland.com
Teaching since: 1978
Top 100 since: 1996
1996 LPGA Teacher of the Year

E.J. PFISTER
Facility: Oak Tree National G.C., Edmond, Okla.
Website: ejpfistergolf.com
Teaching since: 1986
Top 100 since: 2009

DAVE PHILLIPS
Facility: Titleist Performance Institute, Oceanside, Calif.
Website: mytpi.com
Teaching since: 1989
Top 100 since: 2001

CAROL PREISINGER
Facility: The Kiawah Island Club, Kiawah Island, S.C.
Website: carolpreisinger.com
Teaching since: 1986
Top 100 since: 2005

KIP PUTERBAUGH
Facility: The Aviara Golf Academy, Carlsbad, Calif.
Website: aviaragolfacademy.com
Teaching since: 1972
Top 100 since: 1996

NANCY QUARCELINO
Facility: Kings Creek G.C., Spring Hill, Tenn.
Website: qsog.com
Teaching since: 1979
Top 100 since: 2003
2000 LPGA Teacher of the Year

CARL RABITO
Facility: Bolingbrook G.C., Bolingbrook, Ill.
Website: rabitogolf.com
Teaching since: 1987
Top 100 since: 2007

DANA RADER
Facility: Ballantyne Resort, Charlotte, N.C.
Website: danarader.com
Teaching since: 1980
Top 100 since: 1996
1990 LPGA Teacher of the Year

BRAD REDDING
Facility: The Resort Club at Grande Dunes. Myrtle Beach, S.C.
Website: grandedunes.com
Teaching since: 1984
Top 100 since: 2001

BRADY RIGGS
Facility: Woodley Lakes G.C., Van Nuys, Calif.
Website: bradyriggs.com
Teaching since: 1990
Top 100 since: 2007

PHIL RITSON
Facility: Orange County National Golf Center, Orlando, Fla.
Website: ocngolf.com
Teaching since: 1950
Top 100 since: 1996

SCOTT SACKETT
Facility: Scott Sackett Golf, Scottsdale, Ariz.
Website: scottsackett.com
Teaching since: 1985
Top 100 since: 1999

ADAM SCHRIBER
Facility: Crystal Mountain Resort, Thompsonville, Mich.
Website: crystalmountain.com
Teaching since: 1985
Top 100 since: 2009

CRAIG SHANKLAND
Facility: LPGA International
Daytona Beach, Fla.
Teaching since: 1957
Top 100 since: 1996
2001 PGA Teacher of the Year

MIKE SHANNON
Facility: Sea Island Golf Learning Center, St. Simons Island, Ga.
Website: seaisland.com
Teaching since: 1975
Top 100 since: 1996

TED SHEFTIC
Facility: Bridges G.C., Abbottstown, Pa.
Website: tedsheftic.com
Teaching since: 1966
Top 100 since: 2003

LAIRD SMALL
Facility: Pebble Beach Golf Academy, Pebble Beach, Calif.
Website: pebblebeach.com
Teaching since: 1977
Top 100 since: 1996
2003 PGA Teacher of the Year

RANDY SMITH
Facility: Royal Oaks C.C., Dallas, Tex.
Teaching since: 1973
Top 100 since: 2001

2002 PGA Teacher of the Year

RICK SMITH
Facility: Treetops Resort, Gaylord, Mich.
Website: ricksmith.com
Teaching since: 1977
Top 100 since: 1996

TODD SONES
Facility: Impact Golf Schools
at White Deer Run G.C., Vernon Hills, Ill.
Website: toddsones.com
Teaching since: 1982
Top 100 since: 1996

CHARLES SORRELL
Facility: Crystal Lake C.C., Hampton, Ga.
Website: sorrellgolf.com
Teaching since: 1966
Top 100 since: 1996
1990 PGA Teacher of the Year

MITCHELL SPEARMAN
Facility: Doral Arrowwood Golf Resort, Rye Brook, N.Y.
Website: mitchellspearman.com
Teaching since: 1979
Top 100 since: 1996

MARK STEINBAUER
Facility: Carlton Woods, The Woodlands, Tex.
Website: thewoodlands.com
Teaching since: 1977
Top 100 since: 2011

KELLIE STENZEL
Facility: Palm Beach G.C., Palm Beach, Fla.
Website: kelliestenzelgolf.com
Teaching since: 1985
Top 100 since: 2009

TOM STICKNEY
Facility: Bighorn G.C., Palm Desert, Calif.
Website: tomstickneygolf.com
Teaching since: 1990
Top 100 since: 2007

DR. JIM SUTTIE
Facility: Cog Hill G.C., Lemont, Ill.; TwinEagles, Naples, Fla.
Website: jimsuttie.com
Teaching since: 1972
Top 100 since: 1996
2000 PGA Teacher of the Year

JON TATTERSALL
Facility: Terminus Club, Atlanta, Ga.
Website: terminusclub.com
Teaching since: 1988
Top 100 since: 2007

DR. T.J. TOMASI
Facility: Tomasi Golf, Port St. Lucie, Fla.
Website: tjtomasi.com
Teaching since: 1975
Top 100 since: 1999

J.D. TURNER
Facility: The Landings, Savannah, Ga.
Website: jdturnergolf.com
Teaching since: 1965
Top 100 since: 1996

STAN UTLEY
Facility: Grayhawk Learning Center, Scottsdale, Ariz.
Website: stanutleygolf.com
Teaching since: 1986
Top 100 since: 2009

CHUCK WINSTEAD
Facility: The University Club, Baton Rouge, La.
Website: universityclubbr.com
Teaching since: 1993
Top 100 since: 2005

DR. DAVID WRIGHT
Facility: Wright Balance Golf Academy at Arroyo Trabuco G.C., Mission Viejo, Calif.
Website: wrightbalance.com
Teaching since: 1982
Top 100 since: 2005

WORLD GOLF TEACHERS HALL OF FAME

The master class of the Top 100 Teachers in America

PEGGY KIRK BELL
Facility: Pine Needles Resort, Southern Pines, N.C.
Teaching since: 1958
Top 100/Hall of Fame since: 1996/1998
1961 LPGA Teacher of the Year

MANUEL DE LA TORRE
Facility: Milwaukee C.C., River Hills, Wisc.
Website: manueldelatorregolf.com
Teaching since: 1948
Top 100/Hall of Fame since: 1996/1998
1986 PGA Teacher of the Year

JIM FLICK
Facility: TaylorMade Performance Lab, Carlsbad, Calif.
Website: jimflick.com
Teaching since: 1954
Top 100/Hall of Fame since: 1996/2002
1988 PGA Teacher of the Year

DAVID LEADBETTER
Facility: David Leadbetter Golf Academy, Champions Gate, Fla.
Website: davidleadbetter.com
Teaching since: 1976
Top 100/Hall of Fame since: 1996/2007

EDDIE MERRINS
Facility: Bel-Air C.C., Los Angeles, Calif.
Website: eddiemerrins.com
Teaching since: 1957
Top 100/Hall of Fame since: 1996/2008

BOB TOSKI
Facility: Toski-Battersby Learning Center, Coconut Creek, Fla.
Website: learn-golf.com
Teaching since: 1956
Top 100/Hall of Fame since: 1996/1999

DR. GARY WIREN
Facility: Trump International, West Palm Beach, Fla.
Website: garywiren.com
Teaching since: 1955
Top 100/Hall of Fame since: 1996/2007
1987 PGA Teacher of the Year

Get more information on *Golf Magazine's* Top 100 Teachers in America and the Top Teachers by Region, plus exclusive video lessons, tips and drills at

TOP 100 BY THE NUMBERS

31.75
Average years of teaching experience

27
Current Top 100 Teachers and Hall of Famers who have been named LPGA or PGA Teacher of the Year

7
Top 100 Teachers who have been inducted into the PGA Golf Professional Hall of Fame

36,000
Members of the PGA and LPGA of America who are eligible for Top 100 Status

0.28%
Percentage of PGA and LPGA of America members who are Top 100 Teachers

GLOSSARY

Unfamiliar with some of the jargon used by the Top 100?
Consult this glossary so you don't miss a single tip.

ABOVE PLANE Swinging your club above the plane defined by your shoulders.

ACROSS THE LINE Pointing the shaft right of the target at the top of your backswing.

ADDRESS The position you take prior to hitting a shot. According to the Rules of Golf, you've completely addressed the ball when you've taken your stance and grounded your club.

AIM LINE An invisible line that runs from your ball to your target. See also Target Line.

ALIGNMENT The position of your body relative to the target line.

ANGLE OF ATTACK The angle at which your clubhead descends toward the ball on your downswing. A steep angle of attack is the result of an upright swing, while a shallow angle of attack comes from a flatter swing.

APRON The closely mown area encircling a putting green.

BACK LIP The edge of the bunker that's farthest from the green.

BACKSPIN Ball spin in the direction away from the target.

BALL FLIGHT The path and trajectory of the ball from impact to when it hits the ground.

BALL MARK An indentation made in the putting surface where your shot lands on the green.

BALL MARKER A token or a small coin used to spot the position of the ball on the green prior to lifting it.

BALL POSITION The location of the ball relative to your stance width. A ball positioned toward your front foot is said to be more forward.

BALLOONED A ball flight defined by an unreasonably high trajectory.

BANANA BALL A slice.

BASEBALL GRIP Holding the club with all ten fingers.

BEACH A sand hazard.

BELOW PLANE Swinging your club below the plane defined by your shoulders.

BEND The curve on a shot created by sidespin.

BENT GRASS A type of grass characterized by thin blades, found on most courses with varying seasonal climates.

BERMUDA GRASS A type of grass found on most courses located in warmer or tropical climates. Characterized by thick blades and a grainy surface.

BITE The ability of the ball to stop—rather than roll—when it lands.

BLADED SHOT To hit the ball with the leading edge of your iron. See also Skull.

BLAST A shot made from a bunker that displaces a noticeable amount of sand.

BLOCK A straight shot played severely to the right; similar to a Push.

BOUNCE The angle formed between the leading edge of the clubhead and the lowest part of the sole. Clubs with higher bounce angles tend not to dig into the turf and clubs with lower bounce angles tend to dig into the turf.

BREAK The curve the ball makes as it rolls toward the hole on the putting green. Break also refers to the general slope of a green.

BUMP-AND-RUN A shot that's intentionally hit low and short of the target and that rolls substantially after landing.

BUNKER A sand-filled hazard.

BURIED LIE The lie of the ball, typically in a sand bunker, in which most of the ball sits below the surface. See also Fried Egg.

BUTT END The part of the shaft farthest away from the clubhead.

CARPET A slang term referring to the putting green or fairway.

CARRY The distance the ball flies in the air.

CAST Unhinging your wrists too early in the downswing.

CENTER-SHAFTED A putter with a hosel at its center.

CHECK UP A shot that spins and stops once it hits the green.

CHICKEN WING A bent right elbow in the release position. Associated with hitting a slice.

CHILI-DIP A shot in which you hit behind the ball, not moving it very far. See also Fat Shot.

CHIP A short, lofted shot hit near the green.

CHOKE To play badly under pressure.

CHOKE DOWN Gripping the club farther down the handle than normal.

CHOP To hit the ball with a hacking motion.

CHUNK A shot in which you hit behind the ball, not advancing it very far. See also Fat Shot or Chili-Dip.

CLOSED CLUBFACE Your clubface points left of the target when you address the ball, or left of the path on which you swing your club.

CLOSED STANCE Addressing the ball so that your toe line points to the right of the target.

CLUBFACE The area of the club on which contact with the ball is made.

COIL The degree to which your shoulders turn relative to your hips. More shoulder than hip turn usually means more coil and power.

COLLAR A closely mown area surrounding the putting green. See also Fringe.

CROSS WIND A wind blowing across a hole or the course.

CROSS-BUNKER A lengthy bunker in the fairway and perpendicular to the line of play.

CROSS-HANDED GRIP Placing your left hand below your right on the handle when putting. See also Left-Hand Low.

CROWN The top side of your driver, fairway wood or hybrid.

CUT SHOT A shot that moves from left to right.

DANCE FLOOR The green.

DELOFT Subtracting from the loft built into the clubface by leaning the shaft forward or closing the face at impact.

DIMPLE Depression on a golf ball designed to help get the ball airborne and maintain its flight.

DIVOT A chunk of grass taken up by the club during impact. It also refers to the resulting void.

DOGLEG A hole that bends left or right.

DOUBLE CROSS A shot that flies in the opposite direction of the shot you intended to play.

DOUBLE-BREAKER A putt that curves in more than one direction during its roll to the hole.

DOWNSWING The motion of swinging your club from the top position to the point of impact.

DRAIN To sink a putt.

DRAW A shot that starts straight, or slightly right, and arcs gently to the left.

DUCK HOOK A shot that starts straight and curves to the left of the target. See also Snap Hook.

DUFF To mis-hit a shot by hitting the ground behind the ball and then topping the ball.

DUFFER An unskilled golfer.

ELEVATED GREEN A green that sits above your position in the fairway.

EXTENSION Stretching your arms through and after impact.

FACE-BALANCED A weighting system applied to putters that helps keep the putterface square to the target during your stroke.

FADE A shot that generally tends to curve to the right.

FAT SHOT When your club hits the ground behind the ball. This results in high or low shots with a loss of distance. See also Chunk or Chili-Dip.

FIRST CUT Term given to a section of rough (or higher grass) directly bordering a fairway.

FLAGSTICK A movable marker to show the location of the hole.

FLARE OUT To rotate your feet on their heels so that they angle away from the center of your stance.

FLAT SWING Swinging your club under the plane defined by your shoulders.

FLEX A measurement of how much a shaft will bend during your swing. Stiffer shafts bend less than softer ones.

FLIER A shot that flies substantially longer than desired, usually as a result of too much grass between the clubface and ball. Fliers are more common from the rough than from the shorter fairway grass, and are most commonly hit from a Flier Lie.

FLIGHT The path of the ball through the air.

FLOP SHOT A short shot played with an open stance and an open clubface, designed to travel very high in the air and land softly on the green.

FLUB A poorly hit shot usually caused by hitting the ground before the ball.

FLUFFY LIE A ball that's sitting up in grass.

FOLLOW-THROUGH The continuation of your swing after the ball has been hit.

FORWARD BEND The degree to which you bend toward the ball from your hips at address.

FORWARD PRESS Moving your hands toward the target while your club is soled on the ground.

FRIED EGG A lie in a sand bunker in which most of the ball is below the surface of the sand. See also Buried Lie.

FRINGE The grass that borders a putting green. The fringe is typically higher than the grass on the green, but lower than the grass on the fairway. See also Collar.

GAP WEDGE A utility wedge with less loft than a sand wedge and more loft than a pitching wedge.

GRAIN The direction in which the blades of grass on a green grow.

GREENSIDE Adjacent to the putting green.

GRIP The manner in which you place your hands on the club. It also refers to the top part of the club or the material on which you place your hands at the top of the shaft.

GRIP PRESSURE How tightly you hold the club.

GROOVES The lines cut into a clubface to help impart spin. They are either V-shaped or U-shaped with a maximum allowable width of .035 inches.

HACKER A derogatory term given to a player of lesser ability.

HARDPAN An area of the course not covered by grass and defined by hard-packed dirt.

HAZARD Any obstruction on a golf course, such as a lake, pond, fence or bunker.

HEEL The part of the clubhead closest to the hosel.

HOLE HIGH A ball that sits even with the hole but off to one side.

HOOK A shot that starts straight or slightly to the right or left then curves dramatically to the left.

HOSEL The area of the club into which the shaft enters.

HOSELED SHOT A shank.

HOT SPOT The area on your driver clubface between the sweet spot and the crown that's said to deliver the greatest energy transfer.

IMPACT The moment the clubface meets the ball.

INSIDE-OUT Swinging from inside the target line to the outside of the target line through impact. Inside-out swings typically result in either pushes, draws or hooks, depending on the position of the clubface at impact.

INTERLOCKING GRIP A type of grip in which the little finger of your left hand is intertwined with the index finger of your right hand.

KNOCK-DOWN A shot intentionally played low to keep the ball under the wind.

LAG PUTT A lengthy putt, or one designed to simply get close to the hole so the next putt is easily made.

LAID OFF Pointing the shaft away from the target line at the top of the swing.

LAUNCH ANGLE The angle on which the ball comes off the clubface.

LAUNCH MONITOR A device that measures and computes various swing parameters, such as speed and clubface angle, as well as shot data such as distance and direction.

LEADING EDGE The bottom portion of the clubhead closest to the ball when soled at address.

LEFT-HAND LOW Placing your left hand below your right on the handle when putting. See also Cross-Handed Grip.

LIE ANGLE The angle formed between the shaft and the ground when the club is soled at address.

LIP OUT A putt that hits the edge of the hole and does not go in.

LOB SHOT A high, soft shot generally played near the green with a high-lofted wedge.

LOB WEDGE The highest-lofted wedge in your bag. Designed to hit lob shots, flops and to escape bunkers.

LOFT ANGLE The angle of the club's face.

LONG IRONS Your 1-, 2-, 3- and 4-irons.

MID-IRONS Your 5-, 6- and 7-irons.

OFFSET The distance from the front of the hosel to the leading edge of the clubface. More offset gives you more time to square the clubface.

OPEN CLUBFACE Your clubface points right of the target when you address the ball, or right of the path on which your club is swung.

OPEN STANCE Addressing the ball so that your toe line points to the left of the target.

OUTSIDE-IN Swinging from outside the target line to the inside of the target line through impact. Outside-in swings typically result in either pulls, fades or slices, depending on the position of the club face at impact.

OVER THE TOP Swinging outside-in.

OVERLAPPING GRIP A type of grip in which the little finger of your right hand overlaps the space between the forefinger and second finger of your left hand.

OVER-SWINGING Swinging the club past parallel at the top of your backswing.

PACE The speed at which your putt rolls to the hole.

PATH An imaginary line created by the arc of your swing.

PICK To catch the ball cleanly at impact without hitting the ground.

PIN The flagstick.

PIN HIGH A ball that sits even with the pin but off to one side. Same as Hole High.

PIVOT The rotation of your shoulders, torso and hips during your swing.

PLUGGED LIE See Buried Lie.

POP-UP An unintentional high, short shot hit with a driver or fairway wood.

PULL A shot that's hit straight but left of the target.

PULL-HOOK A shot that starts left of target and then curves dramatically to the left.

PULL-SLICE A shot that starts left of target and then curves dramatically to the right.

PUNCH SHOT A shot played intentionally low to avoid wind, trees or other obstacles.

PUNCH-OUT A low shot played from trees that's designed to get the ball back into play.

PUSH A shot that's hit straight but right of the target. See also Block.

PUSH-HOOK A shot that starts right of target and then curves dramatically to the left.

PUSH-SLICE A shot that starts right of target and then curves dramatically to the right.

READING THE GREEN Determining the path the ball will follow during its roll to the hole by analyzing the contour of the putting surface.

RELEASE The point in the downswing at which you unhinge your wrists.

REVERSE PIVOT Swinging to the top of your backswing without shifting your weight to your right foot. Associated with slicing.

ROUGH The grass bordering the fairway that's higher and generally more coarse than the grass in the fairway.

SAND SAVE Escaping a sand bunker and then making the ensuing putt.

SAND WEDGE An iron with a heavy sole and increased bounce that's used primarily to get out of sand bunkers.

SAW GRIP An alternative putting grip that allows you to move your hands along the line of putt during your stroke. The Saw Grip is said to reduce the tendency to putt from outside-in and pull the ball left of the hole.

SCOOP Improperly hitting up into the ball in an attempt to lift it into the air. Scooping is the opposite of Trapping and leads to a variety of bad shots.

SCORING IRONS Your short irons and wedges.

SHALLOW A flat swing plane.

SHANK A shot that's struck on the hosel area of the golf club. The resulting ball flight is generally straight to the right. See also Hoseled Shot.

SHORT GAME The part of the game comprised of chipping and pitching.

SHORT IRONS Your 8-, 9- and pitching irons.

SHORT-SIDED Missing the green on the side that leaves you with the smallest amount of distance between you and the flagstick.

SHOTMAKER A player with the ability to hit a variety of shots.

SIDEHILL LIE A lie with the ball either above or below your feet.

SKULL To strike the top of the ball with an ascending, glancing blow. See also Bladed Shot.

SLICE A shot that tends to start to the left of the target and curve to the right of the target.

SNAP HOOK A shot that starts quickly to the left and angles sharply downward and farther to the left. See also Duck Hook.

SOLE The bottom of the clubhead.

SPINE TILT The degree to which your spine angles away from the target.

SQUARE CLUBFACE Your clubface points directly at the target when you address the ball, or in the direction of the path on which your club is swung.

STANCE The position of your feet at address.

STIMPMETER An apparatus used to measure the speed of a green. Greens with a higher "stimp" are said to be faster.

SWAYING Leaning away from the target during the backswing while turning very little.

SWEET SPOT The dead center of the clubface.

SWING WIDTH The radius of your swing measured from your hands to the clubhead. A wider swing is associated with more speed.

TAKEAWAY The start of your swing.

TAP-IN A very short putt.

TEXAS WEDGE A slang term for a putter used for a non-putting shot.

THIN To hit the ball above its equator.

THROUGH THE GREEN All areas of the course, except for the teeing ground, putting green and hazards.

TIGHT FAIRWAY A narrow fairway.

TIGHT LIE A lie on very short fairway grass or on hard-packed sand or dirt. The opposite of a Fluffy Lie.

TOE The part of the clubhead farthest away from the hosel. A ball hit here is said to be "toed."

TOP POSITION The end of the backswing.

TOPPED SHOT A shot that does not get airborne because the clubface hits the top of the ball at impact.

TRAILING EDGE The portion of the sole farthest away from the ball at address.

TRAJECTORY The flight path of the ball.

TRANSITION The change in momentum from backswing to downswing.

TRAPPED Your clubhead is too far to the inside or behind your body on your downswing.

TRAPPING Correctly pinching the ball against the turf at impact with the face of your iron.

UNDERCLUB To select less club than necessary to produce the needed distance.

UNPLAYABLE LIE A ball hit into a position that does not allow you to make contact or establish a safe stance.

UP-AND-DOWN A situation in which you miss the green, but need only one shot and one putt to finish the hole.

WAGGLE The act of motioning the club back and forth slightly by hinging the wrists before starting the swing. A pre-shot ritual used by many to ease tension or ensure a smooth start to the takeaway.

WEIGHT SHIFT Moving your weight backward or forward during the swing. See also Weight Transfer.

WEIGHT TRANSFER Moving your weight backward or forward during the swing. See also Weight Shift.

WORM BURNER A poor shot in which the ball fails to get airborne.

YANK A shot hit directly left. See also Pull Shot.

YIPS The condition, either mental or physical, in which a golfer cannot make short putts. A short putt that is missed badly is said to be "yipped."

ACKNOWLEDGEMENTS

GOLF MAGAZINE

EDITOR
David M. Clarke

CREATIVE DIRECTOR
Paul Crawford

EXECUTIVE EDITOR
Eamon Lynch

ART DIRECTOR
Paul Ewen

MANAGING EDITORS
David DeNunzio (Instruction)
Gary Perkinson (Production)
Robert Sauerhaft (Equipment)

EDITOR AT LARGE
Connell Barrett

DEPUTY MANAGING EDITOR
Michael Chwasky (Instruction & Equipment)

SENIOR EDITORS
Alan Bastable, Michael Walker Jr.
Joseph Passov (Travel/Course Rankings)

**SENIOR EDITOR, GOLF MAGAZINE
CUSTOM PUBLISHING**
Thomas Mackin

DEPUTY ART DIRECTOR
Karen Ha

PHOTO EDITOR
Carrie Boretz

SENIOR WRITERS
Michael Bamberger, Damon Hack, Cameron
Morfit, Alan Shipnuck, Gary Van Sickle

ASSOCIATE EDITOR
Steven Beslow

ASSISTANT EDITOR
Jessica Marksbury

PUBLISHER
Dick Raskopf

DIRECTOR OF BUSINESS DEVELOPMENT
Brad J. Felenstein

SPECIAL THANKS
Christine Austin, Jeremy Biloon, Jim Childs,
Rose Cirrincione, Caroline DeNunzio, Davey DeNunzio,
Dominick DeNunzio, Lauren Hall Clark,
Jacqueline Fitzgerald, Christine Font, Jenna Goldberg,
Hillary Hirsch, Suzanne Janso, Amy Mangus,
Robert Marasco, Kimberly Marshall, Amy Migliaccio,
Nina Mistry, Dave Rozzelle, Adriana Tierno,
Alex Voznesenskiy, Vanessa Wu,
Hamilton Farm G.C., Old Palm G.C.

Sports Illustrated

EDITOR, TIME INC. SPORTS GROUP
Terry McDonell

MANAGING EDITOR, SI.COM
Paul Fichtenbaum

MANAGING EDITOR, SI GOLF GROUP
James P. Herre

PRESIDENT, TIME INC. SPORTS GROUP
Mark Ford

V.P., PUBLISHER
Frank Wall

SENIOR V.P., CONSUMER MARKETING
Nate Simmons

V.P., COMMUNICATIONS AND DEVELOPMENT
Scott Novak

ASSOC. PUBLISHER, MKTG. AND CREATIVE SERVICES
Charlie Saunders

SENIOR V.P., FINANCE
Elissa Fishman

V.P., FINANCE
Peter Greer

VICE PRESIDENT
Ann Marie Doherty

V.P., OPERATIONS
Brooke Twyford

LEGAL
Judith Margolin

HUMAN RESOURCES DIRECTOR
Liz Matilla

GOLF.com

EXECUTIVE EDITOR
Charlie Hanger

EXECUTIVE PRODUCER
Christopher Shade

DEPUTY EDITOR
David Dusek

SENIOR PRODUCERS
Ryan Reiterman, Jeff Ritter

ASSOCIATE PRODUCER
Kevin Cunningham

Time HOME ENTERTAINMENT

PUBLISHER
Richard Fraiman

V.P., BUSINESS DEVELOPMENT & STRATEGY
Steven Sandonato

EXECUTIVE DIRECTOR, MARKETING SERVICES
Carol Pittard

EXECUTIVE DIRECTOR, RETAIL & SPECIAL SALES
Tom Mifsud

EXECUTIVE DIRECTOR, NEW PRODUCT DEVELOPMENT
Peter Harper

EDITORIAL DIRECTOR
Steven Koepp

BOOKAZINE DEVELOPMENT & MARKETING
Laura Adam

PUBLISHING DIRECTOR
Joy Butts

FINANCE DIRECTOR
Glenn Buonocore

ASSISTANT GENERAL COUNSEL
Helen Wan

BOOK PRODUCTION MANAGER
Susan Chodakiewicz

DESIGN & PREPRESS MANAGER
Anne-Michelle Gallero

BRAND MANAGER
Allison Parker

**THE BEST INSTRUCTION BOOK EVER!
EXPANDED EDITION**
by *Golf Magazine's*
Top 100 Teachers in America

EDITOR
David DeNunzio

ART DIRECTION/BOOK DESIGN
Paul Ewen

IMAGING
Geoffrey A. Michaud (Director, SI Imaging)
Dan Larkin, Robert M. Thompson,
Gerald Burke, Neil Clayton

COPY EDITOR
Gary Perkinson

EDITORIAL CONSULTANT
Michael Chwasky

VIDEO PRODUCTION
Optimism Media Group

A SPORTS ILLUSTRATED PUBLICATION

PHOTOGRAPHY

BOB ATKINS
8 (ML, MR), 9 (M, MR), 13, 32, 42 (L), 48 (L), 48 (MR), 52 (L), 52 (ML), 62 (L), 50 (R), 72-73, 76, 81 (L), 82-83, 87 (R), 91 (B), 95 (B), 104-105, 133 (T), 138, 139 (L), 146-147, 151 (M), 160-161, 165 (L), 166, 168-169, 180, 195, 196, 198-199

NEIL BECKERMAN
61 (L), 112, 113 (L)

D2 PRODUCTIONS
9 (ML), 132, 163 (TL), 175, 182-183

LEONARD KAMSLER
12, 29, 162

SCHECTER LEE
30, 35, 38, 39 (B), 69 (B), 105 (L), 128, 151 (TR)

ANGUS MURRAY
1-3, 5-7, 8 (L, M, R), 9 (L, R), 10-11, 15-23, 26-27, 31, 34, 36, 39 (R), 40 (R), 41, 42 (R), 43, 45 (R), 46-47, 48 (ML, R), 49-50, 52 (MR), 52 (R), 53-60, 61 (R), 62 (ML, R), 63-65, 66 (L, M), 68-69, 70 (MR, R), 71, 73 (R), 74-75, 77-80, 81 (R), 84-86, 87 (L), 88-90, 91 (T), 94, 95 (T), 96-98, 100-103, 106-111, 113 (R), 114-119, 121 (R), 122-127, 129-131, 133 (B), 134-135, 137, 139 (T), 140-145, 149-150, 152-158, 163 (BL, R), 164, 165 (R), 167, 171 (R), 172-174, 177, 179, 184-185, 187, 189-194, 197, 200-213, 224

FRED VUICH
40, 51, 70 (L, ML), 99, 148, 170, 171 (L)

ILLUSTRATIONS

CARLOS ALCANTARILLA
14-15, 23-25, 92-93, 103, 110-111, 131, 143, 151 (B), 159, 175, 178-179, 186, 201

PHIL FRANKE
136-137, 173, 176

ROBIN GRIGGS *(1957-2008)*
43, 83, 120-121, 169, 170-171, 188

PETE SUCHESKI
123

IAN WARPOLE
151 (T)

KEITH WITMER
37

CHARTS/GRAPHICS

KAREN HA
13, 27-31, 33, 35, 37, 39, 44-45, 54, 69, 93, 79, 97, 99, 100, 115, 121 (R), 139, 147, 181, 195, 197, 199, 206-213